SENSIBLE LISTENING

The Key to Responsive Interaction

Fourth Edition
Revised Printing

Paul J. Kaufmann
Iowa State University

Connect Communication Training, Inc.

KENDALL/HUNT PUBLISHING COMPANY
4050 Westmark Drive Dubuque, Iowa 52004

Cover photo courtesy of author

Revised Printing

ISBN 0-7872-7426-7

Printed in the United States of America

10 9 8 7 6 5

❑ Table of Contents ❑

❑ *Preface* ❑

Since we spend half our lives listening, it is important to listen as effectively as possible. As the first chapter of *Sensible Listening* emphasizes, many of life's successes are directly linked to effective listening. This fourth edition of *Sensible Listening* has been revised to optimize listening. With focused effort, my experience has shown that you can apply the information and examples in this book to reach more accurate understanding and rewarding decisions.

❑ *Organization* ❑

The material in *Sensible Listening* is divided into two parts: Part One, "A Background for Sensible Listening," and Part Two, "Practicing Sensible Listening."

Part One, "A Background for Sensible Listening," discusses theoretical bases for listening. In learning any skill, we need to understand the theories and variables involved before we can apply them. For example, as student pilots, we first attend ground school to understand the physics, forces, and rules of flying; as medical students, we would study human physiology before performing surgery. This theoretical understanding comes from reading, discussion, and planned exercises; it precedes solo flight or being in charge of a surgical procedure. Active, responsive listening, like flying or surgery, is accomplished first by understanding the theories, forces, and rules. Consequently, Part One of *Sensible Listening* offers a theoretical overview, and develops an understanding of the theories, forces, rules, and vocabulary related to the process of listening, listening to nonverbal and verbal messages, and listening to ourselves.

Part Two, "Practicing Sensible Listening," applies the information discussed in Part One to five specific listening settings that we experience daily: 1) listening to understand—Comprehensive Listening, 2) listening to help—Therapeutic Listening, 3) listening to make decisions—Critical Listening, 4) listening to purchase—Consumer Listening, and 5) listening to enjoy—Appreciative Listening. The final chapters develop applications for Listening in Partnerships and Improving Listening.

❑ *Awareness Exercises* ❑

The exercises at the end of each chapter are a means of reinforcing and expanding the material to actual listening experiences in your own lives. These exercises provide a structure to focus on personal listening concerns. Reader feedback from the first three editions of *Sensible Listening* strongly confirms the value of these exercises in helping apply listening principles and skills in face-to-face communication settings. I hope you will find these exercises thought provoking and a source of discussion. The "Awareness Database" forms are used for compiling information and investigating various aspects of listening.

❑ *Fourth Edition Features* ❑

The chapters in this fourth edition have been rearranged and restructured for a couple reasons. First, is to clarify message variables in the process of listening. Second, is to end the book with a structured program to improve listening.

With the restructuring, the discussion of message variables goes from general ideas in Chapter 2 to more specific message forms in Chapters 3 and 4. This means Chapter 2 "Listening and the Process of Communication," (which discusses a general view of messages) is immediately followed by the chapter covering nonverbal messages, "Listening Holistically." The next chapter, "Listening to Communication Movement," expands the idea of nonverbal messages as movement forces behind the words. I hope this restructuring clarifies the levels of messages that exist in communication transactions and, of course, messages are all we can listen to.

I put the chapter, "Listening Improvement" at the end, so the reader has easy access to a listening overview. This chapter can be quickly consulted for listening preparation, strategies to use while listening, and debriefing when the listening session is finished.

❑ *Acknowledgments* ❑

The fourth edition could not have been completed without the help of many people. John D., Ellen, Anne, Matt, and Kathryn Kaufmann, Ray Dearin, Martha Atkins, Pat Gouran, Clay Gurganus, Bob Nady, Connie Younger, Bert Miller, Rudy Verderber, Al Paul, Warren Gore, Ted Kennedy, Jr., Dave Palrang, Russ Canute, Dick Warren, Dirk Scholten, Tony Bible, John Fritsch, Dennis Hildreth, Linda Trudeau, and Renee Fosselman—Thank You.

Paul J. Kaufmann

PART ONE

A Background for Sensible Listening

1 Listening in the Organization

The goal of this chapter is to explain the significance of listening as it functions in all organizations. The skills of writing and speaking have been studied for thousands of years; listening, however, has only been examined as an important part of our communication process within the last forty years. It has been in the last two decades that entire texts are devoted to listening. Now, over 400,000 sites are located on one browser alone when a search for "listening" is run.

Active listening—which is *attending with all of our senses to gain meaning*—is central to all organizational communication. No matter what role we take—parent, spouse, manager, lawyer, clergy, physician, teacher, salesperson, technician—we will be listening at least one-half of the time. According to one report, sixty percent of employee time in North American businesses is spent listening.[1] Executives are reported to spend sixty-three percent of their time listening.[2]

In addition, people at all organizational levels express concern about the importance of listening in carrying out their daily responsibilities. A production manager of a large corporation realized that his entire job was anchored in listening:

> I listen to the words, the feelings, the needs of my people; I listen to the current climate. Are workers content? Are new innovations making certain areas of production insecure? Is there dissatisfaction? I listen to the machines. I listen to the flow of the whole operation. My office door is open, and so are all my senses, so I can listen to find the meaning of all the information coming at me.[3]

Managers and executives are increasingly aware that success depends on listening. Lee Iacocca, past Chief Executive Officer of Chrysler Corporation, in his book, *Iacocca,* sums up the importance of listening within his organization:

> I only wish I could find an institute that teaches people how to listen. After all, a good manager needs to listen at least as much as he needs to talk. Too many people fail to realize that real communication goes in both directions.
>
> You have to be able to listen well if you're going to motivate the people who work for you. Right there, that's the difference between a mediocre company and a great company. The most fulfilling thing for me as a manager is to watch someone the system has labeled as just average or mediocre really come to his own, all because someone has listened to his problems and helped him solve them.[4]

Peters and Waterman's *In Search of Excellence*, a classic analysis of successful business cultures, arrives at the simple yet significant conclusion that "The excellent companies are better listeners."[5]

Listening is important for success in family, business, and professional settings. Parents, spouses, corporate leaders, and other professionals express concern about listening, which can strengthen or erode relationships, and save or waste time and money. Listening influences three crucial resources: people, time, and money.

❑ Listening and People ❑

Psychologists emphasize the importance of listening as it develops and maintains relationships, which are essential for organizational success. Carl Rogers, the widely-read founder of Rogerian Psychology, emphasized the importance of listening in establishing and maintaining relationships to achieve productive goals. He believed so strongly in investing in relationships that he developed a specialized form of attending to people called "*empathic listening*" which instructs the listener

> to see the expressed idea and attitude from the other person's point of view; to sense how it feels to him; to achieve his frame of reference in regard to the idea he is talking about.[6]

Further evidence of the importance of listening in building and maintaining relationships comes also from counselors who listen to people's everyday problems. As one counselor stated:

> My profession is to listen and to allow my clients to solve their own problems. So many of their problems have to do with spouses, relatives, bosses, teachers, co-workers, and friends. The single biggest problem that keeps repeating itself over and over is that people don't listen to each other. If I were to start a school of human problem solving, the basic course would be in communicating: with *listening* at its core.[7]

The part listening plays in relationships is difficult to measure, since many human variables are involved. However, one investigation shows consistently that active listening builds productive relationships, and non-active listening weakens relationships.[8]

In this study, participants were interviewed in a one-to-one setting about their future plans. The participants were not aware that active or non-active listening was being examined as an aspect of relationship development. These participants (the interviewees) were asked general questions by the interviewer, and were given time to respond at length. The interviewer did little talking, but listened either actively or non-actively to the interviewee's responses to the questions.

Each interview, then, involved two people: an interviewer, who listened actively or non-actively, and an interviewee, who did most of the talking. *Active listeners* were interviewers who were trained to be 1) relaxed, 2) have appropriate eye contact with the interviewee, and 3) respond verbally to the message being sent by the interviewee. *Non-active listeners* were interviewers who were trained to exhibit tension, have weak eye contact, and offer minimum verbal responses to the interviewee. After an eight- to ten-minute interview session, the interviewees (who did most of the talking) were asked to judge these active or non-active listening interviewers using a scale of descriptive adjective pairs (positive-negative, friendly-unfriendly and so on).

As the table of adjective pairs shows, active listeners were judged to be more helpful and competent, and the interviewees expressed a desire to return for another interview with the active listeners. The interviewees who received non-active listening judged their interviewers to be unlikeable and incompetent, and they did not want to return to that interviewer.

The Effect of Active and Non-Active Listening on Relationships

Adjectives that interviewees used to describe:

Active Listening Interviewers*	Non-active Listening Interviewers**
positive	negative
understanding	ununderstanding
skillful	clumsy
competent	incompetent
decisive	indecisive
conscientious	indifferent
industrious	lazy
secure	insecure
concerned	unconcerned
stable	hostile
friendly	unfriendly
helpful	indifferent

* Interviewees said they wanted to return for another interview.
** Interviewees said they did not want to return for another interview.

Observing people in a variety of organizational settings, from businesses to families, confirms that active listening builds strong relational bonds. Active listening strengthens relationships at all levels in the organization—from family members to customers to vendors to coworkers to managers.

The late Sam Walton, the driving force behind Wal-Mart and Sam's Stores, was one of the biggest success stories in America. Wal-Mart and Sam's Stores expanded to the point that Sam Walton was one of the richest men in America. The key to his success sounds quite simple. Sam Walton cared about his employees and his customers. He referred to his employees as associates, and most important of all, *he listened to them.* Walton would go into his stores, talk with and listen to the clerks and stockers, and see for himself what needed to be changed or improved.

Today, executive offices at Wal-Mart are virtually empty. Managers spend their time walking the floors with employees. Employees at all levels get involved and work together to contribute to Wal-Mart's success. Walton emphasized the empty headquarters rule: "The key is to get into the store and *listen.*"[9]

In a similar vein, Chrysler's Lee Iacocca, also emphasized the principle that active listening effectively promotes involvement and improves relationships. He writes:

> In corporate life, you have to encourage all your people to make a contribution to the common good and to come up with better ways of doing things. You don't have to accept every single suggestion, but if you don't get back to the guy and say, "Hey, that idea was terrific," and pat him on the back, he'll never give you another one. That kind of communication lets people know they really count.[10]

Successful, productive relationships grow inside and outside of an organization from analyzing and getting to know people involved. Listening is the key to this "people analysis." We analyze our relationships with peers, administrators, supervisors, clients, consumers, competitors, and investors. We listen to their attitudes and values over a period of time to determine their concern, confusion, or enthusiasm for particular projects and ideas. From the information gained, we can better adapt to the needs of those involved.

Listening within the organization is a basic step in improving relationships and implementing or improving programs. We listen so we can respond appropriately. We may take a few seconds to listen to the situation and analyze it, or we may need weeks or months of listening to develop an effective and acceptable plan. For example, simply listening to a group during a coffee break conversation can elicit valuable information about the work environment. Or, the listening might be over a longer period of time. One manufacturing organization spent three years in interviews with foremen and workers before implementing a new production strategy.[11] Three years of listening and analyzing ideas generated through these interviews was crucial, because the listening provided needed information for implementing the new production strategy. Additionally, since the employees knew they were being listened to, and were directly involved in the process of change, their ownership of the production plan helped in the successful implementation of the production changes.

Before marketing an idea or a product *outside* the organization, we must listen to recognize and understand the needs and expectations of the client. For example, Digital Corporation relies on its customers to suggest new uses for microcomputers. It is apparent that Digital encourages active listening in its relationships with customers, which leads to innovative uses for their products.[12]

Inside and outside the organization, active listening builds and strengthens relationships and is at the center of any successful organization. Through people analysis, procedures can be implemented and needs met. *Time*, the second crucial resource to be discussed, is also affected by active listening.

❑ Listening and Time ❑

Active listening saves time, certainly a highly valued commodity. In some professions, listening must occur in the shortest amount of time possible. Time is literally a matter of life and death in the case of the nurse answering the telephone at an emergency ward, because this professional must listen to symptoms, addresses, and directions calmly and accurately. A listening error in this demanding time frame could result in a significant loss of time and ultimately the loss of a life.

On a less dramatic scale, imagine situations where non-active listening has cost time and a certain amount of frustration: directions that were misunderstood, or items that were forgotten. These lapses in listening, although not life or death incidents, cost time and make our daily functioning less efficient.

On the job, seemingly short listening lapses can build into substantial lost time. A corporation with 3000 employees who each lose just ten minutes in a given day because of non-active listening, has lost five hundred hours of productive time!

Time is saved by associates who are sensible, active listeners. We meet with them, and we listen to each other. Appropriate questions are asked, and we paraphrase or repeat each other's ideas for clarity. When we leave each other, we are reasonably sure that we understand each other, and as we enter another phase of our work world, we have accurate ideas and plans in mind. Because of effective listening, our time is used productively, and few time-wasting problems will result from misunderstanding.

Communication experts[13] have studied the effects of listening on the *accuracy* of a verbal message, and the amount of *time* taken to communicate the message. Their goal was to determine which *listening* behaviors would achieve accurate understanding of a message in the least amount of time. They developed a message which involved instructions for drawing five rectangles in a specific pattern, and the senders of the message would either listen actively or not listen actively to feedback (questions and comments) from the listener.[14]

In the *non-active listening* part of the study, the sender described the rectangles as well as possible but would not respond to the questions. The receivers were discouraged from commenting or questioning while they attempted to draw the shapes as they were described by the sender. When the sender was finished, the receivers were instructed to write their feelings about the message.

In the *active listening* part of the study, the sender again described a series of rectangles in a particular pattern, but responded to verbal and nonverbal feedback. That is, the sender listened and took time to respond to receiver concerns, which focused on the size and position of the shapes they were drawing. As in the non-listening part of the study, the participants in this part of the study were asked to write their feelings about the message.

This study found that senders who did not listen to feedback were not understood, and few receivers completed their drawings accurately. However, the task was completed quickly. Participants in this non-active listening part recorded feelings of anger, frustration, and low morale, because they felt the sender did not care about their performance during the drawing task.

When the sender describing the rectangle patterns was listening and responding to feedback from the receivers, the accuracy of the message significantly increased. Most of the drawings were correct. The task, however, took substantially more time (three, four times longer) than the non-listening part. The receivers reported that they felt comfortable and confident, and morale was high, because they believed the sender cared about their work.

This study demonstrates that messages are accurately received if the sender listens actively and responds to feedback. However, listening and responding to feedback takes time, so *initially*, increasing accuracy through active listening takes more time. Importantly, as the active listener repeated the directions to different groups, the accuracy of communication remained high, *and the amount of time taken to give the directions became progressively shorter each time the directions were given.* However, even when repeating directions to different groups, *the non-active listening sender never achieved high accuracy.*

What happened in this study? Why did active listening heighten the accuracy of the message and ultimately save time? One answer is that with each message, the sender who actively listens is eventually able to anticipate questions from a new group of receivers, because she has taken the time to listen to the questions and concerns of the previous group. The actively listening sender develops a helpful vocabulary for giving directions, and therefore, eventually anticipates what questions are going to be asked, because she has listened to similar feedback and questions from previous groups.

Listening's Impact on Accuracy and Time
With little or no listening experience

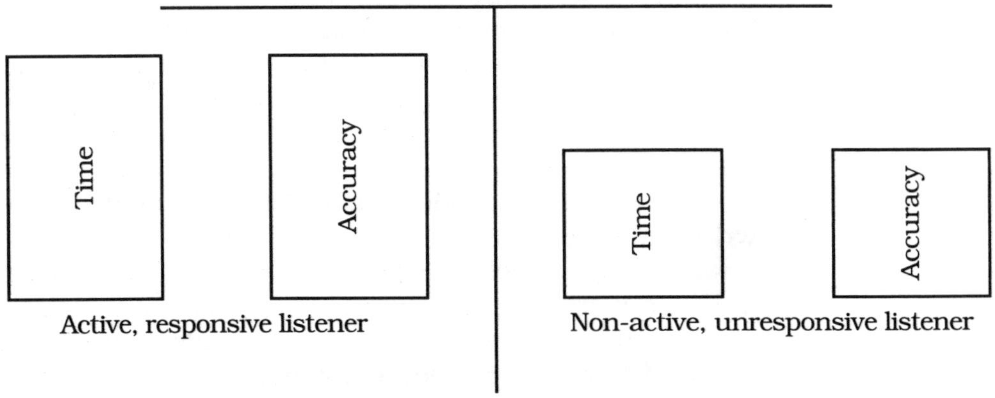

Listening's Impact on Accuracy and Time
With listening experience

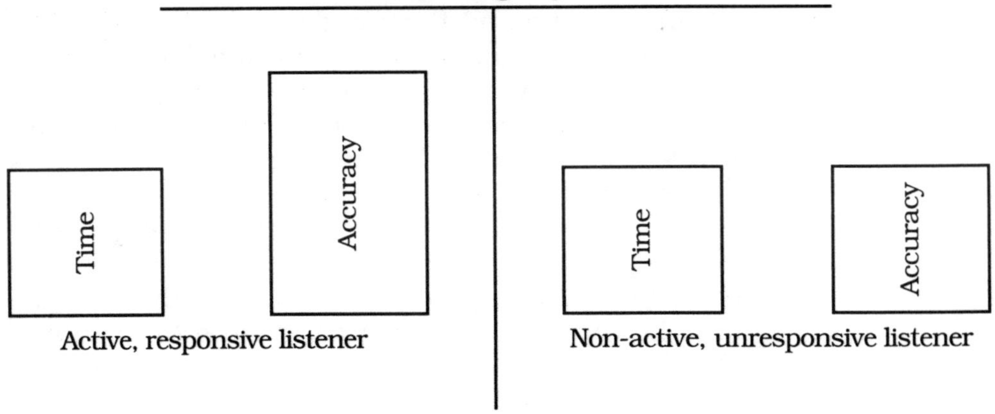

The key finding in this study is this: after each communication experience, the active, responsive listener will communicate more accurately in less time. Eventually, with active listening, the time needed to communicate accurately will shrink to the same amount of time that it takes the non-active listening sender to communicate with little or no accuracy.[15]

What do these findings mean to the organization? The farsighted organization that is concerned with accurate and timely communication should value active listening and encourage feedback. It must take the time to listen actively to new employees and build a culture that values listening. Instances where feedback and active listening have been ignored might result in frustration, wasted time, or improperly completed projects.

One of the differences between active and non-active listening is the crucial resource of time. If the organization is willing to encourage active listening, it will earn the benefits of greater message accuracy communicated in the shortest time possible.

Active listening affects the productivity of people and the effective use of time in the organization. The final resource that will be discussed in this chapter is listening and money.

❑ Listening and Money ❑

Organizations need productive people, good use of time, and adequate money to operate effectively. Generally, money is one measure of an efficient, productive organization. In a newspaper article entitled, "Poor Listening is Big Problem for Business," the chief executive officer of Sperry Corporation is quoted:

> Poor listening is one of the most significant problems facing business today. Business relies on its communications system, and when it breaks down, mistakes can be very costly. Corporations pay for their mistakes in lower profits, while consumers pay in higher prices.[16]

This Sperry Corporation executive acknowledges that the breakdown in the communication process is attributed to a lack of listening skills, and because of this poor listening, profits go down and prices higher. Sperry is one of several major international organizations that recognizes the value of active listening in determining profit margins.

American Airlines saved money by listening to a flight attendant who noticed that the olives on passengers' salads were not being eaten. Not a single passenger complained when they stopped serving olives, and American Airlines saved $40,000.[17]

In its thorough examination of effective organizations, the authors of *In Search of Excellence* describe a store in Norwalk, Connecticut, called Stu Leonard's Dairy. At the time of the documentary, this store carried 750 items, while the average store carried 16,000 items. Leonard's store grossed $1.5 million per week; the average store grossed $200,000 in a good week. Leonard's store grossed $80 million per year; the average store, $10.5 million per year. Compared to the average grocery store, Leonard's store was small, yet yielded much higher profits. Clearly, the operators of this little store were doing something different; they were actively listening to customers' needs and as a result earning substantially more money.

Stu Leonard attributed the success of the little store to listening. "I went around to the customers' side of the table; I keep an ear to the ground and keep listening to customers. I keep listening and doing what they say." Since the time he adopted the philosophy of actively listening, profits have grown, and he has made twenty-four additions to his store.

Stu Leonard carried out his philosophy of active listening by listening to his customers as they shopped in the store, and, in addition, he arranged special meetings to listen to them. Every other Saturday, customers met in the store conference room to share their views of procedures and products. Stu Leonard and his associates listened to them and, whenever possible, put their customers' suggestions into practice. In addition to these face-to-face meetings, customers had the opportunity to use a suggestion box for written feedback.

Clearly, Stu Leonard believes that customer relations are the number one priority; he and his associates listen to the customers for needed information and give them what they want. Regarding revenue, this active listening helped Stu Leonard's Dairy gross nearly 70 million dollars more than the average comparable grocery store.[18]

The examples with Sperry Corporation and Stu Leonard's grocery show that active listening can increase profits and help expand an organization. Non-active listening can have the opposite effect; it can erase profit and diminish the effectiveness of an organization.

Non-active listening, which ignores feedback, has resulted in major human and financial disasters. The oil tanker *Exxon Valdez* running aground in Alaska, the Union Carbide plant explosion in India, and the Bay of Pigs invasion in Cuba are tragic incidents which resulted from faulty listening. The captain of the *Exxon Valdez* did not listen to his crew or to the sea and terrain; instead, he remained in his cabin, allowing the first officer to pilot the ship; the plant operators in India did not listen to employees' warnings of danger; the group planning the Bay of Pigs invasion did not listen to the facts and figures involved.

Two other tragedies that occurred as the result of faulty listening are described in more detail here. The first describes listening errors between a flight crew and air traffic control. The second highlights listening problems between engineers and management involved in the *Challenger* space shuttle project. Both ended in a loss of lives and monetary resources.

On March 27, 1977, KLM flight 4805, a Boeing 747 carrying 248 passengers, began its take-off on runway 1-2. At the same time Pan Am Flight 1736, another 747 with 335 passengers aboard, came out of the fog and mist at the end of the same runway. The resulting crash was the worst in aviation history: 576 people lost their lives; two multimillion dollar 747s were destroyed, and damages reaching into the hundreds of millions were incurred because of faulty listening. This is the sequence that led to the crash of two airplanes that never became airborne.

The air traffic control tower told the Pan Am 747 to taxi to the third ramp—ramp C-3—but perhaps the Pan Am crew understood "first" instead of "third." The taped control tower voice reiterated: "The third, sir. One, two, three—the third, third, *third*." The instruction was then confirmed by the co-pilot. The Pan Am 747 taxied to ramp C-3, but the crew found a problem turning into that exit so they continued taxiing on the runway to ramp C-4, perhaps thinking they were to go to the third free exit.

The control tower told KLM to taxi to runway 1-2's holding position. KLM did, and replied, "We are now at take off."

Meanwhile, Pan Am was taxiing on the same active runway toward the KLM 747 to reach exit C-4. At that time KLM requested clearance to take off, and the control tower answered, "Okay, stand by for take off. I will call you." Apparently the KLM crew thought they had been given clearance to take off, because the KLM 747 began accelerating.

As they were moving toward exit C-4, Pan Am told KLM, "We'll report when we're clear [off the runway]," but this message apparently did not warn KLM that Pan Am was still on the runway. "We'll report when we're clear," were the last words before the impact. By the time the pilots realized that they were on a collision course, the KLM plane was going too fast to avoid the taxiing Pan Am ship.

The investigation of the tragedy acknowledged that the cause of the accident was faulty listening and interpretation on the part of the KLM captain, a man with 39,000 hours of flying time.[19]

On January 28th, 1986, the *Challenger*, a United States space shuttle, exploded thirteen seconds after launch. Nine astronauts were killed. Roger Boisjoly, a shuttle engineer, describes how the events that led to the tragedy were a mix of technical and listening flaws.

According to Boisjoly, the joint seals that caused the explosion had shown problems early in 1985. His team found that colder than normal temperatures allowed hot gases to flow freely into the joint and burn the O-ring seal: "At this time, we knew we had a serious problem, but officials said the information was 'too sensitive to tell anyone.'"

Boisjoly was outraged by this response, especially after he found a joint seal totally destroyed after a January, 1985 flight. He was so concerned that the next month, he and his partner presented a report detailing a solution to the joint seal problem. However, the committee that could have solved the problem did not act because, in Boisjoly's words, *"No one would listen to the material that we presented!"*

In a formal memo dated July 31, 1985, Boisjoly wrote: "If we do not take immediate action . . . we will lose a flight and possibly a launch pad." No response was made to this memo.

On January 27th, the eve of the *Challenger* flight, Boisjoly had his final chance to stop the flight. At an emergency meeting, he and his partner, Artie Thompson, presented a report with graphed data to emphasize the importance of redesigning the joint before another flight.

But the failure to listen continued. According to Boisjoly, "The officials were guilty of one of the most unethical decisions in history because they misconstrued and even ignored our findings in order to keep the shuttle on schedule." One official told them their data were "inconclusive." Again Boisjoly and Thompson warned against launching at low temperatures and showed the committee members photographs of destroyed joints from the January, 1985 flight. They would not listen.

Since no one had listened to his concerns and taken corrective action, Boisjoly's fears mounted: "I vowed not to watch the space shuttle launch that next morning." However, at the urging of a colleague, he did watch and after a successful launch remarked, "We have just dodged a bullet." Thirteen seconds later, the shuttle exploded.

Twenty-four hours afterward, Marshall Space Flight Center knew from pictures of the launch that the joint seals had caused the disaster. Boisjoly targeted faulty listening as the problem: "We were led down blind alley after blind alley and were told cold temperatures had nothing to do with it, when indeed this was exactly the cause."

During the Presidential Commission hearings, Boisjoly and Thompson told of the information they presented the night before the explosion, and how it was not listened to by the decision makers.[20]

❑ Summary ❑

Listening—attending with all of our senses to gain meaning—is central to the success of any organization. Successful leaders spend a substantial amount of their day listening, and they study and practice active listening to optimize the productivity of the three most important organizational resources: people, time, and money.

People are central to any organization, and they are most productive when their ideas and concerns can be expressed in an accepting, active listening environment. Effective listening in the organization establishes strong, satisfying relationships and encourages people to be a part of the organization. Actively listening to people outside the organization allows adaptation to new markets and new uses for products and programs.

Time, the second resource, is optimized by active listening. An effective organization will encourage active listening and feedback, which will initially take extra time. Ultimately, however, the active listening will result in the saving of time and an increase in the accuracy of communication.

Active listening increases the potential to generate money. Successful large international and small local organizations adhere to the idea that active listening increases business activity and revenue. Non-active listening not only lowers profit margins but can also result in disastrous losses of money.

A Consumer Support Management Magazine article carried this sub-title that encapsulates the importance to listening in an organization. "In this day and age the last thing you want to do is turn a deaf ear to your customers. If your company is not proactively listening, it's not customer-centric."

Awareness Exercises, Chapter 1

Name ______________________________ **SS#** _____-____-_____

Before responding to these exercises, spend some time paying attention to your listening and the listening of others. Pay particular attention to the amount and type of listening you do and to how others listen to you. Note how much time you spend listening.

Listening awareness exercise. Please answer these questions thoughtfully.

1. How many effective listeners do you know? _________
2. What do they do that makes them effective listeners?
3. How many poor listeners do you know? _________
4. What do they do that makes them poor listeners?
5. How do you rate yourself as a listener?
6. What do you do as a listener to earn this rating?
7. How much training have you had in listening?
8. What are the nature of the problems you have had because of faulty listening?
9. How many times in a week do these problems occur? _________
10. What are the nature of the rewards you have had because of effective listening?
11. How many times in a week do you feel you have listened well? _________
12. In what situations do you feel you listen well?

13. In what situations do you feel you listen poorly?

14. What percentage of your waking day do you spend listening? _________

15. Do you feel you are effective at understanding and remembering information? (A lecture, getting directions) Why?

16. Do you feel you are effective when listening to someone's problems? Why?

17. Do you feel you are effective when listening to make a decision? Why?

18. How much time in a day do you spend listening to enjoy? (Watching TV, movies, theatre, concerts, records, tapes, stories, jokes) _________

19. What is your most comfortable situation for listening? (one-to-one, small group, large group)

20. What do you do to make your listening more effective?

21. What people in your life have been the best listeners?

22. When do you find it difficult to listen?

23. Name an organization where active listening is emphasized.
    A. What behaviors tell you that listening is emphasized?

    B. What is your connection with this organization?

24. Name an organization where active listening is not emphasized.
    A. What behaviors tell you this?

    B. What is your connection with this organization?

2 Listening and the Process of Communication

Accurate and thorough communication is essential in any organization. It is the only means we have for understanding people and situations. This ability to communicate is the key to success in our business, professional, and personal lives.

In the example below, Donald F. Craib, Jr. saw a need to restructure the Allstate Insurance Company. For this major change to succeed, he realized the necessity for complete employee involvement. In this description of the restructuring, notice the emphasis he puts on employee involvement through communication:

> Right off, he announced his intention to reorganize the company.
>
> Then he did an even more remarkable thing: He asked employees—yes, employees—to tell him how to do it. . . .
>
> The effort wouldn't have succeeded had it not been for the emphasis that Mr. Craib placed on employee communication. That was a priority from the start. He beefed up Allstate's internal media and used them—*along with his own tireless face-to-face sessions with employees* (emphasis mine)—to inform his workforce of the details of the business, the increasingly competitive environment Allstate was operating in, and the firm's problems and opportunities.
>
> Ironically, amid all the signs of new sophistication, many employee-communication programs nevertheless are putting increasing stress on old-fashioned face-to-face communication.
>
> It may be primitive, but it can still be effective. Surveys reveal that employees prefer to get information firsthand from their bosses. Thus, many companies are emphasizing communication skills in their training courses for middle and line managers.[1]

This example illustrates that successful management involves talking with and *listening* to employees, and that these communication skills should be a central part of management training. Consequently, to meet these communication concerns, this text offers principles designed to improve listening in five of the most common settings: comprehensive, therapeutic, critical, consumer, and appreciative. Before discussing these listening settings, we first need to understand the process of communication and listening. In order to accomplish this understanding, this chapter defines communication and describes the process of communication witih a descriptive model.[2]

❑ Communication Defined ❑

Simply put, communication is the act of connecting with someone to share ideas. The *connecting* is through any of our five senses—sight, sound, touch, smell, and taste. The *someone* may be ourselves, another person, or a small or large group of people. *When we have communicated effectively, we have created a shared understanding of ideas, facts, or feelings.*

This complex process of communicating is one of the most important aspects of our professional and personal lives, and becoming an effective communicator takes knowledge and practice. The example below helps us understand the complexities of what appears to be a relatively simple communication situation. Notice the detailed decisions that seem to come so easily and naturally in this scene with an experienced and expert communicator—Lewis Lehr, past Chief Executive Officer of 3M Company. In this description of a morning meeting, Lehr increases the efficiency of the communication with his employees by 1) preparing for their physical comfort by arranging for refreshments and 2) preparing for their psychological comfort by sharing a pleasant environment, using preferred names, and creating a comfortable atmosphere for *listening.*

> They came at 8, the caller and five fellow production workers. On the top floor of the 14-floor headquarters of the 3M Company. Lehr was waiting for them in his office, with a pot of coffee. To put the men further at ease, he took them to the window, which covers the entire east wall, pointing out 3M's 435-acre industrial complex below and the Mississippi River beyond.
>
> Before the sugar was passed around, everyone was on a first-name basis. The men got to the point—a festering problem at their plant.
>
> Lehr listened hard. As 3M's chairman and chief executive officer, he was into his major responsibility to the corporation's 85,000 employees: communicating.
>
> "If you can't speak openly about your problems," Lehr contends, "then your problems shouldn't be attended to. And if, as a supervisor or manager, you can't listen to the problems, then you shouldn't be a supervisor or manager."
>
> The fact is that Lehr, 63, presents such an unaffected, easy-to-talk-to sociability that all echelons of employees in the giant manufacturing corporation feel free to stop him in the hall or in the parking lot for a chat.[3]

An analysis of this face-to-face communication shows some of the many details that an effective communicator considers in order to make a meeting successful. The details include planning the time of the meeting, establishing a supportive, friendly climate—both physically and psychologically—developing an openness to listen, and sharing on an equal, first name basis.

Communication consists of a number of elements, and if any one of the elements is missing, effective communication will not occur. Consequently, using a model of the communication process will help us examine the basic elements involved when we communicate. A model cannot completely replicate the act of communication. However, it will help us identify, understand, and adapt the communication process to meet our needs.

❑ A Communication Listening Model ❑

Before we can discuss and analyze the aspects of listening, we need to understand the fundamental elements operating during the process of communication. The discussion consists of two divisions of the model. The first division discusses four elements that are necessary at the most fundamental level of communication: sender, message, listener, and feedback. The second division of the model addresses three intervening variables: climate, culture, and noise.

Sender

Communication occurs between people or things. Because our main concern is with *people*, we will limit the discussion to people as senders.

Basically, the sender puts ideas into symbols. This means that the sender is primarily responsible for planning, encoding, and transmitting (through air, light, and touch) a message. The sender has the central role in the communication process. In a one-to-one or small group communication situation, the sending role may go back and forth between two people or quickly change from person to person as the tempo of the communication requires. In a one-to-one or small group situation, sender planning time may be brief, and the message may be no more than a sentence or a nod.

In a presentational or public speaking situation, the focus usually remains on the sender, who may spend weeks in the planning of a message which might last five minutes to an hour or more. Whether in the one-to-one, small group, or presentational situation, the sender is *primarily* responsible for planning, encoding, and sending a message. However, sender responsibility is not limited to those functions, because the sender is also a *listener* who decodes messages coming back from the receiver of the message. These returning messages from the receiver to the sender are called feedback.

Communicators have dual roles: the sender functions as a listener, and the listener functions as a sender. *This unique capability to carry out simultaneous sending and receiving in a face-to-face situation allows the potential for constant monitoring for accuracy and understanding of meaning.* The sender is responsible for planning, encoding, and transmitting a message. At the same time, the sender is responsible for listening to the feedback coming from the receiver of the message.

Message

The message is created when the sender puts ideas into verbal and nonverbal codes and transmits them to a listener. The listener decodes the message and attempts to create ideas in his mind that represent what the speaker intended. Since we are incapable of mind merging (for example, Mr. Spock of the *Star Trek* series, who could put his hand on someone's head and read thoughts) with other people, we use shared symbols—words and nonverbal cues—to express our ideas. The sender's process of putting ideas into shared symbolic codes is called *encoding*. The listener's process of changing the codes back to ideas is called decoding, and what is being encoded and decoded is the *message*.

A message may be intentionally or unintentionally shared with listeners. An intentional message is encoded by the sender with the intent of reaching a specific goal. The message might be made up of information, questions, repetitions, demands, and affirmations. Even though the sender has a goal she hopes to reach through the intended message, the sender might also be encoding unintended messages that distract the listener from receiving the intended goal.

For example, an intentional message might be to encode approval of a plan that has been proposed: "Yes, I've thought it over, and I think we should adopt the new plan." The unintentional message might come from the tone of voice and facial cues: no eye contact with the listener, and a lack of enthusiasm, or even a hint of doubt in the voice. ". . . I *think* we should adopt the new plan." Several nonverbal messages may be occurring here. Perhaps the facial cues and lack of excitement in the tone of voice, which contradict the meaning of the words, send additional information of insecurity or uncertainty about the idea, or maybe the nonverbal movements are pushing the listener to make a decision. (The discussion of nonverbal messages and communication movement is expanded in Chapters 3 and 4.)

Listener

The listener's primary responsibility is attending to the sender's message, decoding it, and attaching meaning as accurately as possible. Similar to the sender role, listener responsibility in the one-to-one or small group situation will shift back and forth or from person to person. In the presentational or public speaking situation, the listening audience member usually remains in the listening role, and feedback is primarily nonverbal.

The listener's primary responsibility is attending, decoding, and understanding the message. But just as the speaker listens while speaking, the listener is simultaneously sending messages while listening. We have all experienced listeners who send messages while listening: a smile, a frown, a puzzled look, a nod of affirmation, or even a question to clarify understanding or a paraphrase of the message content.

Feedback

Feedback is the nonverbal and verbal information the sender receives from the listener. The nonverbal feedback can be transmitted from the listener simultaneously, or the feedback may come after the sender has finished the message. In the one-to-one and small group situation, feedback is likely to be verbal in the form of questions and interjections as well as nonverbal—nodding, grunting, smiling. In the presentational or public speaking situation, feedback during the presentation is usually confined to nonverbal messages—nodding, smiling, frowning, looking puzzled, applause, laughter, or even sleeping. However, feedback time might be allotted during the presentation or at the end of the presentation in the form of a question/answer period.

Communication Model

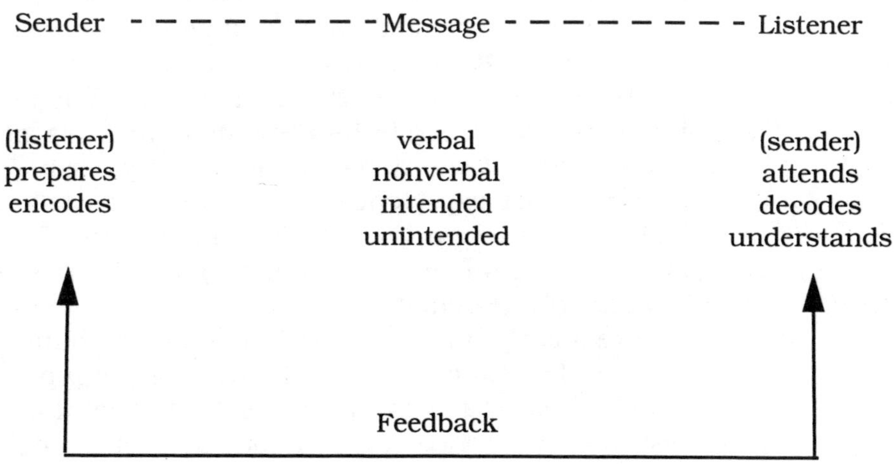

The first part of the model is comprised of the four parts. These are the central elements in our communication model. Communication will not occur if one of these four elements is missing: 1) the *Sender*, who originates, encodes, and transmits a message; 2) the *Message*—intended or unintended—which is made of verbal and nonverbal codes; 3) the *Listener*, who attends, decodes, and attempts to understand or replicate the message; and 4) *Feedback*, which is a message that goes back to the sender from the listener.

In addition to the four fundamental elements, there are three intervening variables that are present during the process of communication. The three intervening variables are 1) Climate, 2) Culture, and 3) Noise. These variables comprise the second part of the model.

Climate

We usually think of *climate* as closely associated with weather. We can measure many of the weather conditions such as temperature, humidity, barometric pressure, precipitation, and wind that combine to make the climate. These conditions, when combined and measured, give us an overall picture of the climate, which we can evaluate. When we judge the climate as beautiful, perfect, ideal, lousy, or ugly, we are taking an overall view of the conditions and judging them by our expectations.

For example, judging a weather climate "ugly" perhaps is a conclusion drawn from observing the temperature and precipitation as cold, sleet, and snowing. Our judgment that the climate is "ugly" comes about because the weather conditions are not what we desired. Perhaps we had hopes of skiing, cutting fire wood, traveling, or taking a walk.

Ironically, depending on our expectations, these same weather conditions could be judged "beautiful." For example, for mountain vacationers who are ready to relax by the fire in a well-supplied cabin, the conditions might be judged "beautiful." The duck hunter would see these same conditions as "ideal."

Similar to the weather, effective listeners attend to the communication climate or mood which is also a combination of events and human expectations. As members of families as well as the business and professional world, we listen to the communication climate and realize that the climate might also be judged as ugly, uncomfortable, or ideal, and we remember it can change like the weather.

An example of the effect of climate happened recently when an industry experienced some major dismissals at the highest management levels. One department manager who survived the shuffle, described her experience of the climate as follows: "Until things settle down, I'm taking a low profile. You can literally *feel* the tension in the air. Sometimes I wish I were invisible." The manager was describing an uncomfortable climate.

Frequently, unexpected circumstances happen that can change the climate. For example, the climate might change abruptly to a positive mood when you hear the news that, "Hal got an 'A' on that English test," or "We landed the BIG contract," or it might change to a negative mood with the news that "The stock market has crashed," or "There will be no Christmas bonuses," or "The first shift is canceled for Monday," as you interpret the positive and negative climate. Therefore, climate is an intervening variable that affects the sender, message, listener, and feedback.

Culture

Culture is the second intervening variable that we need to consider in the process of communication. Culture is a strongly held system of shared values, traditions, legend, and folklore. Unlike climate, culture is more permanent in the organizational setting. Where the *climate* might vary on a daily or even hourly basis, the culture remains a stable set of behavioral guidelines within the organization.

Every country, every town, every family, and every organization has its own distinct culture. *Culture is a system of shared values and expectations initiated and maintained by the leadership in the organization.* Peters and Waterman's *In Search of Excellence* illustrates the reality of culture in businesses and professions:

> All the companies we interviewed, from Boeing to McDonald's, were quite simply rich tapestries of anecdote, myth, and fairy tale. And we do mean fairy tale. . . . Nevertheless, in an organizational sense, these stories, myths, and legends appear to be very important, because they convey the organization's shared values, or culture.

Culture is not only present in the business and professional setting, but it also has significant impact on the *communication* within the organization. Peters and Waterman continue their discussion of culture by describing how it becomes the structure for effective communication.

> . . . the stronger the culture and the more it was directed toward the marketplace, the less need was there for policy manuals, organization charts, or detailed procedures and rules. In these companies, people way down the line know what they are supposed to do in most situations because the handful of guiding values is crystal clear. One of our colleagues is working with a big company recently thrown together out of a series of mergers. He says: "You know, the problem is *every* decision

is being made for the first time. The top people are inundated with trivia because there are no cultural norms."[4]

Culture can have a very specific impact on communication in a variety of ways. For example, one professional leader has developed the cultural value that clients are the top priority. Consequently, a shared cultural norm is that employees in her organization will always be positive and accepting. In this merchandising enterprise, the customer is so highly regarded that one of the shared cultural values is that no one comes to the job in a bad mood. In fact, coming to work in a good mood is part of the job description. Needless to say, with this expectation as a cultural value, the employees are always positive and helpful to the customers.

These examples further demonstrate that culture is a system of shared values and traditions that are unique for every business and professional setting. Culture, as a variable in the communication model, affects who communicates to whom, how they communicate, and even the comfort level of the communication.

Culture and climate are intervening and interdependent variables that function along with noise within the communication process. Noise, the third variable is any interference in the communication process.

Noise

Noise is any interference in the communication system. It can stop communication, so that no understanding takes place. For example, two people may become so angry that they walk away from each other, or the noise can be minimal in an effective communication situation, where people put their feelings aside and exchange information. Much of our communication energy is spent in reducing noise, which might enter externally or internally in the sender, listener, message, feedback, climate, and culture.

Sender/Listener Noise

Although speaking and listening focus on two different communication roles in the communication process, much of the noise that affects both sender and listener is common to both. Noise affects the communication of the sender and the listener externally and internally.

External sender/listener noise is any outside distraction. External noise might be noticed with any of the senses: competing sounds coming from machines or voices, interruptions, or visually distracting movements, gestures, or colors. Some other less common sources of external noise could be odors, uncomfortable temperatures, or cramped and confining spaces. We have all experienced external noise in rooms that are too warm or cold, or where chairs are uncomfortable.

Internal sender/listener noise is distraction within the sender or listener. The noise might be physical, or psychological. Physical noise could be hunger, headache, lack of sleep, a cold, a sore throat, pain, or any physical discomfort that competes for our attention. The physical noise might be mild, taking little energy and concentration to overcome, such as being thirsty or a bit hungry, or the noise might be severe, a migraine headache or sharp pain, making any meaningful communication difficult or impossible.

In addition to physical internal noise, is psychological noise, which is in the mind. Psychological noise can range from minor internal messages—"I've got to give Arnie a call about Jan's marketing plan," or "Did I leave my keys in the car?" In the cases of minor internal noise, the psychological messages can be dismissed and the sender or listener can attend to the message. However, severe psychological noise can effectively stop communication. Internal concerns like: "Dad's health is going downhill fast, and I feel so helpless," or "I'll have to fire my friend Bill if he continues his heavy drinking," or "Jake's been avoiding me, I wonder if he's seeing someone else?" can become so distracting that communication can stop. Psychological noise, like physical noise, pulls the attention of the speaker or listener away from the communication focus and lowers efficiency.

Message Noise

As noted above, external and internal physical and psychological noise can affect the speaker's and listener's encoding and decoding of a message. The effects of this dysfunctional encoding and decoding result in message noise.

For a number of reasons, message noise might lie in the words or the nonverbal cues being encoded. The words may be technical jargon, or words that are not part of the listener's field of experience; therefore, the listener might decode them differently from the sender's intended meaning. Common words that we use to designate meals can be misinterpreted. For example, "supper," "lunch," and "dinner" might carry different meanings to different people in terms of meal time and amount of food being served. For example, *Supper* to some people means a light meal served in the evening. To others, *supper* means a large meal served at noontime; others think of *supper* as an afternoon snack between the noon meal and the evening meal.

Noise can also enter the message with words that have changed over a period of time. For example, computer technology has created different meanings for "hardware," "software," "on line," and the word "down." Time has also changed the meanings of words such as "pot," which has changed in meaning from a vessel to carry water to a plant that is smoked, or "cool," which used to be an aspect of temperature, but is now a measure of desirability.

Noise can distort the message nonverbally. One type of nonverbal noise occurs when the sender encodes mixed messages. For example, the words may be giving a message of calm reassurance, while at the same time, the gestures, facial expressions, and tone of voice are sending messages of concern and anxiety. The nonverbal messages of calmly, quietly, and politely saying, "I'm very angry," or in a flat, monotone saying, "That was fun," or "That was a good idea," might send confusing, mixed messages where the words do not match with the vocal emphasis. In these examples, the sender has encoded two different messages. The words are the intended main message, but the accompanying nonverbal cues create noise by presenting a message

that is inconsistent with the words. Therefore, the listener is confronted with the different meanings of two messages: the verbal message and the noise of the nonverbal message.

Message noise can be verbal or nonverbal. Verbal noise comes from jargon, words from different fields of experience, and meanings that have changed over time. In addition, noise can be created by mixed messages where the nonverbal and verbal meanings are in apparent disagreement.

Climate Noise

As discussed earlier in this chapter, climate is a combination of conditions and expectations. Climate can be a source of noise and cause dysfunction in communication when the atmosphere changes unexpectedly or does not meet expectations. For example, you arrive at your office with plans to review a complex procedural change with a colleague. When you arrive at your office door, you are surprised to see it has been covered with balloons and messages of "Happy Birthday." The whole climate in the office is one of festivity, and this climate certainly changes the communication with your colleague, at least for the time being. Another example of climate noise occurs when you are at a store discussing a purchase that you have been considering for a month. To your surprise, the manager announces that the store will be closing in ten minutes; that they have shortened their day by an hour. Your discussion becomes rushed and confused, and you delay your purchase.

In both of these examples, climate noise disrupted the communication. In the first example, the unexpected, festive, birthday climate made serious discussion difficult or impossible, for the time being. In the second example, the unexpected early store closing precluded meaningful discussion of the purchase, and the shortened time created pressure that caused delay of the purchase. In both of these cases, climate noise made communication dysfunctional.

It should be remembered that communication climate is not always noise. In fact, climate can encourage functional communication, and how we choose to deal with the climate can determine how effective the communication will be. An example of building a comfortable communication climate is discussed in an article entitled, "The Manager's Open Door and the Communication Climate," which focuses on the impact of climate and how it can support or threaten communication.

> In general climates are on a continuum from supportive to defensive. Supportive exchanges invite openness, but defensive remarks result in resentment or lack of communication. We would venture that traditional principles of management unintentionally reinforce or initiate defensive climates.[5]

This example emphasizes that climate can encourage or discourage communication. It also points out that we typically want to be supportive of effective communication, but we need to look carefully at the climates we create to determine if they are actually supportive.

Culture Noise

We have defined culture as long-term shared values, traditions, and expectations within an organizational unit, and that culture is generated by the leadership. When the cultural values are not shared, understood, or known, or when they conflict with other shared values from another culture, inefficient communication results.

Through organizational leadership, every group establishes its culture: its own set of values and expectations. We are effective in our communication if the rewards and punishments are consistent within the culture.

Cultural noise exists when there are conflicting cultures. For example, in manufacturing organizations, there are sometimes differing cultures between salaried positions, which are usually supervisory employees, and employees paid by the hour, who are typically involved in production. Noting these cultural differences, one supervisor remarked that when he was visiting with another supervisor in a one-to-one situation, he was relatively comfortable and at ease; however, when a production worker was present, neither supervisor felt comfortable, and the communication became dysfunctional because of the differing cultural values. The supervisors went on to disclose how the differing cultural expectations hampered effective communication:

> It was as though we couldn't be ourselves. We shared some important ideas about the job and the company, but the ideas and values that we were interested in were somewhat different from the concerns of the production people. One difference I remember was emphasized in a remark I made about a new marketing strategy we were considering which I thought was terrific. The man in production had just the opposite view. He felt the marketing idea would just cause massive procedure changes and do nothing but hurt production output. We certainly didn't share the same values on that topic, and our communication stopped immediately.

From this example, we see that the supervisor and production cultures differed greatly. One value difference dealt with marketing programs. The supervisors saw the new marketing idea as making the product more visible and increasing sales. The production worker saw it in terms of difficult machine changeovers and revised procedures.

Culture is a stable part of an organization. When the leadership at any level changes a valued tradition, it will create communication noise. For example, one large manufacturing organization had, for twenty-five years, given its employees a turkey before the Christmas holiday. One year, with no explanation, the week of the Christmas Holiday arrived without the expected turkey. A tradition had been broken. As a result, rumors, speculation, and low morale created cultural noise that affected the communication in the organization. Communication broke down because of value differences. The employees speculated that the withheld turkey was punishment for any number of difficulties which ranged from low production and poor quality control, to high numbers of accidents. However, management simply believed the tradition was outdated and not important any more. The cultural value that made the communication confused was based in the idea that the employees had come to value information as a cultural expectation, and management had failed to inform them that the outdated tradition of giving a turkey was going to be stopped: it was not a punishment; it was just not important any more. *From this example, we can see that cultural noise occurs when values or traditions are abruptly changed or ignored*, and the resulting dysfunctional communication can spread throughout the entire organization.

At this point, our communication model looks like this:

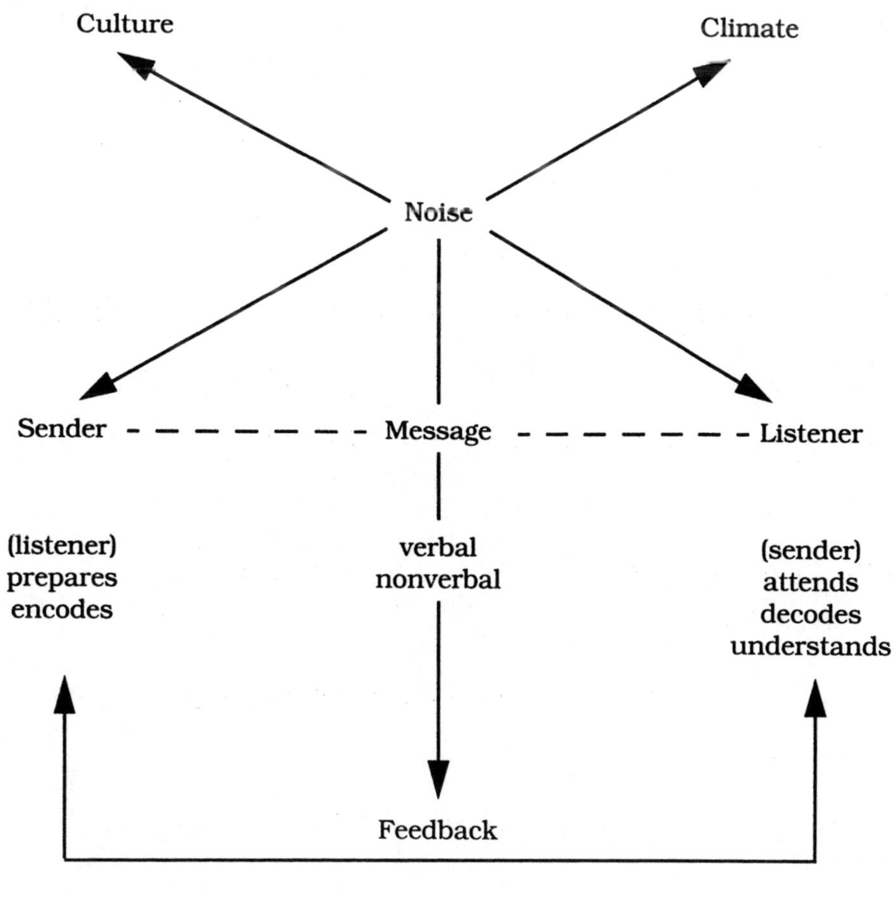

❑ Summary ❑

This chapter discusses the complex process of communication and defines communication as the act of connecting with someone to share ideas. To help understand the process of communication, a model elaborating on the communication elements and intervening variables is developed. The elements are: Sender, Message, Listener, and Feedback. The intervening variables are: Climate, Culture, and Noise. Noise is discussed as any internal, external, physical, or psychological interference in the communication process. Noise brings dysfunction into the communication process at any point it occurs.

In Chapter 3, the idea of nonverbal messages is expanded by exploring *holistic* listening, which is listening with both brain hemispheres and all five senses.

Awareness Exercises, Chapter 2

Name ______________________________ **SS#** _____-____-_____

Before responding to these questions, spend some time paying attention to your listening and the listening of others. Notice the amount and type of listening you do and to how others listen to you.

1. Define Communication noise.

2. List three examples of external noise that have interfered with your listening in the past week.

   Example #1

   1. Source of noise

   2. Situation

   Example #2

   1. Source of noise

   2. Situation

   Example #3

   1. Source of noise

   2. Situation

3. List three examples of internal physical noise that have interfered with your listening in the past week.

Example #1

1. Source of noise

2. Situation

Example #2

1. Source of noise

2. Situation

Example # 3

1. Source of noise

2. Situation

4. List three examples of psychological noise that have interfered with your listening in the past week.

Example #1

1. Source of noise

2. Situation

Example #2

1. Source of noise

2. Situation

Example # 3

1. Source of noise

2. Situation

5. Give an example where a confusing word interfered with your listening.

6. Give an example where a mixed message interfered with your listening.

7. Briefly describe someone who gives you clear feedback.

8. Briefly describe someone who gives you vague feedback.

9. Describe a communication situation where climate noise existed.

10. Describe a communication situation where cultural noise existed.

11. Give three cultural values of an organization in which you are involved. Name of organization:

____

Values

a. ____

b. ____

c. ____

3 Listening Holistically

The goal of active listening is to gain as much meaning as possible from each message. Examining holistic listening can help us reach this goal. The term *holistic* is frequently applied to medicine. It implies that health is the product of a number of factors which include genetics, diet, stress, exercise, and environment. At a given time, any one of these factors may affect health more than another, but generally, health as a whole is greater than the sum of these interdependent parts. Listening, like health, is holistic, and it also is the product of factors working interdependently. The factors in listening are the five senses and both hemispheres of the brain. When we listen, the five senses and the hemispheres of the brain are working to assign accurate meaning from the sender's input. Also, like health, any one of the senses or either hemisphere of the brain might have a substantial effect on listening, but generally, the whole meaning derived from listening is greater than the product of these individual factors.

The following narrative offered by a city manager exemplifies the power of holistic listening.

> On a city council I was working with, there were five members: a physician, an attorney, a teacher, a businessman, and a factory worker named Joe. During the course of a meeting, Joe said little, but he listened. He listened to the words, spoken and unspoken, and the flow of the meeting; he took it all in. When Joe finally spoke, usually at the end of the meetings, everyone gave him full attention, because his comments incorporated the important ideas and feelings of the whole group. Because Joe listened, he could put his finger on the heart of the problem and come up with helpful, acceptable solutions to their problems.[1]

Holistic listening is defined as *assigning meaning to all sense input, using both brain hemispheres*. This definition means that we listen to messages through our senses: ears, eyes, noses, skin, and tongues, and we interpret and evaluate the messages with the right and left brain hemispheres to create meaning. This chapter examines the concept of holistic listening by first discussing the role of the left and right brain hemispheres in the listening process, and second the role of the five senses in the listening process.

❑ Listening with Both Sides of the Brain ❑

In our society, we are educated to use primarily the left side of the brain. The creative demands of holistic listening, however, require that the right side be activated as well. Consequently, listening is difficult because by choosing to listen actively, we have decided to activate the less used right hemisphere of the brain to work together with the regularly used left hemisphere.

A comparison of left and right hemisphere characteristics will help explain the brain functions as they relate to holistic listening.[2] While reading the left brain/right brain comparisons below, notice that the left brain hemisphere functions are practical, rational, logical, evaluative, and concerned with symbols in the form of words, gestures, numbers. The right brain hemisphere is spontaneous, aware of the whole scene, creative, nonevaluative, playful, unconcerned with symbols, and intuitive. In short, the left hemisphere is logical and evaluative; the right hemisphere is creative and nonverbal.

Left	**Right**
Verbal: Using words to name, describe, define.	*Nonverbal*: Awareness of things, but minimal connection with words.
Analytic: Figuring things out step-by-step and part-by-part.	*Synthetic*: Putting together to form wholes, aural sounds.
Symbolic: Using a symbol to stand for something.	*Concrete*: Relating to things as they are, at the present moment.
Abstract: Taking out a small bit of information and using it to represents the whole thing.	*Analogic*: Seeing likenesses between things, understanding metaphoric relationships.
Temporal: Keeping track of time.	*Non-temporal*: Without a sense of time.
Rational: Drawing conclusions based on reason and facts.	*Non-rational*: Willing to suspend judgment, fun loving, playful.
Digital: Using numbers as in counting.	*Spatial*: Seeing where things are in relation to other things, and how parts go together to form a whole.
Logical: Drawing conclusions based on logic: one thing following another in logical order—for example, a math theorem or well-stated argument.	*Intuitive:* Making leaps of insight, often based on incomplete patterns, hunches, feelings, or visual images.
Linear: Thinking in terms of linked ideas, one thought directly following another, often leading to a convergent conclusion.	*Holistic*: Seeing whole things all at once; perceiving the overall patterns and structures, often leading to divergent conclusions.

As this left-right hemisphere comparison shows, each side of the brain is primarily responsible for processing different types of input. The left side responds to structured information in an analytic and logical way using numbers and words. The right side is creative and processes nonverbal input working mainly in images and pictures.[3]

To some extent, our culture and educational systems emphasize the logical and sequential left brain functions. For example, emphasis is placed on developing knowledge in mathematics, grammar, science, and logic, as opposed to the right brain functions of music, art, poetry, creative writing, and dance. Consequently, through conditioning and habit, the left hemisphere is used more than the right hemisphere. The fact that 80 to 90 percent of meaning is created in the right hemisphere from nonverbal input,[4] helps us understand the importance of right hemisphere activity when listening.

As an example of the importance of nonverbal, right hemisphere listening, picture a morning scene at your workplace. Your usually upbeat, energetic secretary says the words, "Good morning," as expected, but something is uncomfortable in the *way* the words are said. Her tone of voice connotes a somber feeling. How do you interpret this? In actuality, the nonverbal message in the voice has more impact than the words, "Good morning." Your right hemisphere is sensitive to this nonverbal message and creates a meaning that something is wrong.

What if a secretary or co-worker says nothing when a greeting is appropriate or expected? In this instance, the entire message is nonverbal. The right hemisphere attempts to attach some meaning to the silence, so we respond internally by asking ourselves, "What is wrong with Debbie today?" Then we may do a quick mental search of personal interactions: "Did I do something to cause her to react this way?" or, "Were there procedural changes that could have been responsible for the uncomfortable atmosphere in the office?" "Is she having problems at home?" The point is that holistic listening involves assigning meaning from *all* senses, not just hearing, and as the last example demonstrates. Sometimes there is nothing to hear, yet several meanings are generated from the silence.

Holistic listening relies on all working senses for input. People who are totally deaf can listen. For example, even though they cannot hear sound, they give meaning to input by listening to their other working senses—sight, smell, touch, and taste. The idea that listening is holistic means that listening is the integration of all of our working senses and seldom relies on assigning meaning from only one sense.

Holistic listening is a combination of the five senses working together. Listening holistically processes significantly more information input than senses working independently, because our senses and brains are functioning cooperatively, giving a more reliable meaning to the message-receiving process. Listening holistically can be compared to a basketball team. Each of the players represents one of the five senses: sound, sight, smell, touch, taste. The patterns and movements of the players are interdependent, and there is a rational and emotional bond between the players, similar to the bond between the right and left brain hemispheres. The players, like our senses, come together to form a team which accomplishes tasks which none of the players would achieve if playing independently on the court.

To emphasize further the concept that we listen to more than words, imagine yourself as a plant manager. A forty year old woman who was fired yesterday by one of your supervisors tells you the following:

> Yesterday I was talking with one of the punch-press operators when my boss storms in and begins raking me over the coals for a work stoppage I had nothing to do with. I stood there in shock. I was so angry that I wanted to yell back at him, but I kept my cool. But all day I couldn't get it out of my mind. No matter what I was doing, it haunted me. I finally got so angry that I burst into his office and told him just what I thought

> of him. I even let him have it for a few lousy things he's done in the past. He fired me on the spot. Last night I was pretty depressed, and all day today I've been trying to figure out where I can get a new job or maybe how I can get my old job back.[5]

What is missing that would help us get a better understanding of the situation? Would we get more meaning if we could listen to the tone of the voice? If we could listen to the facial expressions? If we could listen to the gestures and movements? It is frustrating not to be able to include these other nonverbal listening cues in the listening process, because we know how crucial they are in helping to form *complete* meaning.

❑ Listening with All the Senses ❑

It is estimated that sixty-five to ninety percent of our listening is directed toward nonverbal messages.[6] We listen to the space around us, to touch, to smell, to dress, to the environment, to time, to facial expressions and eye movements, to bodily movements and gestures, and to the tone of voice. The successful professional is actively listening to the verbal and nonverbal cues of a client, co-worker or employee. The professional listens for the meaning beyond the words.

Holistic listening is the process in which we actively obtain meaning from information received from all of our working senses, as we consciously use the right and left hemispheres of the brain. In addition to listening to sounds and words with our ears, we also listen to visual messages with our eyes, to smell with our noses, to taste with our tongues, and to touch with our skin.

Listening with Our Ears

The sense most commonly connected with listening is hearing—using our ears—and certainly hearing is an extremely important part of holistic listening. Hearing is sometimes called "the watchdog of the senses," because when we are asleep or daydreaming and the other senses are not actively listening, we can still be awakened by a smoke detector, a child's cry, or a siren. When crossing a street, we remind children to, "Stop, look, and listen." In this reminder the word "listen" means using the ears to function along with the eyes. The warning before crossing the street would actually be more accurate in the holistic sense if it were stated, "Stop, listen with your eyes, and listen with your ears."

Hearing is the mechanical and neurological process of noticing various incoming signals. *Listening* takes the incoming signals to another level and *assigns meaning to the signals.* To increase our understanding of the process of listening, we need to recognize the function of semantics and vocalics in order to assign meaning to these sounds.

Semantics

While signals have been thoroughly studied and understood as parts of communication, meanings are the least understood and analyzed, because a substantial difference between signals and meanings exists. Signals—particular words, sentences, or gestures—can be recorded on audio or video tape, but the meanings of these signals cannot be recorded, since meanings are inside the listener and are much more complex and subjective than signals.

Meanings we give to signals are psychological and learned from culture.[7] The study of meanings is called *semantics* and focuses on how situations, social systems, and cultures form the meaning we put on language. A primary function of listening with our ears in a face-to-face interaction is to listen to words and put an accurate meaning on those words. However, in addition to the semantic meaning we give words, we use our ears to listen beyond the words. The *voice itself* which is saying the words contains messages that may or may not be related to the dictionary meaning of the words themselves. In addition to using our ears to hear signals, we also use them to hear vocal intonations which add meaning to the signals. These added meanings which come from the voice are called *vocalics*.

Vocalics

The vocal aspects of holistic listening are called *vocalic paralanguage* which means there is vocal meaning embedded in the words themselves (we hear the words, but what is the voice saying?). We have all listened to messages where the meaning of the words changes completely because of the tone of the voice. Someone saying, "That's just a *wonderful* idea," with a sarcastic vocal emphasis on the "wonderful" can completely reverse the meaning of the sentence. Vocalic meanings are derived from voice volume, pitch, rate, pauses, quality, and vocalization.

Volume. Volume is the strength or loudness of the voice. A message sent very quietly might convey a meaning of secrecy—this is just for you, or it might convey the meaning that the sender is shy, or the receiver might infer that the sender has a cold. A loud message might mean that the sender is angry or wants others to hear the message, or the sender is hard of hearing and cannot adjust the volume appropriately.

Pitch. Pitch, the highness or lowness of the voice, also carries meaning. A higher than usual, tight sounding voice might imply a nervous, tense sender. A lower pitched, relaxed, steady voice might be more believable and credible. For example, newscasters with their trained voices speak at a lowered and less varied pitch in order to deliver an objective message.

Rate. Rate, the speed at which the sender speaks, carries meaning. For example, someone who speaks at a slow rate can give the additional message of being thoughtful, slow-witted, or tired. Consequently, as with any paralanguage, the slow rate of speaking may mean nothing at all—this person just talks slowly. Words that are spoken at a rapid rate can carry the meaning that this person is busy, is intelligent, is hyperactive, is angry, is a compulsive talker, is non-thinking. These are just a few examples of how rate can affect the meaning of a message.

Pausing. Pausing is defined as one to five seconds of silence, and these pauses in the delivery of a message create the additional meaning of speaking at a slow rate. We might attach a meaning of wisdom or thoughtfulness, slow thinking, or lack of preparation to the person who pauses frequently. Long periods of silence, which are more than a few seconds, might send the message of anger, boredom, comfort, thoughtfulness, or nervousness.

Quality. Through time and repetition, a person's voice can be recognized by its unique sound. For example, a child can recognize a parent or family member's voice quality, and eventually, grows to identify friends' unique voice qualities. The voices become extensions of personalities. The low voice with little variety might be perceived as more authoritative and masculine. A high pitched voice with variation might be perceived as artistic, or feminine.

Vocalizations. Vocalizations are signals that are not specifically categorized as words. "Hmmm," "uh huh," "uhm," and "ugh" are sounds that might offer some meaning. "Hmmm" and "uhm" might indicate that the sender is thinking; "Uh huh" might signal agreement, and "ugh," distaste or physical effort.

Vocalics is listening with our ears to the vocal aspects of loudness, pitch, rate, pauses, quality, and vocalizations. Listening actively to vocalics can add greatly to the meaning of the message being received. Moreover, vocalics can help us determine if someone is telling the truth. Research indicates that voice pitch is a better indicator of lying than facial expression.[8] Perhaps this is the reason the statue of justice has the eyes covered.

Listening with Our Eyes

Our eyes, listen to space—*proxemics*, body movement—*kinesics*, physical appearance, *artifacts*, and facial expressions and eye movement.

Proxemics

Proxemics is a general term for space. Proxemic listening is assigning meaning to space. In listening to space, we are first concerned with the organization of space, placement of objects and the directions and distances between people and objects. The general meanings derived from space usually lie in one of two categories: affiliative or private. With affiliative space, we might listen to the space and decide that the sender wants to connect with people around him; s/he uses space to say "I'm interested in you. Won't you join me?" On the other hand, we might listen to the space and assign the meaning that the sender wants some privacy, or some distance. This private space is saying, "Don't get too close." "Leave me alone." "I need some time to myself." Space can be manipulated and managed to be affiliative or private.

Observing how space can be managed is very informative. One Chief Executive Officer (CEO) of a large manufacturing organization thoughtfully arranged his office space. The CEO placed a large, tall desk and heavy leather padded chair in the back of the office near picture windows overlooking wooded hills. The desk faced the office door. A few feet in front of the desk stands a glass covered table that is short and round. The table is surrounded by short, plush looking chairs.

Upon entering this office, one might observe through listening to the organization and placement of objects in the space that this man is powerful, big, and distant. A person invited to have a seat in one of the plush low chairs at the low round table might find that this position has the effect of exaggerating the CEO's size. This same person standing in front of the desk, finds himself eye-to-eye with the sitting CEO. Eventually, the visitor sits in a short, plush chair and finds himself looking three feet up to the CEO. Consequently, depending on the nature of the discussion, the CEO might stand, walk around his desk, and sit with the person in one of the low seats at the round table. This change in space is dramatic. Proxemic listening at this point might tell us that this man is not so powerful, but very average in many ways, and friendly.

Territory is space that includes ownership of specific locations or geographical areas. All animals, as well as humans, have a need to control and sometimes defend territory to achieve a balance between their affiliative and private needs. Individuals set up their homes, studies, offices, or rooms to meet specific needs. Affiliative or public territories would include a booth at a lounge, a place at the lunch table, a table at the restaurant, or a seat in a breakroom. Private needs would include offices, study rooms, and parts of the home.

We listen with our eyes to determine if people have *marked* or laid claim to some territory. The mark may be as obvious as a name plate on a door, or in the case of public space, territory may be marked by the placing of personal possessions which say, "This place is mine at this time." If one were to walk into a lounge and put a briefcase on a table and coat over the back of the seat at the table, she would have marked that territory as "hers." If she left for a moment, she would be surprised and perhaps a little disturbed to return finding her case and coat had been moved to another table. In this situation, the person who moved the belongings either did not listen carefully enough to the visual mark of the territory, or the meaning was ignored and the items were moved anyway.

Personal space is another aspect involved in proxemic listening. This is space that we, as senders and listeners, carry with us. Personal space is like an array of circles around us. We stand in the middle in a tight circle around us and the diameters of the circles become greater as they get further from us. Imagine personal space as a stop action picture of waves after a stone has been thrown in the water. We are the stone, and the waves are personal space which move with us wherever we go.

We allow someone to enter our personal space depending on the situation and the relationship, and, of course, as listeners, we assign meaning to personal space. If we were to view the same people—same clothing, same room, in different situations—we could probably determine accurately whether they were being inducted into an honor society (a formal situation), or whether they were attending a family reunion. One of the variables used in making this determination would be listening visually to the personal space.

Just as we develop different languages in different cultures, and even different meanings for the same words within a culture, the meanings we attach to personal space become part of our culture, and the meanings can vary from culture to culture. Within family cultures, some members can function comfortably at close range and some function better at a greater distance. That is, members of one family may speak softly and closely, while members from another family might speak more loudly at greater distance. When members of these different families get together for the first time, they are likely to listen to the space and misinterpret it—assign inaccurate meanings. A family member who is accustomed to close interactions might think, "S/he is certainly unfriendly;" a family member who is accustomed to more distant interactions might think, "S/he is pushy; a little too friendly." Therefore, it is best to observe and listen to the proxemics for awhile in order to receive a more accurate meaning.

Becoming aware that holistic listening includes visually assigning meaning to space, helps us realize that space affects communication. We assign meaning to space as it involves the arrangement of an office, the type of territory, and the distance we create between people. We also listen with our eyes to body movement or *kinesics*.

Kinesics

Kinesics is the name given to body communication. We can imagine walking into our supervisor's office. She smiles and offers a chair. As the conference begins, we notice that she is relaxed, and we interpret this relaxation as a sign of her security and self confidence. We also notice that she is attentive because she is leaning slightly forward, facing us directly. We interpret this posture as showing interest, involvement, and even respect.

In another scene, we imagine ourselves walking into our supervisor's office. She glances toward us and waits for us to sit. As we begin the conference, we notice she is fidgeting with her pen and darting her eyes around the office, and we interpret this nervousness as a sign of insecurity. We feel that she is not paying attention because she is leaning away and is facing her desk. We interpret this posture as showing disinterest, uninvolvement, and disrespect.

In both instances we are listening with our eyes and assigning meaning to body communication, particularly body movement. We listen to the way people move when we are interacting with them, but we also form impressions of people when we are not interacting with them. For example, we put meanings on walking styles. Long, solidly planted strides might indicate confidence and security. Short, choppy steps, might indicate uncertainty and insecurity. Heavy, rocky steps might convey toughness.

Physical Appearance

Physical appearance and artifacts are also observed with the eyes. We listen to physical appearance in terms of body build and condition, as well as artifacts: clothing, make up, jewelry, and hair style. Some of the labels we assign to body build might include wrestler, football player, basketball player, gymnast, runner, swimmer, or model. Some meanings from body build might be expressed as: "She really must feel good about herself. She stays in shape and keeps her weight just right." "He must be having problems, look at the weight he's put on."

In addition to physical appearance, we listen to artifacts. Most artifactual listening lies in clothing and accessories. The style of clothing and accessories a person chooses can tell much about his or her organizational culture. For example, International Business Machines, IBM, has a white shirt, tie, and leather briefcase culture. Apple Computer Corporation artifacts are a blue jeans, sweatshirt, and tennis shoes culture, which indicate freer values and traditions in that organization. These written or unwritten dress codes tell us something about the formality and expectations of the culture. Moreover, on a daily or weekly basis, we listen to the meaning derived from the clothing worn at certain restaurants or theatres—some are casual, relaxed, and informal; some are formal.

Many job roles we play require a uniform. For example, a woman in an airline stewardess uniform quickly informs us of her role. In fact the symbolic impact of some uniforms carries such strong meaning that the occupation becomes synonymous with the uniform. For example, a badge is closely identified with a police officer, as is a fire hat with the firefighter, or a mail bag with the mail carrier. The businessperson's suit, and the mechanic's coveralls, although not as strictly defined, are also uniforms that give occupational meaning.

Just as we can assign inaccurate meanings to words, we can also process inaccurate meanings for artifacts. For example, some years ago—a friend of mine—a twenty-five-year-old man named Ron, was getting ready to go to a wedding. In those days, one fashion that was popular for young men was to wear a black turtleneck sweater and black pants. Accompanying this outfit, the appropriate jewelry was a gold or silver medallion about three inches in diameter (it usually looked like a sunburst or rays radiating from a circle) dangling from a chain around the turtleneck.

At the wedding reception, Ron was dressed in black with the medallion hanging from his neck. Another man of a different generation, age about sixty, listened with his eyes to Ron's appearance. To this older man, the medallion, which looked somewhat like an Olympic medal, meant something: Ron must have won that medal. So he approached Ron with a question:

Man: "What did you win it for?"

Ron: "Win what for?"

Man: "That medal." Pointing to the medallion.

Ron: "Oh, that. No, it's just some jewelry."

Man: "Come on, pal. Really, what did you win it for?"

Ron: "Seriously, nothing. It's just a decoration."

In the older man's world of meaning when a man wore something that large around his neck, it was a medal, and it *had* to be an award. The older man had listened with his eyes and had assigned meaning. However, the meaning was wrong; it was inaccurate, and as is often the case with inaccurate communication the miscommunication caused some discomfort and frustration. In fact, as the festivities progressed through the evening, the gentleman became more insistent on knowing the nature of the award. To put an end to the questions, Ron finally invented an act of heroism to satisfy the older man's certainty that the medal was won for something.

Facial Expressions and Eye Movements

We listen to facial expressions and eye movements, and when we do not have access to this visual input—when we are on the telephone, for example or on the Internet—we lose an important source of listening input. Facial and eye expressions supplement, clarify, and amplify interpretation of spoken words. This additional input is called *metacommunication*, which is messages about messages.

As holistic listeners, we can look at the other person's face and eyes to determine the intensity of what is being expressed. For example, an emotional expression, like a smile, is probably the most obvious, and when linked with direct eye contact, a smile can show genuine warmth in the accompanying words. Along with facial expression, the eyes can have a powerful metacommunication impact. During the 1960's struggles for racial equality, people identified what they called a "hate stare," which was an expression of intense eye contact that furthered the intensity of hate, by focusing on another person as a *thing*.

Women and men communicate differently with their eyes and faces. Generally, women are more expressive than men. They tend to smile more frequently, and their messages are more pleasant and positive. Consequently, when a woman's eyes and facial expressions are somewhat unpleasant or negative, she is viewed as much more harsh than a man who sends the same kinds of unpleasant and negative eye and facial messages.[9]

The eyes and face also send meanings that can coordinate interaction between people. Imagine yourself sitting across from a friend at a table in the library, and an acquaintance sits one chair away from you. You know something about the newcomer and want to share this information with your friend. To get your friend's attention, you quickly connect your eyes with hers, and she knows you want to talk to her. You both casually walk over to the drinking fountain where you can converse.

Changing amounts of eye contact can also have meaning. Decreased eye contact might mean, "He doesn't want to talk to me anymore." or

"Something is distracting her from our conversation." You may be conversing with your supervisor and notice that she is shifting her eye contact away from you. From this change in eye contact, you arrive at the meaning that it is time to close this meeting, so you thank the supervisor, and leave. At another time you may be in your supervisor's office when a secretary enters quietly and puts a memo on the side of the supervisor's desk. Neither you nor your supervisor gives the secretary acknowledgment through eye contact; instead you continue your conversation. This unspoken agreement not to establish contact with the secretary is called *civil inattention*, and it allows the secretary to function without disrupting the communication. In addition, increased eye expression can help us determine whose turn it is to listen and whose turn it is to speak. As the sending role is ending, the sender will begin to look at the listener more. These increased eye signals tell the listener that it is his turn to speak.

We have discussed holistic listening as a whole brain activity that processes meaning from ear and eye input. The next sense input that adds to meaning is *haptics*, which is listening to touch.

Listening with Our Skin

Tactile or touch communication is called *haptics*. Touch communication may be the basis for all communication, because without direct or indirect touch, we cannot send or listen to one another. For example, with speech, the sender's vocal bands vibrate the air, and the air is formed into words by the articulators (the tongue, teeth, lips, and nose). These words go through the air, and the vibrating air *touches* the listener's eardrums and sends them into motion. The mechanical energy of the vibrating eardrums is converted into neurological energy and presents itself as sound to the brain. In the process, if the air is removed, we can no longer hear the sound, since the air is an extension of the sender. The air, then, is a means for the sender to touch the listener.

Visual communications is also based on touch. Light is reflected from the sender and *touches* the cones and rods of the listener's eyes. This touching vibrates the eye receptors and presents a visual image to the brain. As with air touching the eardrum, the light touching the eye is an extension of the sender. If the light is removed, as in a totally dark room, the sender can no longer touch visually, and the input is lost.

Direct sender-receiver touch also communicates, and this narrative highlights the fundamental nature of tactile communication:

> I went through high school and college with a good friend named Greg. I knew his family well and spent a good deal of time with them. Our senior year in college, Greg's father died. When I arrived at the funeral home, there was Greg with his brothers and sisters standing at the coffin. As I approached Greg, words would not come. So without thinking, I took his hand and held it tightly. As I look back on this spontaneous act, I realize that touching is the basis for all communication; that is, direct physical touch works when no other communication channels seem appropriate or available.

Touch is a basic means of communication, and even though the channels of air and light are available as extensions to touch, other variables in the communication setting might require direct touch for effective communication. For example, a father hears the baby crying;

picks the child up and cuddles and soothes her through touch. It would be unreasonable for a parent to attempt to reason with the baby or discuss the situation—"What seems to be the trouble? Does your diaper need to be changed?" Instead, the parent communicates to the child by comforting her through closeness and stroking. When touch through air and light is removed as an extension of the sender, the only communication option that remains is direct person-to-person touch, which is a central part of communication.

The rules that regulate touch are defined within every culture; consequently, the meanings assigned to various touches are different from culture to culture. One researcher proposes that there are five categories of touch. Each category is described by the quality of touch, the body area that is touched, and touch response from the listener.[10] The five touch categories are: 1) Functional-professional, 2) Social-polite, 3) Friendship-warmth, 4) Love-intimacy, and 5) Sexual-arousal.

1. Functional-professional touches are basically without relational meaning; they are an expected part of the profession. The barber or hairdresser cutting, styling, and shampooing; the doctor touching to diagnose, and the tailor fitting clothing are examples where touch has no meaning beyond accomplishing a task.

2. Social-polite touches are regulated by the expectation of the social situation. Examples of social-polite touches would be an approving pat on the back for a job well done, or a social hug as a greeting.

   One of the most common social-polite touches is the handshake. Some researchers report that they can assign categorical meanings to different handshakes. These categories of handshakes and the meanings they give are self-explanatory: Bone Crusher, Pump Handle, Limp Digits, Dead Fish, No-release, and Winning.[11]

3. Friendship-warmth touches occur between family members and good friends. The relationship is not sexual, but it is one of deep caring. Depending on the situation, the friendship-warmth touch could be misinterpreted as a relational advance beyond that of friendship.

4. Love-intimacy touching progresses from the friendship-warmth relationship. This touch communication occurs between very close family members and lovers.

5. Sexual-arousal is touching that leads to and occurs during lovemaking.

Listening to touch can be extremely rewarding, because touch messages are usually connected with professional and social behavior, friendship, love, and sexual behavior.

The next sense is listening to smells, *olfactics*. Listening to olfactics is responsible for providing us witih substantial meaning, but it has not been as thoroughly researched as have other areas of holistic listening.

Listening with Our Noses

Listening to smell, *olfactics*, is one of the most basic senses, and it consumes a good deal of our time and money. Americans spend millions of dollars every year on changing how they smell and how their territory smells. Mouthwashes, deodorants, perfumes, colognes, sprays, furniture polish, and air fresheners are some of the marketed items designed to alter smell.

Three general meanings are given to smell: identification, identification/attraction, and attraction. Moreover, smell is also closely related to taste.

We listen to smell for *identification*. To identify leaks and the possibility of danger, utilities distributors put the "gas" smell into natural gas which is odorless. Chemists and physicians smell various compounds to determine the formula or composition. Certainly, if all of our other senses were not functioning, we could identify a musty basement, or a hospital, or a spring rain shower.

We may listen to smell and assign a combined meaning of *identity and attraction*. We identify the smell of caramel popcorn coming through a shopping mall, and we are attracted to the store to buy some. We smell a hint of hardwood smoke, and we are attracted to the fire in the living room; or to the roast turkey in the kitchen, as the aroma moves through the home.

We might also identify a smell and be repulsed by it—the smell is so foul that we are repulsed, and not attracted to it. The smell from a bus or a car burning oil might be easily identifiable as something wc want to avoid. One smell that is repulsive is that of cigarette smoke. Our society is educating us to have increasing negative reactions to it. Some families and businesses do not allow smoking in their homes or offices because of the immediate infiltration of smoke and because of the residual smell long after the smoker is gone. Most government buildings have banned smoking altogether.

Listening to some smells creates meanings which are attractive or repulsive. The smell may be coming from an unknown source, yet it conveys meaning: "I don't know what they're cooking in there, but it sure does smell good." "Mmmm, I really like the smell of what you're wearing." On the repulsion end, "By the smell of things, there must be a culture in its golden age living in the refrigerator. I think we have liquid lettuce again"; "There's a real bad odor coming from the sewer in the basement."

A final thought about listening to smell lies in the fact that *smell is closely linked to taste*. We listen to the taste of food with our tongues, and if our ability to smell is impaired, taste is also impaired. Consequently, the variables that apply to smell also apply to taste, and we put meanings of identification, attraction, and attraction or revulsion with certain tastes.

Identification is as simple as tasting and noticing, "This has onions in it." Attraction comes from a good tasting meal, and might reflect meaning about the cook: "He is a good cook," or "She cares about me because she cooks my favorite meals." Revulsion is also a possibility with taste: "What! garlic in the chile again?" The taste of garlic might mean, "He doesn't care about *my* dislikes." Someone might take a sip of wine and notice: "This wine tastes watered down." To the taster, the weak taste of the wine means, "Man, is he tight with his money." We listen to taste and assign meaning.

❑ Multi-Sense Listening ❑

We have discussed how we listen with our ears, our eyes, our skin, and our noses. The final aspect of holistic listening is applying multisense holistic listening to four aspects of our daily lives: time (chronemics), immediacy, power, and responsiveness.

Chronemics

Listening to time can be a visual interaction with a clock, a calendar, an appointment book, or the familiar list of things to do. Time also can be intrapersonal. For example, "When is the best time for me to do this?" "My best time to put together an outline for my report is in the morning; I can concentrate better then." Listening intrapersonally, people learn that efficient use of time will vary. Some people wake up ready to begin a project; others slowly gain momentum as the day moves along. We listen to time with our eyes and we listen to time intrapersonally.

We listen to interpersonal or interactive time with our eyes and ears. When two people are going to have a meeting, they need to coordinate their views of time. They listen to each other's concerns and commitments about time to decide if they are going to meet in the morning, afternoon, or evening. Having determined when they are to meet, they need to decide the length of the meeting. For example, if someone is willing to meet, even though the particular time is not optimal for that person, we might assign the meaning: "She's really interested in this project, and really wants to get it finished." Moreover, if someone says, "No, I can't meet with you tonight, I have to do my hair," you might assume that the project is not one of her higher priorities."

Listening to interactive time gives meaning about our interpersonal relationships. For example, when someone in a relationship wants to spend the best quality time in the relationship, a listener might conclude that the relationship is important to that person. However, if someone in a relationship wants to spend his or her best quality time outside the relationship with other people or projects, the listener might conclude that the relationship is not the highest priority for that individual.

Often, people cannot choose how to use their time. Jobs, family responsibilities, and various other commitments determine the use of time. However, when the use of time can be chosen, the listener can observe what choices are made and draw conclusions. Observing how people choose to use their time can give a great deal of meaning about what they value. The idea that time use indicates priorities is illustrated in the following narrative:

> When I was working on my doctorate degree twenty-five years ago I was involved in some demanding statistical analyses. Fortunately, one of my committee members, Dr. Warren was an expert statistician who was willing to give me some of his much sought-after time. He would meet with me on Saturday mornings and Sunday evenings, and whenever he could squeeze me in. Today, I cannot recall the specific problems we

discussed, but I remember him fondly for sharing his time and helping me. By giving me his time, he was telling me that I was important, and he believed in me.

When we listen to how people choose to use their time, we can begin to understand their personal priorities. When we listen to how people respond to cultural expectations of time, we can gain insight into their willingness to conform and adapt to cultural pressures. The North American culture is time conscious. If someone arrives late for a meeting, we might assign a negative, neutral, or positive meaning: "He doesn't care about this project," or "He's not prepared for the meeting," or "He must have had car trouble," or "He's probably been busy on something more important." Also, if someone keeps us later than the expected time for a meeting to end, we might assign the meaning, "She sure is insensitive," or "Doesn't she know I have to be in the shop now?" or "She cares enough about my understanding this procedure that she's willing to go overtime to explain it," or "I respect her for not being overconcerned about the time pressure to finish the report."

Time, when listened to carefully, gives additional meaning to intrapersonal, interpersonal, and cultural communication. Internally, it might tell us when it is best to perform a certain task. Interpersonally, listening to time can give meaning to the quality of a relationship and what someone values. Culturally, time gives us insights into a person's view of cultural pressures in relation to other values and expectations.

The three final multi-sense aspects of holistic listening are, immediacy, power, and responsiveness.[12]

Immediacy

Immediacy describes attraction, and it is measured by approach or avoidance behaviors. When listening holistically for immediacy, we are processing sense input that might indicate attraction or avoidance. For example, note the immediacy in the following statements: "He really likes that car"; "She seems very fond of that puppy"; "They seem really attracted to each other," and "She loves her job." There are conclusions drawn from listening to sense input that indicate attraction or approach behaviors, resulting in high immediacy. The following statements indicate avoidance behaviors and low immediacy: "She certainly keeps him at arm's length"; "He hasn't been inside a church for ten years"; "He wouldn't buy one of those if it were the last one on earth."

Power

Power is the amount of control a person has in a situation. It can be physical, psychological, or both. Physical power is determined by the use of strength and skill. We can listen holistically, for example, and come to the conclusion that one team or person overpowered the other. In relationships between adults or children, physical power is sometimes used to control. Psychological power comes from arranging and manipulating situations to gain control. It attempts to control through offering rewards or punishments which can be quite subtle. As listeners, we might assign meanings of power to a large office, a person's title—president, doctor, manager, supervisor, CEO, and the amount of space and money a person controls. A subtle message from a person with a large, expensively decorated office would be: "If you go along with my ideas and plans, I can reward you"; "If you don't go along with me, I can punish you."

Responsiveness

Responsiveness conveys the idea that someone is alert to what is happening. A responsive person is someone who is listening actively and effectively. When we listen to someone who is reacting to others quickly, adjusting eye contact appropriately, and attending in movement and gestures, we come to the conclusion that this person is alert and aware of what is going on. This person is listening with a high level of responsiveness, and responsiveness is the highest priority in active listening. Conversely, when we observe someone who is not listening attentively, who is slow to react, whose comments do not reasonably follow the flow of ideas, and whose eye contact and gestures are not appropriately adapted to the situation, responsiveness is low. Holistic listening requires us to combine the senses working interdependently with the effects of time, immediacy, power, and responsiveness. In fact, responsiveness is the most important aspect of listening—the title of this book, *Sensible Listening*—listening with common sense and all of our senses—leads to responsive interaction—the ultimate goal of human connecting. In turn, one can obtain an accurate meaning to the messages.

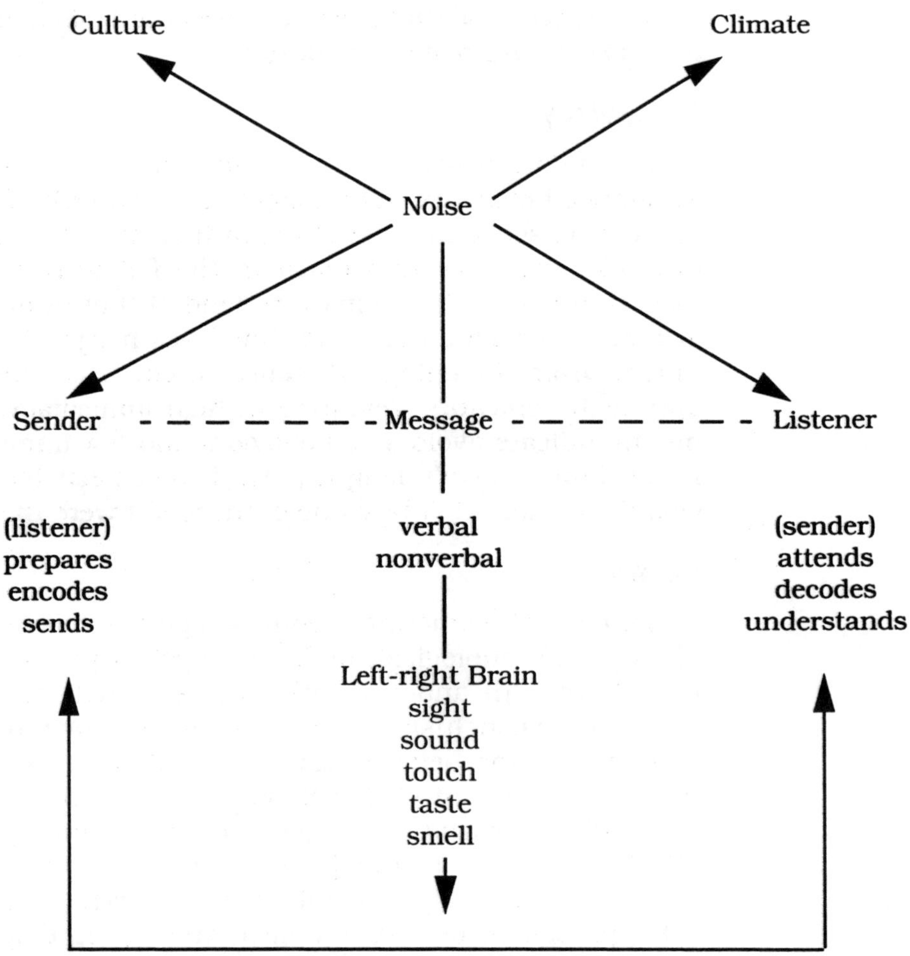

Summary

This chapter defines holistic listening as a creative process using both the right and left hemispheres of the brain and all sense input to assign meaning. It discusses the differences in right and left brain functions, noting that the left hemisphere is responsible for the logical and practical, while the right hemisphere is responsible for the creative and nonverbal.

The chapter examines the principles of holistic listening skills using all of the senses: sound, sight, touch, smell, and taste. Auditory listening includes semantics, vocalics, vocalizations, and silence. Visual listening includes proxemic, kinesics, artifacts, facial and eye movement. Haptic and olfactic listening include the meaning of touch and smell. In addition, holistic listening requires that we apply our multi-sense meanings to four aspects: chronemics, immediacy, power, and responsiveness, and responsiveness is the goal of face-to-face human interaction.

Holistic listening principles provide us with an awareness of how we use all of our senses in the listening process to make it more effective. We listen with all senses and process information with all of our abilities to gather information to create complete and detailed meanings. Therefore, if we apply holistic listening, we will achieve the success which comes with clear and complete understanding.

Chapter 4 "Listening to Communication Movement" completes our discussion of the listening process by applying the principles of holistic listening to communication movement.

Awareness Exercises, Chapter 3

Name Jennifer Sorensen **SS#** _____-____-_____

Before responding, spend time paying attention to the holistic aspects of your listening and the listening of others.

1. Describe someone you know who listens holistically.

2. Describe an office that uses space to communicate.

3. Describe an instance when you assigned an inaccurate meaning to a nonverbal message.

4. Describe an instance when you assigned meaning to olfactics.

5. Describe an instance when you assigned meaning to chronemics.

6. Describe an instance when you assigned meaning to vocalics.

7. Describe an instance when you assigned meaning to haptics.

8. Describe an instance when you assigned meaning to territory.

9. Describe an instance when you assigned meaning to proxemics.

10. Describe an instance when you assigned meaning to artifacts.

11. Describe a right brain hemisphere activity you enjoy.

12. Describe a left brain hemisphere activity you enjoy.

13. Give an example when you listened to smell for identification.

14. Give an example when you listened to immediacy.

15. Give an example when you listened to responsiveness.

4 Listing to Communication Movement

In Chapter 2, we explored the four fundamental elements of communication: Sender, message, listener, feedback, and three intervening variables: climate, culture, and noise. In Chapter 3, we extended the topic of messages by discussing nonverbal messages from sight, sound, touch, taste, and smell. This chapter focuses on the last aspect of messages—*communication movement*,* which is the energy or force behind a message. Communication movement is part of every interaction, and it adds substantial meaning to the message. This chapter will first explain the general idea of communication movement; second, define and explain the five communication moves, and third, relate movement to holistic listening.

❑ Communication Movement ❑

If we try to communicate with someone who is unconscious, or in a deep sleep, we quickly rcalizc that somc sort of movement is necessary for a response. If the unconscious person is capable of even slight movement, we can listen and assign some meaning to the movement. The smallest muscular twitch can give some cue, some signal that could be the basis for interaction. For example, there are stories where a paralyzed person's movement is so limited that all he can do is blink once for "yes" and twice for "no" in response to questions. In this situation, some minimal communication can take place. However, where there is *no* movement, there is no meaningful interaction. Consequently, a reasonable conclusion is that movement is required for interacting with others.

The idea that human behavior is predicated on some kind of muscular movement cannot be overemphasized, because *listening to movement gives significant meaning to the total message.* People will use the phrase, "Make some moves on someone," to indicate they are going to attempt to relate to someone by *moving on* or *moving toward* that person.

To understand the importance of this communication movement, it will help to start at the beginning. Philosophers argue that a thing is alive when it moves by itself. A fetus begins to move on its own long before the mother can feel it move. Ultrasound pictures show it constantly in motion, turning over, gesturing with its arms and legs, and opening and closing fists.

---

* Material related to Communication Movement copyright © 1972 by Ted Kennedy, Jr. Reprinted with permission.

The movements of the fetus, however, are undirected and involuntary. Even after birth, the infant behaves randomly, only slowly learning to bring muscles under control. Kicking, squirming, and grabbing evolve from reflexive to purposeful movements. The baby learns that certain movements help in picking up desired objects or in knocking down blocks or in getting a cracker to her mouth. Movement of vocal muscles comes early. At first cries may simply register general discomfort, but by degrees they soon indicate specific needs: food, diaper change, attention. Through arms and voice the baby discovers a world to move on and a world which moves on him or her.

As children, we learn to move more effectively as social beings. That growth continues through adulthood, where we learn more sophisticated behaviors that are based upon both physical and vocal moves.

As this discussion points out, in early life, movement is random. Later, it becomes purposeful, and it is used to communicate goals and desires. As we grow to maturity, a variety of verbal substitutes is developed to replace some of the physical movements used in infancy. Among these substitutes are words. As babies, we might throw a rattle out of the playpen for attention, but as adults, we would simple say, "Please come here for a minute." The goal would be the same. With maturity, we substitute words for gestures or touch. Adults communicate with infants through physical movement, which is the only language babies understand. The seven-month-old might get a touch on the hand for pulling an electrical plug; the two-year-old might be *told* not to touch it. In the latter case, the words are a verbal form of physical movement on the two-year-old.

By replacing words for physical movement, we reach goals. In effect, words function as physical muscular moves, but words are more efficient. For example, picture a father wanting his daughter to drive the car into the garage. He could say, "Please put the car away." This is more efficient than taking her hand and leading her to the front door, taking her to the car, opening the door, pushing her into the car, and finally getting her to drive the car into the garage. Saying the words gets the same results with much less energy. Yet in saying, "Please put the car away," the father is efficiently moving on her. It is apparent, then, that speech is a form of movement: speech enables people to move on others, causes them to change, and causes them to behave. In short, speech is the most common movement in interacting with others.

Speech, or verbal moves, often takes the place of silent, physical moves. Moreover, verbal moves often accompany and emphasize silent, physical moves. A teacher might place her hands on a student's shoulders while saying, "Sit at your desk." A more physical teacher might force the student to sit without using any verbal move.

We listen to silent moves in many situations: athletic events, music performances, art, drama, and just watching people in various settings. An example where silent moving occurs can be seen at some auctions where the bidders substitute subtle physical moves for verbal ones: a tug at an ear, a nod, a finger at the forehead. A verbal move, "I'll give $200," could be used, but in this case, silent moves are used instead. So, verbal and nonverbal messages grow from movement. Early in life the movement is random and unmeaningful, but later it becomes goal oriented.[1]

❑ Definition of Communication Moves ❑

Communication movement, then, is inherent in the communication process. Consequently, awareness of the five basic move categories—the PLACE move, the PUSH move, the PAUSE move, the PLEASE move, and the PULL move—will lead to a more complete understanding of the message.

The Place Move

The place move places ideas, facts, or feelings in front of the listener. It is usually a non-controversial move, and the goal in placing is to inform, describe, explain, and add to the listener's understanding. Below are some examples of Place moves that might be made during a conversation. In the Place move pairs, the first is placing of an idea or fact; the second is placing a feeling.

PLACE:

Idea or fact—"Maybe I'll go fishing later this week."
"A bolt on the landing gear of the tow plane is broken."

Feeling— "I'm *delighted* with the new procedure."
"I am *angry* because John ignored my suggestion."

Just as with physical objects, facts and feeling can be placed near or far from us. Imagine yourself as the listener, and listen for the removed, distant nature of these Place moves:

Distant PLACE:

Idea or fact—"I think I'll wax the car this weekend."
"The low temperature a year ago was 41."

Feeling— "I'm *upset* about the new bus schedule."

Again, as a listener, listen for the closeness of these Place moves:

Close PLACE:

Idea or fact—"The product flow might be smoother if I eliminate your division."
"Your work crew is the most efficient in the unit."

Feeling— "I'm *confused* about the procedures that came down from your department."
"I'm *impressed* by the effort you put into this project."

Of course communication movement is not confined to conversations. It exists in all settings, including speeches. Listen to the repeated Place moves of fact and belief at the beginning of this speech entitled "Restructuring America: Focus on the Core Business." Notice that each sentence is a place move.

> My talk today is about Corporate America's problems and what I see as solutions to those problems. Corporate America is in the middle of a major overhaul that is long overdue.
>
> We are seeing a transformation of Corporate America. We're seeing a new focus now that's where it should have been years ago. It's a focus on results, where size becomes meaningless. The emphasis is on creating value instead of empires.
>
> Corporate America's problems started soon after World War II with the emergence of professional managers. The professional manager was trained to minimize the risk and maximize the upside.[2]

Place moves do not ask or demand; rather, the sender is objectively placing facts or feelings for the listeners' understanding.

The Push Move

The Push move is just that—an attempt to exert force or pressure on the listener. Instead of physically pushing, the sender puts directional energy behind words and nonverbal symbols. Push moves are muscling, compelling, pressuring, or insisting. In the examples below, compare the dynamic energy of the Push move with the calm static feeling of the Place move:

Push—"Okay, get out on that floor and play the second half like you did when you beat Iowa!"

Place—"We have fifteen minutes of game time left."

Push—"Please shut the door."

Place—"The wind is blowing all the papers off my desk."

Push—"Drop everything, and put all your people on this project."

Place—"We're two days late on this shipment."

Push—"Get out of bed!"

Place—"It's already 7:30."

Push—"Let's try to beat last quarter's excellent record."

Place—"I see that our productivity is on the rise."

Push—"You start getting here on time, or you're OUT!"

Place—"I notice you're been late the last five days."

Push—"Stop, or I'll shoot!"

Place—"I'm pointing a loaded pistol at you."

Push—"Would you please come here?"

Place—"I'd feel better if we could discuss this."

There is a definite feeling of directional force in the Push move when compared to the Place move, and not only can we Push people in a lateral direction—"Check the mail," or "Preflight the plane," but we can also push upward or downward. An upward Push affirms someone; it is a type of Please move. It encourages: "Keep up the good work!" "Great, just one more page, and we'll be finished."

A downward Push is discouraging and can lower self-esteem: "Can't you come up with anything better than that?" "Any third grader could solve that problem."

To help understand the directional force of the Push move in a speech, we turn to the speech cited earlier, "Restructuring America: Focus on the Core Business." Recall that in the introduction, the speaker used mainly Place moves. Now, near the end of the speech, he moves away from the Place moves and starts Pushing for action. Notice his plan—Push and then Place the direction he wants his listeners to take.

> Let's go back to the transformation we are witnessing in Corporate America. [Push] There's a group that's fighting change, and they're being left at the station. This crowd is easy to identity. [Place moves] Watch for them in your proxy material. [Push] They have very little stock. They have a big salary, they have a big bonus and they have a big mouth about the many "constituencies" of the corporation. [Sarcasm—Pushing downward] They make a lot of speeches about short-term and long-term strategies [Place].[3]

The Pause Move

The Pause move is actually no movement in relation to the listener. The Pause is *intentionally* being unaware, ignoring, not responding, not reacting, letting things go, or not consulting. Here are some Pause examples:

Pause—You are conversing with a co-worker about a job related subject, when he makes an untrue and inappropriate comment about one of the secretaries. You Pause the comment by continuing the discussion, so you can reach your initial goal—agreement on the job related subject.

Pause—You are passing a string of traffic on the Interstate, and another driver moves up quickly and follows you closely. Your goal is to pass comfortably and get into the right hand lane, so you Pause the car behind and continue passing at your chosen speed.

Pause—You are involved in a discussion with three other people. One of them keeps interrupting one of the other speakers. You Pause the interrupter by keeping your attention focused on the interrupted speaker. Your goal is to give an equal chance for everyone to talk.

Pause—In your office you are having an important discussion with your oldest daughter, a college freshman. Your phone rings; you Pause the phone caller by shutting off the ringer, and continue toward your goal of working toward a solution to her problem.

Pause—You are a department manager responsible for making a decision that will greatly impact nine of your people. Your goal is to get the decision finalized fast, so you Pause discussing it with the nine and make the decision quickly by yourself.

We have discussed the three basic communication moves. Place, Push, and Pause. The intent of the Place is to inform by placing fact or feeling close or distant from the listener. The intent of the Push is to energize the listener to act, agree, or conform. The intent of the Pause is to ignore and avoid reacting. Two other moves, the Please and Pull are subcategories of Place, Push, and Pause.

The Please Move

The Please move is often a subcategory of the Place move. It is an idea, fact, or feeling that is positive or helpful to the listener. It can be a compliment, an affirmation, sharing, understanding, showing friendship, listening, or making things easier. The Please move attempts to establish a positive connect between the sender and the listener. Below are some Please moves that are subcategories of Place moves:

Please (place)

Idea or fact—"I want to work on this project together."

"All indications show that you did an excellent job."

Please (place)

Feeling— "I feel confident that you can handle the plane by yourself now."

The Please move can also be a subcategory of the Push move when it directs that listener toward a desired goal, or it pushes upward in a friendly manner:

Please (push)

"Keep up the good work!"

"Let's show them what *we* can do."

The Please move can be a subcategory of the Pause move. Pausing something that might be embarrassing or uncomfortable is a Please move:

Please (pause)

Someone ignores (pauses) the fact that I'm wearing braces.

Someone ignores (pauses) the fact that I'm a half-hour late.

As with any of the moves, the Please move is not limited to conversation. Listen to the please moves at the beginning of this speech, "The Truth About Savings and Loan Institution." One can almost feel the sender patting the listeners on the back for their good work.

> As I look around this room this afternoon I see people who have devoted their working lives to the savings and loan business—successful managers who can be proud that, day in and day out, they deliver on the promise that is the savings institutions charter: To make it possible for American families to realize the dream of home ownership.
>
> Ours is a worthy, necessary pursuit and one that has made this nation the best-housed of any in the world.[4]

The Pull Move

The Pull move is a special type of Place or Pause move. It is a move that arouses curiosity, and attracts the listener. A Pull move might be offering a reward, inducing, hinting, seeking elaboration.

Pull

(Place/Idea or fact)—"I've been thinking . . ."

(The listener is Pulled in ". . . About what?")

"I have a plan that might get us out of this mess."
(The listener is Pulled in "Let's hear it.")

"Number two engine is really acting strange."
(The listener is Pulled in "How? In what way?")

"I need a favor." In question form:
"Would you do me a favor?"
(The listener is Pulled in "How can I help? What is it?")

"I wonder why you made that decision." In question form: "How come?"
(The listener is Pulled in "Well, I just thought . . .")

"You'll never believe what's going on at the Johnson house!"
(The listener is Pulled in "What *is* happening over there?")

"I'm curious to know what you said in response." In question form:
"And you said . . .?"
(The listener is Pulled in "Well, I started by mentioning the incident last May, when . . .")

Sometimes conjunctions by themselves are Pull moves:

"And . . ."
(The listener is Pulled in ". . . and I overshot the runway.")

"So . . ."
(The listener is Pulled in ". . . So I told her what was on my mind.")

"But . . ."
(The listener is Pulled in ". . . but it quit ringing before I could get to it.")

Pull moves are sometimes difficult to identify, because they are frequently questions. However, all questions are not Pull moves. Sometimes questions are Push moves where the sender is trying to push answers out of a listener: "Will you *please* tell me what has been going on?!" is pushing, not pulling, for a response.

In addition to words and questions, being silent and not reacting might be a Pause move, but the silence also can Pull the listener toward a goal. Maybe the goal is to keep someone talking to find out what happened, or get another view of a situation. Examples of silent pull moves are in this conversation between two pilots:

1. "The howling got louder and louder."
2. "-----------------silent pull--------------."

1. "Well, I don't know what it was."
2. "------------------silent pull-------------."
1. "So . . . I shut it down."

All messages fit into five basic move categories—Place, Push, Pause, Please, or Pull. Consequently, we could record all of our conversations and speeches, and put each sentence into one of the Basic Communication Move categories:

Instructor, Placing: — "We need to know the wind velocity and direction."

Student, Placing: — "Well, an hour ago it was twelve knots, out of the South."

Instructor, Pausing: —---------------silent----------------

Student, Placing: — "I guess we should use runway one-nine."

Instructor, Pulling: — "Well, I . . ."

Student, Pulling: — What . . .?"

Instructor, Placing: — "There's that construction at the south end."

Student, Placing: — "Just some little dirt mounds; the machines are gone."

Instructor, Placing: — "Yes, that's right, the big stuff is gone."

Instructor, Pushing: — "Preflight the ship."

Student, Placing: — "Okay."

Instructor, Placing: — "I'll check the traffic."

Instructor, Pleasing: — "You're coming along pretty well."

Instructor, Pushing: — "Hang in there!"

Now with the moves identified, we can expand our understanding of listening by discussing the role of movement sender, listeners, climate, culture, and noise.

We have seen that communication movement adds meaning to the message. In addition, movement functions with the sender and the receiver, as well as the other elements and variables in the communication process. Below are some examples of this functional relationship.

Sender/Listener

Movement enters the communication process as the sender prepares and encodes the message, and as the Listener decodes and understands the message. The sender may *intend* to Place, Push, Pause, Please, or Pull, or not even think about the moves s/he is making, but whether intentional or unintentional, the movement is there. Below are some examples of movement's relationship with the sender and listener.

Sender, Placing: "It's about ten after six." Listener recognizes that the information has been placed in front of her.

Sender, Pushing: "Please clean-up this work area." Listener recognizes that he has been pushed to clean-up the work area.

Sender, Pausing: Does not acknowledge that the listener has entered the room. Listener recognizes that she has been paused (ignored).

Sender, Pleasing: "Your report was excellent!" Listener recognizes that she had been pleased.

Sender, Pulling: "I'm out of ideas for promoting this project." Listener recognizes that he is being pulled for some ideas to help with the promotion.

Noise

Movement can become noise in the process when it is misunderstood by the listener. For example, noise is increased when a manager intends a Place move, "I appreciate employees who get to work on time," but an employee, who has been late a few times, misinterprets the intended place move and feel uncomfortably Pushed. Consequently, movement is noise when the sender's intended move is misinterpreted by the listener. Below are some examples of noise caused by misinterpreted moves.

Sender, *intends* a Place move: "It's getting late, and I have a 4:00 appointment."
Listener, *interprets* a Push move: "He wants me to help him finish."

Sender, *intends* a Push move to get some help: "It sure is awkward for one person to carry this."
Listener, *interprets* a Place move: "Yes, I'll bet it is difficult to carry."

Sender, *intends* a Pause move by ignoring the salesperson.
The salesperson *interprets* a Pull move and continues to explain the qualities of the products.

The sender *intends* a Pull move: "I'm not sure what to do next."
The listener *interprets* a Place move: "I have trouble deciding what to do sometimes."

Climate

Communication movement can create the climate. We can listen to the relatively objective, matter-of-fact climate of a discussion where Placing is the predominant move. We can listen to the heightened energy in the climate where Pushing is the main move. We can listen to the controlled pace, and measurable timing where the Pause move is a common part of the climate. We can comfortably listen to the climate that is supportive with Please moves. Finally, we can sense when we are being Pulled in a certain direction. An example of a Pull climate is a meeting where the leader establishes open, non-judgmental communication. She offers a background to a problem to be addressed and uses questions to prompt ideas and suggestions. The climate is one of pulling for solutions. Below are some examples of movement and climate:

Place Climate

> As I walked into the board room, I could sense the tone of the meeting. There was not a great deal of excitement or irrelevant talk. The speaker was just placing some information and some ideas for us to look over in the next two weeks. The atmosphere of the meeting turned into a factual exchange, and a large amount of information was shared.

Push Climate

> Just listening to his footsteps in the hall told me we were in for a real "motivating" meeting. The latest information had clearly shown that deliveries were catching up, but not fast enough. Some clear-cut directives were on the way—they would be heavy handed and blunt: "We will put every available person on loading and shipping." "If we need to work overtime for the next three months, we will do it!"

Pause Climate

> We watched as she read the report and waited for her reaction to the problem. But there was no reaction. She thanked us for coming to the meeting and told us we were free to go. A month later, she told us that she knew we were working on the project as well as possible, so she paused it and put her thinking on other matters.

Please Climate

> As soon as I walked through the door I felt a warm, almost festive mood. The big computer print-out read "HAPPY B-DAY, JIM!" I could smell the goodies and hear the relaxed conversations. The mood was warm and pleasing, and we all stayed and visited for over an hour.

Pull Climate

> The supervisor began the meeting by detailing the deadlines we were under. Then she gave us a hand-out with the deadline information, spread her arms with hands open and said, "What do you think?" This open gesture and question encouraged us—pulled us—to give feedback, and whether we did or did not give feedback, we all felt obligated to try to offer some suggestions.

Culture

Communication Movement is a cultural value. The movement that is valued by the leadership becomes ingrained in the culture. One need only look at the leadership of one of America's most successful men, the late Sam Walton. Walton emphasized the Please move culture in his Wal-Mart stores. He believed in pleasing the customers by developing the attitude with his employees that the customer comes first. This please move culture keeps the customers coming back to the stores.

The place move culture exists in the law firm where the founding partners valued giving and obtaining information. As a client enters the firm, s/he is acknowledged by a receptionist who places, "Mr. Benson is with another client and will be free in five minutes. You may hang your coat and have a seat if you wish." The receptionist then announces,

"Mr. Benson will be out in a moment to show you to his office." Mr. Benson then arrives and places, "Good morning. I'm ready to discuss your case. I have coffee and tea in my office."

When in the office, Mr. Benson places, "I'm interested in listening to the facts involved in this case. I'd like you to start at the beginning." The client responds by placing the facts and events that are pertinent to the case.

The push move culture is experienced in a clothing store where the salespeople are on commission. Since they are paid a percentage of each item they sell, the management encourages pushing articles of clothing to be purchased. The push culture is noticed by such comments as: "Take that one into the dressing room and try it on." "You can't possible get along without that." "I'll get the green tie that goes with that." "You can't wear that skirt with those high heels, put these flats on." "Oh, that hat is YOU; you just can't get out of the store without it."

The pause move culture is experienced in another clothing store. At this store, the salesperson greets the customer and says, "If you have any questions, I'll be happy to help out." After that, the salesperson responds only if the customer requests help or information.

A pull move culture can be found where there are attempts to draw us into the organization by arousing our curiosity. Probably the most commonly experienced pull cultures are shops and stores with window displays and entries that attract our interest. Once pulled inside, other messages might tell us, "Elegance at an affordable price," and we are pulled to find out the price, or "Unequaled power and performance," might arouse our interest in an automobile's performance figures. Simple messages reading, "Ask us about our low interest rates," pull us toward the possibility of making a credit purchase.

These examples show that movement is a basic part of organizational culture. Even though the leaders that formed the culture may not have consciously decided to create a Place, Push, Pause, Please, or Pull culture, a culture valuing one or more of the moves evolved under their leadership. As listeners, we need to be aware of the movement that the culture values, so that we can adapt to it when necessary.

The listening model is now complete.

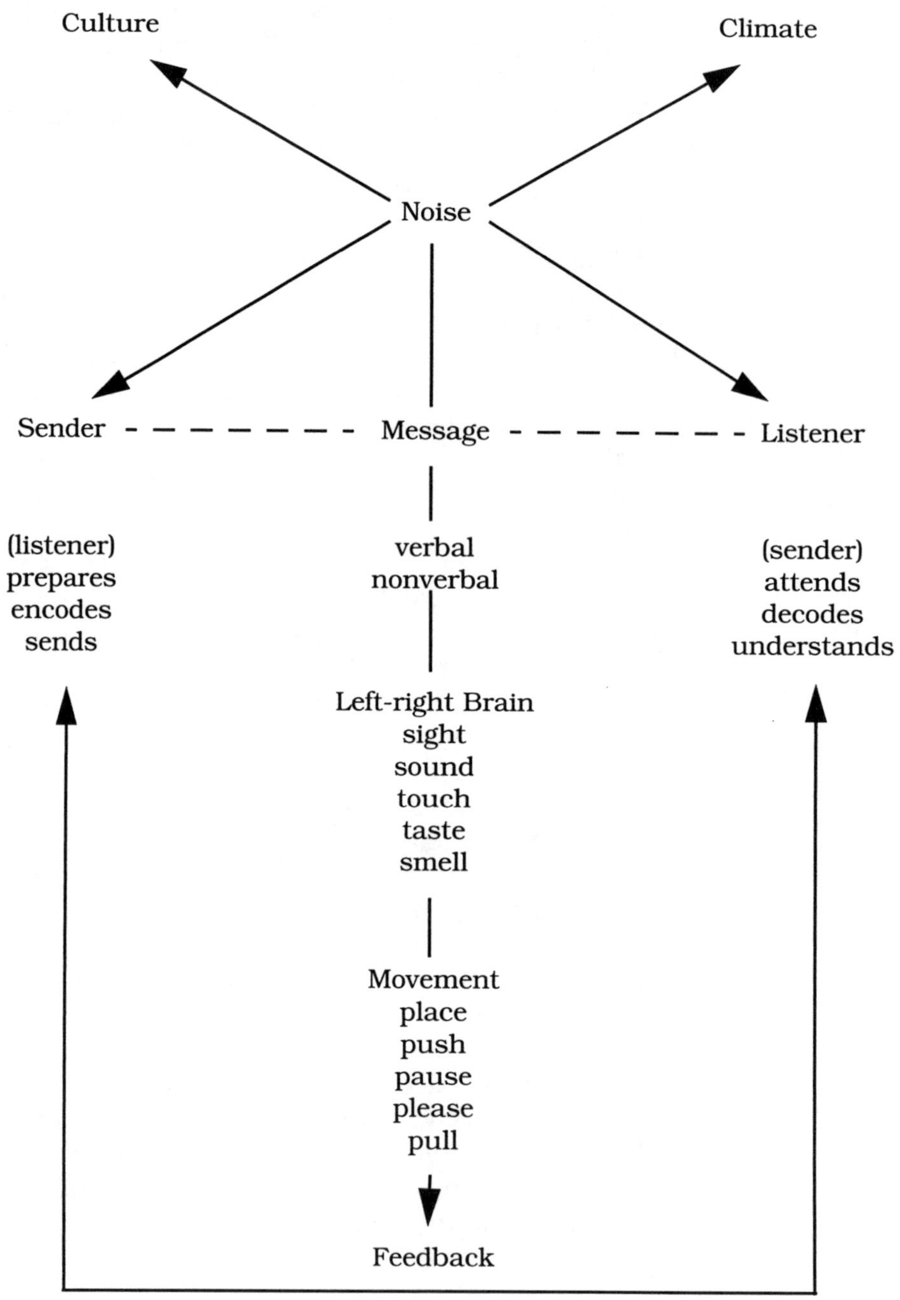

Summary

Movement is the last variable to be discussed as part of the communication process, and it is a basic component of human interaction. Listening to movement, which occurs in the form of gestures and speech, can add substantial meaning to a message. Movement is broken down into five categories: 1) the Place move, 2) the Push move, 3) the Pause move, 4) the Please move, and 5) the Pull move. Moreover, movement affects each element and variable in the process of communication: Sender/Listener, Noise, Climate and Culture.

Awareness Exercises, Chapter 4

Name ______________________________ **SS#** _____-____-_____

1. Write three Place moves.

   A.

   B.

   C.

2. Write three Push moves.

   A.

   B.

   C.

3. Describe a situation where a Pause move is used.

4. Write three Please moves.

   A.

   B.

   C.

5. Write three Pull moves.

   A.

   B.

   C.

6. Explain how movement might be a part of a culture.

7. Explain how movement can be a source of noise.

8. Explain how movement can effect the communication climate.

9. Briefly describe a time when you listened to Place moves.

   A. The setting

   B. The Place moves

10. Briefly describe a time when you listened to Push moves.

    A. The setting

    B. The Push moves

11. Briefly describe a time when you listened to Pause moves.

    A. The setting

    B. The Pause moves

12. Briefly describe a time when you listened to Please moves.

    A. The setting

    B. The Please moves

13. Briefly describe a time when you listened to Pull moves?

    A. The setting

    B. The Pull moves

14. Describe five instances when noise occurred because of misunderstood moves.

    A.

    B.

    C.

    D.

    E.

Awareness DataBase, Chapter 4

Name Jennifer Sorensen **SS#** _____-____-_____

Identify the predominant move.

A. Place B. Push C. Pause D. Please E. Pull

1. Would you please shut the door?
   A. B. C. D. E.

2. The oil isn't at running temperature yet.
   A. B. C. D. E.

3. There's something very interesting going on in the production manager's office.
   A. B. C. D. E.

4. The mail just came.
   A. B. C. D. E.

5. You put on an excellent program.
   A. B. C. D. E.

6. Smoking is not allowed in this building.
   A. B. C. D. E.

7. We've got to move; jump in!
   A. B. C. D. E.

8. Look. I'll do my job; you do yours.
   A. B. C. D. E.

9. Can I give you a hand with those packages?
   A. B. C. D. E.

10. The power just went off.

A. B. C. D. E.

11. This stew is terrific!

A. B. C. D. E.

12. Wait till you see what they've done to your office.

A. B. C. D. E.

13. I feel relieved that the whole business is finished.

A. B. C. D. E.

14. Would you mind getting that knife for me?

A. B. C. D. E.

15. I'm so angry I could spit!

A. B. C. D. E.

16. Your department's final report was clear and thorough.

A. B. C. D. E.

17. I think you'll find the solution very interesting.

A. B. C. D. E.

18. Last year we put on four ground towing workshops.

A. B. C. D. E.

19. Start the engine.

A. B. C. D. E.

20. We'll be in your office at half past ten.

A. B. C. D. E.

5 Listening to Ourselves

Before we can give our complete listening attention to another person, we must first listen to *our own needs* and attempt to satisfy them or pause them until they can be satisfied. This in*tra*personal listening (listening to ourselves) is the basis for effective int*er*personal (listening to others). In this chapter, we will discuss 1) the intrapersonal listening role, 2) listening to personal needs, 3) self-esteem and listening to others, and 4) changing internal messages.

❑ The Intrapersonal Listening Role ❑

The int*ra*personal listening role involves shutting out external messages and *listening to ourselves.* This personal listening time allows us to become aware of our own needs, and if they are unmet, to plan to satisfy them either immediately or in the foreseeable future. Satisfying personal needs is like putting our house in order for visitors. When our house is in order, we can shift our attention to the visitors. Similarly, when our personal house is in order, that is, when our needs are met, we are free to give our listening energy to others. The idea that recognizing and meeting personal needs precedes listening to others is illustrated in this narrative, told by a supervisor. Notice how the employee, Russ, is unable to listen effectively to his supervisor because of Russ' unresolved personal needs:

> A few years back I was in charge of a department with eleven employees. I had gotten to know each of them fairly well, and we seemed to be getting along fine. One morning, one of them, a man named Russ, walked past my office door, and I gave a loud and friendly, "Morning,

Russ!" He shot a glance in my direction, didn't say a word and went on to his office. I was puzzled and thought about what the problem might be.

I reviewed his job assignments and requests for time off and vacation time but found nothing that would prompt his disturbing behavior. The next morning's encounter really took me back. My "Good Morning," this time was warmly returned, and the next thing I knew he was in my office with a cup of coffee and all sorts of chatty news. His behavior was just the opposite of the day before.

After several more experiences with Russ' responsive and nonresponsive mornings, I came to realize that *I had nothing to do with his responses to my, "Good Mornings."* What Russ was listening to inside himself was affecting how he listened to me.

It turns out that Russ was having some serious personal problems, and on the mornings when these problems were bothering him the most, he was so preoccupied that he couldn't listen to my simple greeting. On the mornings when he had apparently thought about his problems and had either solved them or put them aside, he could listen to my "Good Morning," and we would visit.

These experiences with Russ taught me that what's going on inside people directly affects how they listen to those around them.

Intrapersonal listening takes place at any time: when we first wake up and begin to assess how we feel, and what needs to be satisfied; when we are alone and removed from work and other responsibilities; or when we take a short break to determine how we are feeling when we are with other people.

We are in the intrapersonal listening role whenever we listen to our feelings, which are reactions to physical or emotional needs that have been met or unmet. Examples of physical reactions are: "My stomach was churning when she called my name." "This pain in my left shoulder is getting worse." "I wanted to get into some warm clothes and rest." Some emotional reactions are: "I felt a glow of joy when I saw the kids having such a good time." "I smiled to myself as I realized how much fun the ride was." "Now, more than ever, I had to get out of there and make some decisions of my own." "I wanted to talk to her about the loss." "I really need to get this done on time." In each of these intrapersonal messages, some reaction to personal needs is being expressed.

Just as individuals listen intrapersonally to determine need satisfaction before listening to others outside the self, successful business organizations listen internally before reaching out to serve others. Before an organization can successfully adapt to the needs of those it serves, it must listen to its own internal needs to be sure it is well organized and running smoothly and has high organizational self-esteem. After this internal listening, it can listen to the expectations, problems, and needs of those to be served. Listening and adapting to those being served comes *after* listening internally.

The importance of internal organizational listening is highlighted in the sequence of internal listening events that led to the establishment of a very successful restaurant:

Gina, the owner and manger of a popular and financially rewarding restaurant, decided to open another restaurant with totally different menu offerings—she was going from a meat, French fries, and salad menu to an array of Mexican offerings. She had surveyed other Mexican restaurants in the area and had a good sense of the competition. Moreover, her years of experience had taught her to listen internally to her organization before attempting to open the doors of her second restaurant to the public.

She listened carefully to the *internal* needs and limits of her current staff of cooks, servers, washers, managers, and other support personnel. She then organized the new staff around a core of her experienced employees. Listening to the needs and limits of her cooks, she began with a very small menu which consisted of a combination of only eight items, and because of her staff's uncertainties about the new business, she began by serving dinners only. Setting up for lunch service would come when her listening told her the organization was ready.

By listening carefully to internal needs, she opened a restaurant with a confident, well organized staff and a small but competently prepared menu. Listening internally helped her build a smooth and well organized operation which made it possible to begin the process of *external* listening to customers' additional requests and needs.

Internal listening, whether it is personal or organizational, is the first and most important step toward effective external listening. The discussion now turns to need areas which must be considered when listening intrapersonally.

❑ Listening to Personal Needs ❑

To the extent that our personal needs are met, we will be effective listeners. For example, before I can concentrate on what you are saying, I must satisfy my need for food and shelter. If I were hungry, wet, and cold, I would find it difficult to turn my listening energy to you. However, if I am relatively comfortable, well fed, and warm, I can more easily listen to you. Intrapersonal listening is the first step in recognizing and satisfying needs. Once these needs are satisfied, we can listen more effectively to others. To structure this discussion the needs are numbered from one to five; however, number one is not necessarily the most important, because the relative importance of the needs will vary with each individual. Consequently, for some people, need five, the need for fun, will be more important than need number one, the need for survival. The needs are: 1) to survive, 2) to belong—to love, share, and cooperate, 3) to have power, 4) to have freedom, and 5) to have fun.[1]

Survival

The first need to be discussed is survival. We listen to ourselves for physical survival to determine our state of nutritional satisfaction, environmental comfort (temperature, humidity, noise, and light), and health (amount of energy, pain, ability to rest, or physical well being). Intrapersonal messages related to physical survival are: "I'm feeling hot." "The noise of that train is giving me a headache." "I find the waves washing on the shore relaxing." "I feel rested and ready to finish the painting."

In addition to physical survival needs, we also listen to emotional needs, which include feelings about relationships—family members, spouses, lovers, parents, friends—feelings about decisions or events which affect self-worth, success, and failures, and our general outlook on life. Intrapersonal messages that relate to emotional survival needs are: "I'm happy he sent me that birthday card." "I feel great about the raise I got." "I think I'll stay away from her; I'm not worth anyone's time." "I feel like crawling in a hole and disappearing." "I'm glad mom and dad called this morning." "It was a tough decision, but I feel good about it."

Love and Belonging

The second need is to love and belong. This need is satisfied when people or projects that we care about help us feel comfortable and welcome. The need might be satisfied through family and friends whose company we enjoy, or through people who share the same hobby such as boating, jogging, basketball, tennis, flying, writing, or quilting. The need for love and belonging is not met when a person has chosen to spend time where there is little love and sense of belonging: a family setting where nothing in common is shared, a work environment where there is no sense of caring or belonging, and the only reward is a paycheck (which *does* help satisfy the need for survival). In this case where the work environment does not meet the need for love and belonging, it is reasonable to conclude that the worker's listening energy will not go beyond the minimum to get the job completed.

By intrapersonal listening, we become aware of what needs are being met and unmet. Moreover, we discover that at any given time different needs will be important. Sometimes the need for survival might be more important than the need for love and belonging as in the case of the worker who puts up with a cold, uncaring environment for a paycheck. As we survey our personal needs and how they impact our listening, we need to keep our priorities in mind. In the description below, imagine how the person describing the priority of his need for love and belonging might listen to others:

> As I look inside myself, I find that the need for friends, family, and love—best described as the need to belong—occupies as large a place in my mind as the need to survive. It may not be as immediate as thirst or hunger, but if, over the long pull, I did not have the close, loving family and friends that I almost take for granted, I think that the idea that life is hardly worth living would come occasionally to mind. Even if we have friends and family, many of us also enjoy a sense of belonging with pets, plants, and even an inanimate object like a "beloved" boat or computer.[2]

From this example, we can understand that depending on circumstances, needs will have varying importance in our lives. The person who wrote this description gives listening attention to people he loves. If his situation were to change, or if he were from a country where war is a constant threat, his concern for survival would become a high priority, and he would shift his listening focus to matters of survival.

Power

The third need, the need for power, has a clear and strong impact on how we listen to others. This need to control other people and our environments can be felt on a daily basis. Concerns for power range from physical to psychological. From a physical stand-point, men and women, just in the simple routine of preparing for a day outside the home are concerned about how they appear in comparison with other people. A number of popular books exist on dressing for power, and they address questions like: "How do I look?" "Am I in style, well groomed?" "Do I have the *right* shoes?" "Good looking?" Moreover, people will exercise to become a physical model of strength and what they think they should look like. When people are comfortable intrapersonally with how they look, they increase the probability of listening to someone else comfortably, because they have satisfied their needs for physical power.

Psychological power needs are concerned with emotional and mental control of the situation. Someone exploring this power need might ask herself: "Are my feelings calm and positive about this matter?" "Can I let go of the anger I feel about this?" "Can I control the happiness I have about this?" "Do I have the information I need for this discussion?" "Is my mind alert and ready to think?"

As with the needs for survival and love and belonging, the need for power varies with each individual. Some people have little concern for physical power, either in appearance or strength. Some have little interest in psychological power, but whatever the need level, power, like the other needs, must be met for the individual to function as an effective listener.

Freedom

Freedom is the fourth need. As physical creatures, we need freedom of movement to stay alive and to communicate. At the most basic level, freedom of movement allows us to find shelter, prepare food, and to express our ideas. At a higher level is physical freedom to gain access to social and educational opportunities. Organizations are realizing the importance of this need and are making their facilities available to those whose physical freedom is impaired.

As physical freedom increases, effective listening increases. One well known example of this lies in the story of Helen Keller, who early in life lost her sight and hearing, which at the time ended her freedom to listen and express. With the help of her nurse and her parents, Helen learned to communicate through touch, and was able to listen to her needs and ultimately listen to others and express herself.

In addition to physical freedom, we need psychological freedom. We have all observed youngsters growing up and asserting themselves for their "freedom," as well as parents who need the freedom that "being away from the kids" occasionally gives them. Sometimes people feel psychologically trapped in a relationship or an occupation.[3] Their listening loses effectiveness, and their intrapersonal messages tell them they need some time away from each other or a vacation away from the job.

Fun

The fifth need is the need for fun. Fun is doing something for enjoyment—something that gives pleasure without hurting anyone else. As Mark Twain wrote, "Fun is what you do when you don't have to do it." Our culture, which is based on the Puritan work ethic, at times views fun as unacceptable behavior; it tells us that fun is all right for kids but not for adults. However, fun is an important need which can keep our lives balanced, help us learn, and help us become better listeners. In a lecture entitled "Listening and Counseling," Dr. Russ Canute, a counselor for thirty-five years, offered these ideas about fun and listening:

> People who have a life balanced with fun are better listeners. They listen to their own need for fun, and even though the work is piled sky high, they decide to leave it for awhile and have some fun. (And, by the way, when they get back to it, they're better at it.) And whenever they have fun, they're learning something. Think of the last time you had fun. What did you do? Did you go waterskiing? What did you learn from that? Did you go to a movie or a play? What did you learn from that? Did you run, walk, play basketball, swim, play chess? What did you learn from that? Did you go visit with some friends? What did you learn from that? Did you go to the library and read some journals? What did you learn from that? I honestly don't think you can have fun without learning something. And, in order to learn, you have to listen with your ears and your eyes. But keep the fun thing in balance. There are things in life we need to do that we don't like, but when you can, listen to your need for fun, it'll make you a better listener to the people and things around you.[4]

Listening intrapersonally for these five basic needs: survival, love and belonging, power, freedom, and fun, is the first step in satisfying these needs. Satisfying these needs raises self-esteem and allows us to listen effectively to others.

❑ Self-Esteem and Listening to Others ❑

Intrapersonal listening gives us a grasp of what needs are being satisfied, and to the extent that they are satisfied, our self-esteem is formed. If we listen to ourselves and find that our own needs are satisfied, we can listen to others in a comfortable and responsive manner. If we listen to ourselves and find conflicting needs and discomfort, we cannot reach out to someone else's world and listen to them.

The type of internal messages we listen to stem from a complex catalog of perceptions we have about ourselves. Depending on how well we are working to meet our needs, these perceptions fall into two categories: first, the amount of *value* we have for ourselves, and second, how *competent* we perceive ourselves to be. Our self-esteem is anchored in our sense of *value* and *competence.*

If we experience a high sense of personal value, we see both our strengths and shortcomings. We accept who we are and work to improve those shortcomings. So when we value ourselves, we send positive messages to ourselves. Although not in so many words, these messages say, "I like who I am"; "I'm not perfect, but I'm a good person who's getting better all the time." Valuing ourselves means we accept ourselves, and this acceptance frees us to accept others as they are.

When we experience a low self-esteem, we do not value ourselves, and listening effectively to others becomes difficult. In the listening setting we may become defensive in order to hide our nervousness, fear, feelings of insecurity, or inadequacies. Many of these defensive messages are rooted in the feeling that we are not of value in this situation: "I've always been lousy at this," "No one really cares about how I feel, anyway." Defensive messages come from a hidden belief that we are bad, unlovable, unworthy, and not respected for who we are.*

So instead of listening attentively, a person with low self-esteem might avoid the situation all together: "Well, I don't want to talk to her; she never has anything interesting to say"; "This report's going to be stupid. I can't ever figure out what he's getting at." If already in a listening setting, a person with low self-esteem might be internally saying, "You're just talking to me because you have to"; "You don't really care if I understand this or not; you're just here to show how much you know and how little I know."

A listener with high self-esteem listens attentively without becoming defensive. People who respect themselves do not need unhealthy defenses, because defenses are put up to protect weaknesses; they are not needed where there is strength and adequacy.[5] With high self-esteem, the listener's internal messages might say, "Sure, I'll listen to her; I usually learn something interesting from her"; "This guy's vocabulary is difficult to understand, but I'll take good notes and figure out what he's getting at," or "I'm not sure why John came in to visit, but I'll keep listening to see what's on his mind."

The sense of value we have for ourselves at any given time has some impact on the message we listen to internally. Our image of our level of competence also plays a role in our internal messages.

Imagine the following office scene: Behind a large walnut desk sits an executive, about forty-five years old, white shirt, dark tie, and suit coat. A new employee comes and is introduced by a secretary. The executive looks the new employee in the eye, reaches over the desk and shakes his hand.

The executive appears confident, but for some reason he does not seem to *feel* confident. Sometimes we are fooled by false confidence, but at this time, the nonverbal messages show the executives's discomfort. Maybe a hesitancy, an exaggerated gesture, or some visible tension reveal a lack of competence and confidence. Perhaps the handshake was a bit too long and tight; the voice too loud; the eye contact too direct and mechanical.

At the time, the executive's internal messages might be saying, "I'm not good at this"; "I hate meeting new people," or "I can't let this guy get the best of me." The executive is giving the *appearance* of confidence rather than *being* confident, and his internal feelings of insecurity come to the surface and lower the effectiveness of the communication.

Listeners who are sending themselves messages that say, "I'm not competent" or "I'm really afraid," find it particularly important to appear competent and courageous on the outside. However, listeners who send realistic internal messages of, "I'm nervous, but I can handle this" or "I'm looking forward to this interaction," have no need to present a flawless image to others, because they accept themselves as they are.

Listening to ourselves honestly will give us a realistic picture of who we are. We will find that we are worthwhile and competent in some areas and that we fall short in others. What is important is that we recognize our strong characteristics and face our weaker ones and work to improve them.

---

* The goal here is not to detail all of the types of defenses linked with self-esteem—there are volumes that do that in detail; rather, the purpose is to discuss some common defensive messages in order to raise awareness of their impact on listening.

How we value ourselves, self-esteem, determines how we will behave with others. If we feel positively about ourselves, we will have more self-confidence and will communicate with people effectively. If we are feeling negatively about ourselves, we will shy away from others; our communicating will not be effective.[6] Moreover, people who feel good about themselves, that is, people with high self-esteem are willing to take risks: they will try new things, meet new people, listen to new and unusual ideas because they are secure within themselves to the point that what they might learn from the new experience is worth the risk. They see involvement with the world around them as an exciting opportunity to learn.[7]

To increase the effectiveness of our listening to others, then, we need to listen to ourselves to determine the kinds of *intrapersonal* messages we are sending. In general, to the extent that these internal messages tell us that we are meeting needs, and are likable, worth-while, competent, and confident we will be more effective listeners.

❑ Changing Internal Messages ❑

Our self-concepts, that is, how we view ourselves, grow and change throughout our lives. We take on new tasks, new responsibilities, and we experience some degree of success and failure. Since self-concepts are learned, we can unlearn parts of our self image and learn about new needs and aspects of ourselves.

To raise our self-esteem, we must have positive experiences. As adults, we can look back on our parents and our upbringing and praise or possibly criticize some of those experiences. This looking back to understand why we are what we are is healthy and normal, but it probably will not change our listening behavior. What *will* help, however, is listening to ourselves as we are *today*.

The one person in the world we should not avoid is ourselves. So we listen to ourselves, and if we find aspects that we feel need improvement, we can decide to make some changes. Maybe there are certain listening settings where we feel less confident. We all know professionals who seem confident and at ease in a meeting, but in a social setting appear uncomfortable and seem to wish they were somewhere else.

To be effective listeners, we need to operate confidently in a variety of settings. If we do not feel comfortable in a particular setting, the first step in changing how we feel is being *aware* that the discomfort exists.

Facing internal discomfort is important. For example, a person may be fearful of a staff meeting where a particular idea she has been promoting will be discussed at length. Because of the amount of thought and time put into the proposal, she feels personally attached to it, and she is concerned that the idea might not be accepted. She is afraid and does not even want to go to the meeting.

After recognizing her fear about this meeting, the next step is accepting it: "I'm afraid to walk into that meeting room," and after accepting her fear, it is no longer the threat it once was; it no longer controls behavior. Now, she is free to imagine the people and the situation as they really are. In facing and accepting the fear, she feels better about herself, because she has taken the time to listen to herself. Now, even if the reality of the upcoming meeting is dreadful, she can accept that and face the meeting with dignity and listen carefully and thoughtfully, because she has faced her internal concerns and put them aside. One author comments on the power of facing internal realities as a way of accepting and controlling unwanted feelings:

> We are always stronger when we do not try to fight reality. We cannot make our fear go away by yelling at it, or yelling at ourselves, or indulging in self-rebuke. But if we can open to our experience, stay conscious, and remember that we are larger than any one emotion, we can at minimum begin to transcend unwanted feelings, and often we can dispel them, since full, sincere acceptance tends, in time, to dissolve negative or unwanted feelings such as pain, anger, envy, or fear.[8]

So, we must first listen to our needs to put our own feelings in perspective before we can listen to others. These four steps offer a structure for listening to ourselves:[9]

1. How is my self-esteem? How am I feeling about myself? Are my needs of survival, belonging, power, freedom, and fun being met?
2. How do I treat these feelings? Do I accept them as my own, or blame someone else for how I feel? Do I cover up my feelings or do I pretend I have feelings that are not there?
3. When I feel this way, how well do I listen to others? How well do I communicate?
4. How comfortable am I in this new listening situation? Am I comfortable enough within myself to take the risks of listening to others?

To illustrate this four step process, we can look at a professional, Nancy, a junior vice president of a bank, who goes through the process herself to improve her listening effectiveness.

Nancy is thirty two years old, and she works with two other junior vice presidents, three senior vice presidents, and of course, the bank president. In addition, there are three loan officers and fifteen other employees working as tellers and performing miscellaneous jobs around the bank.

Nancy is a college graduate who has been with the bank for six years. In this relatively short time, she has advanced through the ranks of teller, to loan officer, to junior vice president. Her performance reviews consistently highlight her effective communication skills, particularly her listening, as the key to her promotability.

Nancy acknowledges that listening was a failing in her performance on her last job, so she took it upon herself to work consciously on improving her listening skills. This is her narrative of the process when she first started her job at the bank:

> Step 1. How is my self-esteem? Are my needs of survival, belonging, power, fun, and freedom being met?
>
> In the morning, while I was getting ready for work, I would assess how I was feeling about myself today. Usually, I felt fairly worthwhile and confident, and needs were being met. But there were some areas of

uncertainly. This bank job was new, and I wanted to do well. One consistently recurring feeling I experienced had to do with meeting with the other junior vice presidents. One VP was a woman eight or nine years older than I; the other, a man of about my age. I had just started as a teller, and the first meeting I had with those VPs was not comfortable, to say the least.

Without going in to irrelevant detail, let me say that the first meeting was at best intimidating. I left that I had no power in the situation, and it certainly allowed me no freedom or *fun*.

At this first meeting, we met in Mrs. Borman's office, and instead of taking the form of a meeting, it was more like a military briefing. I sat while the *both* of them stood and explained the policies I would be following.

But that first meeting was a long time ago, and this morning as I faced another meeting with them, my feelings were ones of anger and fear, and I didn't want to go to the meeting. I was a little disappointed in myself, too, for letting these feelings take control, but I had felt so powerless and restricted the last time!

Step 2. How do I treat these feelings? Do I accept them as my own, or blame someone else for how I feel? Do I cover up my feelings or do I pretend I have feelings that are not there?

My next reaction, after admitting how I felt, was to blame the two VPs for their insensitivity, lack of preparation, and demeaning behavior at that first meeting. I was saying to myself, "It's *their* fault that *I* feel this way." This was an old rule from my past—put the blame for my feelings on someone else. But this morning I threw that old rule out, and simply acknowledged, "I feel angry and afraid. I DO NOT want to go to that meeting." No putting my feelings on someone else; no blaming someone else; just "These are my feelings. I needed to face them, period."

Step 3. When I feel this way, how well do I listen to others? How well do I communicate?

At this point, I decided not to communicate my feelings directly to the VPs, but rather to imagine the reality of the meeting, put my anger and fear aside, and concentrate solely on LISTENING to the information. Instead of communicating my feelings of powerlessness and frustration, I decided to communicate my interest in the information they were to give me. Information that might help my job performance.

Step 4. Am I willing to take the risk of actively listening when I feel like I don't belong in this intimidating, and restricted setting?

This was a new and different approach for me. It was risky, because in the past, I used to go through all the motions of listening—fake listening, I guess—just to make the meetings bearable and make myself look good. Now I put my feelings of frustration and anger aside, and didn't worry about anything except listening to and understanding the information.

> My anger and fear aside, I was able to focus on the positive aspects of listening—"I'm good at it"; "I'm able to attend to them and understand what they are saying to me." I faced the reality of the situation—simply, what was expected of me was to listen—and played the role of a listener, and it worked! I came out of the meeting with some helpful information, and the VPs actually thanked me for my attentive listening.

Listening to ourselves is the first step in developing effective listening with others. Understanding needs, the conflicts they can bring, and how we solve the conflicts to meet these needs will help us develop a background for understanding others. Intrapersonal sensitivity and awareness will give us confidence to listen to others in a variety of settings and learn from our communication experiences.

As we listen to ourselves and work to meet needs, we grow in self-esteem, and high self-esteem allows effective communication with others. Effective listening comes from a firm personal sense of confidence and self knowledge. As we get to know who we are and come to terms with ourselves, we form the foundation for comfortable and effective listening with friends, family, and coworkers.

Dr. William Glasser, author of *Control Theory*, provides an insightful summary of the importance of listening intrapersonally to needs, so we can listen effectively to those around us. He points out that we emphasize different needs in our lives, and if we listen to ourselves we can begin to understand these needs and listen with respect and understanding to the needs of those around us:

> To gain effective control of our lives, we have to satisfy what we believe is basic to us and learn to respect and not frustrate others in fulfilling what is basic to them. All you will ever know is what drives *you*, just as I will know only what drives *me*. We cannot look into other people's heads and see what drives them. We can listen to what they tell us and look at what they do, but we should not make the mistake of assuming that we *know* what drives them. This means that we can never be sure of satisfying anyone else no matter what we do. It is reasonably safe, however, to assume that what drives us is similar to what drives other people, so there is no harm in trying to satisfy another person. But if what we do does not work, we should be careful not to persist or we run the risk of losing that person for a friend or lover.[10]

Dr. Glasser is advising that we probably will never reach a perfect understanding of another person. If, however, we listen sensitively to ourselves, we can begin to listen to others to understand their motivations and feelings.

❑ Summary ❑

Intrapersonal listening is listening to ourselves, and it is the first step in becoming an effective listener. As we listen internally, we can determine which of the five needs: survival, love and belonging, power, freedom, and fun, should be satisfied before we can turn our energy to listening to others. Need satisfaction results in higher self-esteem, and the more we value ourselves as competent individuals, the easier it becomes to listen to others. Finally, a four step process for improving intrapersonal communication and listening effectiveness is discussed: first, listening internally to feelings; second, deciding what to do with these feelings; third, determining how these feelings affect communicating with others, and forth, taking the risk to listen actively.

Awareness Exercise, Chapter 5

Name ____ **SS#** ______-_____-______

Before responding to these questions, spend some time paying attention to your intrapersonal listening and how you listen to others.

1. Describe a listening situation that is uncomfortable for you.

2. What messages do you give yourself to make the situation bearable?

3. What listening situations do you avoid if possible?

4. What listening situations do you enjoy?

5. When are you most aware of listening to yourself?

6. Describe a survival need that you have (either physical or psychological):

   A. satisfied

   B. not satisfied

7. Describe a love and belonging need that you have:

   A. satisfied

   B. not satisfied

8. Describe a power need that you have:

   A. satisfied

   B. not satisfied

9. Describe a freedom need that you have:

   A. satisfied

   B. not satisfied

10. Describe a fun need that you have:

    A. satisfied

    B. not satisfied

11. Describe someone you believe has high self-esteem.

12. Describe someone you believe has low self-esteem.

13. How does self-esteem affect your listening?

PART TWO

Practicing Sensible Listening

6 Listening Comprehensively

❑ Listening Roles ❑

In the first part of this book, we discussed the importance of listening in the organization, the process of communication, listening holistically, listening to movement, and listening intrapersonally. With the background from these chapters, we can now prepare for specific listening roles.

Identifying and understanding listening roles is necessary for effective listening. This chapter and the following four chapters define and discuss the five listening roles that are part of daily interaction. This chapter focuses on the comprehensive listening role; chapters 7, 8, 9, and 10 discuss the therapeutic, critical, consumer, and appreciative listening roles. This chapter discusses six aspects of comprehensive listening: *information, vocabulary, concentration, memory, notetaking, and questioning.*

❑ The Comprehensive Listening Role ❑

In the comprehensive listening role we listen to understand and remember information from briefings, reports, seminars, conferences, oral papers, and other presentations. When in the comprehensive role, we are focused on what we can gain from the sender; we are being selfish in a healthy way. We have succeeded if the message we have created in our minds is the same as the message that was intended by the sender. In the academic setting comprehensive listening is a necessity. However, when listening to a 10-minute lecture, most students are only listening with a 25 percent level of efficiency. After longer periods of time, less is remember or comprehended.[1] Understanding and retaining information are the first concerns of comprehensive listening.

Information

Information is found primarily in three parts of the message: 1) the main points, 2) material that supports, explains, or proves the main point, and 3) inferences.

Main Point

Main points might be obviously stated: "My first point is . . ." The main point might be indirectly presented: ". . . the answer to the question is . . ." "There are two approaches to this problem." "The topic this morning is . . ." "In summary, keep in mind . . ." "So we can conclude that . . ." The main points may be indicated by transitions, which are sentences or phrases that connect one main point to another. Examples of transitions are, "Now that we've discussed the importance of factor A, let's turn to factor B." "An additional item should be looked at now."

Supporting Material

Supporting material proves or clarifies the main points. Examples are: illustrations, statistics, stories, analogies, visuals, or quoted material. Phrases that indicate supporting material are: "For example . . ." "To illustrate this idea . . ." "Looking at the compared data . . ." "There's a story that might illustrate this idea. . . ."

Inferences

An inference is an unstated or implied conclusion. Sometimes a sender might infer a point that is important but not directly state it. In addition to the words, the sender's tone of voice, looks, and movements might offer clues to inferred or implied messages. The sender might say, "Wouldn't you really rather have freedom of choice on this matter?" The inferred answer might be, "Yes, of course I would." Or the sender might ask, "Do we want economic growth or a stagnant economy?" As a listener, you listen to the words and tone of voice and infer the point the sender is trying to make

We must be sure the inferences drawn are legitimate, and that they are intended by the sender. We need not *agree* with the intended inference, because *as comprehensive listeners our goal is only to understand the intended message and not to make judgements about it.*

To help clarify listening for main points, supporting material, and inferences, this speech entitled, "The Light Side of Listening" is presented with comments.

> I chose the title, The Light Side of Listening, because when discussing listening I usually focus on the dramatic effects of listening errors and the crucial nature of listening in business. But this evening, as we approach the holiday season, I've shifted my focus to some of the more fun aspects of listening, and I'm glad I did, because the lighter side of listening is something that I haven't often focused on.
>
> [*Before going into the body of the message, the speaker previews the four main points to be discussed, and the comprehensive listener should attend to these points.*]
>
> This evening, I first want to give you my definition of listening; second, I'll discuss the idea that listening can be fun and rewarding; thirdly, a lot of humor comes from listening mix-ups, and finally, listening inspires our imaginations. First, let's take a look at my definition of listening: Listening is using all of our senses to gather information and then give meaning to that sense input. [*The speaker has stated his first point—the definition of listening—and now offers supporting material to help the listeners understand the definition.*]
>
> This definition tells us that we listen with more than our ears. A deaf person can listen. In fact, we listen with our eyes and our noses. We listen to touch and to taste, also.
>
> [*Now, the speaker transitions to the next main point. He alerts the listener that he is finished with the first point, and he previews point number two.*]

Now that we've an understanding of the nature of listening, let's look at how listening can be fun and rewarding.

Everyday listening can be fun and give us personal rewards. [*The speaker supports this point by giving examples and illustrations.*] Many of us enjoy the outdoors—hunting, fishing, or taking pictures. [*In the next four examples, the speaker through words and tone of voice,* infers *the fun aspect of listening.*] Imagine yourself standing in a quiet spot listening to a beautiful autumn scene. Imagine listening to carolers on a clear, frosty, winter evening. The crunch of snow under your shoes. Listening to little kids *actually* getting along. [*The speaker finishes point two and transitions to point three.*]

So the lighter side of listening is fun and rewarding. Next, let's look at some of the humor that comes from listening.

A good deal of humor comes from listening mix-ups. [*The speaker offers three examples as supporting material for this assertion.*] Humor comes when someone *thinks* he's listening and assigning the correct meaning, and he's not. Humor comes when someone listens and is unable to assign accurate meaning. Humor comes when someone listens and assigns the wrong meaning because of stereotyped thinking.

[*The speaker transitions to his fourth and final point by summarizing points one, two, and three and previewing point four.*] We've discussed a definition of listening, talked about the idea that listening is fun, and adds humor, now let's look at the final point. Listening inspires our imaginations.

[*The speaker concludes the message by summarizing the main points.*] My goal this evening was to provide a little diversion from the important discussions and decisions you are involved with and also help us prepare for a holiday season that will be full of opportunities for listening. I also hope we leave with a higher awareness that listening is hard work because it involves all of our senses, and that there is a light side of listening: it can be fun and rewarding; a lot of humor can come from listening, and listening can inspire our imaginations.

In addition to listening for main points, supporting material, and inferences, we listen to *specific* vocabulary for information.

Vocabulary

The comprehensive listening role is focused primarily on the words of the sender, and it is important to be aware of the impact of words on understanding the message.

We have four vocabularies: the reading vocabulary being the largest; the listening vocabulary being the second largest; the writing vocabulary being the third largest; and the speaking vocabulary being the smallest.[2]

As adults, on the average, we possess reading vocabularies of 20,000 words, out of the possible 800,000 to one million words in the English language. However, our listening vocabularies average only 12,000 to 15,000 words.[3] The problem in comprehensive listening is that we do not all know the same 15,000 words, so there is a possibility of assigning an incorrect meaning or no meaning at all to the words being sent.

It seems reasonable, then, the larger the vocabulary we have, the better the chance of comprehending and attaching accurate meanings to the words. One way to increase the probability of accuracy is to develop an interest in words. We might make a note of words and word combinations that are new to us, and use them, so that they become part of our listening vocabulary, because the more words we understand, the better the chance of assigning accurate meaning when listening.

Concentration

To comprehend we must concentrate, and concentration is hard work. Research ranks inattentiveness—lack of concentration—as one of the most important listening barriers,[4] and this lack of attention or concentration is substantially affected by time, and internal and external distractions.

Time

One of the most significant distractions to effective comprehensive listening in our culture is time. While on the phone, we might be splitting our concentration time by writing a note or reading a short article. While listening to a lecture or a report, we might be giving time to that overdue project, reading a newspaper, or giving time to the people around us that we could visit with after the session.

Our culture puts a premium on time, and often we feel that we cannot give our total time to one message, so we focus on several different messages at the same time. The message becomes like a camera out of focus—we get some of it, but lose the subtle fine points that can be significant to our understanding of the information.

Time pulls our attention away from effective, focused comprehensive listening and so does weak concentration on the central message being sent. We lose our concentration because of internal and external distractions.

Internal Distractions

Internal reasons for weak concentration might come from our own self-esteem. Intrapersonal communication sets the stage for listening and all other interpersonal communication, and it is smart to remind ourselves that all communication begins with the self. If we are focusing on our own behavior or self-esteem while trying to listen to someone else, we will be comprehending only a portion of the external message.

We might be attending to internal noise: the headache we have, our hunger, or what we are going to say next. We might be thinking, "I know what he's going to say; I've heard this before; It's the same old stuff."

External Distractions

External noise which interferes with our concentration might be a siren, the ringing of a clock chime, a hot room, or the person next to us. We may also be focusing on the sender rather than the message, but the sender's tone of voice, clothing, and mannerisms are our concern only insofar as they enhance the information in the primary message.

When in the role of comprehensive listener, we need to realize that the average human mind can process about 500 words per minute, but the average speaker talks at only 140 words per minute. Therefore, a 360-word-per-minute concentration slippage exists in the listening/speaking system; that is, our minds could process 360 more words per minute than are being spoken. Because of this thought-speech differential, we can take trips while the sender is speaking. If these mental trips away from the sender's message get longer and longer, the listener may not come back, and lose a substantial portion of the message.[5]

A way to remedy these mental trips is to focus on every word being said until we become reengaged in the listening process. In addition, the listener might spend the extra processing to create examples and illustrations based on the content of the message.[6]

Memory

The effectiveness of comprehensive listening is measured by recall and understanding. If one could recall and understand one hundred percent of a message, that would indicate perfect comprehensive listening.

Certainly comprehending information without remembering it is not effective listening. One program designed to help us remember suggests four steps: 1) Consciously make the choice to remember, 2) create a visual picture of the message you want to remember, 3) associate the message with something familiar to you, and 4) repeat and discuss the message to yourself or others.[7]

1. *Choose to remember.* You might be listening to a presentation about the function of control surfaces on airplanes. You want to remember this information, so you tell yourself, "I want to remember this; it is important."
2. *Create a picture.* As the sender talks about the effect of the *elevator* and the *pitch* of the airplane; the *ailerons* and the *roll*; and the *rudder* and the *yaw*; you visualize these maneuvers.
3. *Associate with familiar.* Now you connect these control surface functions to something you have experienced like riding a bicycle or steering a boat. Or you can make other creative connections. You might think of an elevator which goes up and down, and connect it to the idea of *pitch* which raises or lowers the nose of the plane; you could connect the fourth and fifth letters in ailerons as the first letters in *ro*ll; and you might change the spelling of *rudder* to *yudder* to remember *yaw*.
4. *Repeat and discuss.* Finally, you repeat and discuss the ideas: elevator/pitch; ailerons/roll; rudder/yaw, until they become familiar. If you diligently keep these listening exercises active, you will remember the information.

A number of mental devices can help us remember and understand information. One is called a *mnemonic* device which is frequently used to make acronyms. (An acronym uses the first letter of a list of works, to make a name.) For example the acronym HOMES can be a key to remember the Great Lakes—Huron, Ontario, Michigan, Erie, and Superior. While listening, we can make mnemonic associations that are simple, but help us remember names or dates. The mnemonics might be silly and outrageous, but nonetheless can aid in remembering.

Another memory helper is the *link* system where the listener links or associates vivid images to the information being sent.[8] Again, the link can be as ridiculous as it needs to be to remember it. For example, imagine being at a meeting, and being introduced to Harry Jackson, a car salesman. To remember his name and what he does you link his name to a car with hair (Harry) growing all over it; the trunk open, exposing the spare tire and the jack (Jackson). Sitting in the car is the man you just met. The next time you need to communicate with him, there is a good probability that you will remember his name and what he does. Or you are listening to a talk about the workings of the human eye, and the sender notes that the rods sense the lightness and darkness, and the cones sense color. You link rods and light with lightning rods, and the letter "C" (Cones) with the "C" in color and remember the information for future reference.

Additionally, when we listen we can link in with numbers. For example, the telephone number, 322-7743 has a natural link with the number seven. The obvious link is with the two sevens, but there are two other links—322 adds up to seven and so does 4 and 3. Linking can become an effective way to help comprehensive listening and remembering.

As a final thought, researchers in memory indicate two ways to improve memory that will help in preparing for the comprehensive listening role: 1) be motivated. Have a strong desire to remember. Ask yourself, "What's in it for me?" 2) Focus your concentration on remembering.[9]

Notetaking

Taking notes increases involvement in the listening process, and it can help in understanding and remembering messages in at least three ways. First, studies have found that notetaking helps us focus our concentration, by increasing our involvement and our attention to the message. This heightened attention and involvement increase the chances of recalling the message at a later time.[10] Second, notetaking raises our awareness of the structure of the message. It helps us visualize the flow of the message. We can see how the main points develop the thesis of the presentation; how the supporting material clarifies our understanding of these main points, and how the sender transitions from point to point. The third value of notetaking is that we have a "hard copy" of the message. When we need to review the message, we can look over the notes, and research on recall has found that notetakers remember messages in more detail than non-notetakers.[11]

As soon as possible after the presentation, the listener should read the notes and make any changes for clarity and completeness. Highlight any misunderstandings and try to make sense of them by asking questions or researching for answers. Developing a reliable and accurate system of notetaking will result in fuller understanding and retention of information, greatly increasing our effectiveness as comprehensive listeners.

Questioning

Questioning is a part of active listening, because it can help ensure accuracy of meaning and help us remember messages. Questions not only help the listener clarify messages, but they also give the sender a chance to correct unintended or confusing information. Necessarily, questions should be relevant to the message being sent. We need to keep in mind that our purpose in questioning is to help clarify and retain the message. Off-topic questions or questions that go beyond the sender's intended goal can disrupt the communication and ultimately lessen the amount of information exchanged. Questions should be thoughtful and to the point. They should be an attempt to clarify the sender's message and not become a forum for the listener to express her or his own views.

Summary

Identifying listening roles, and accurately determining which listening role we are taking, are the first steps in preparing to listen effectively. This chapter focuses on comprehensive listening, which is listening to understand and remember information. Comprehensive listening is centered on information which is found in the main points, supporting material, and inferences. Vocabulary, concentration, and memory are discussed as three key elements affecting comprehensive listening.

Concentration in the comprehensive listening role can be improved by focusing our time and energy on the message and removing internal and external distractions. Memory is improved by mnemonic devices and linking, and, when possible, note-taking.

Awareness Exercises, Chapter 6

Name ______________________________ **SS#** _____-____-_____

Before responding, spend some time paying attention to your own comprehensive listening and the comprehensive listening of others. Notice how much time you spend listening comprehensively.

Listening awareness exercise. Please answer these questions thoughtfully.

1. List and describe three comprehensive listening settings you have been involved with in the last month.

   A.

   B.

   C.

2. Describe an inference that you made which was incorrect.

3. Describe an inference that you made which was correct.

4. Describe a misunderstanding that came about as the result of an incorrect meaning of a word.

5. Describe a comprehensive listening setting where you used your time efficiently.

6. Describe a comprehensive listening setting where your mind wandered.

7. Describe a comprehensive setting where your mind did not wander.

8. Describe a mnemonic device you have used to help you remember a series of facts.

9. Describe a link, or association, you have used to remember a fact or series of facts.

10. Outline a procedure for preparing for the comprehensive listening role.

7 Listening Therapeutically

The therapeutic listener offers an upset person the chance to talk about a problem. When discussing the comprehensive listening role, the major concern is for *the listener to understand and remember the message*. In therapeutic listening, our primary concern is with the sender's *feelings* about the content being expressed. We are there not primarily to gain and remember information, but to allow the sender to express feelings.

In this chapter we will discuss the therapeutic listening role, listening for feelings, and therapeutic listening guidelines. Before beginning the discussion of the therapeutic listening role, imagine yourself a listener in the following situations:

A friend that you jog with comes into your office and tells you that she will not be able to work out today. You ask her, "What's up? Is there a problem?" She replies,

> Well, Hank (her husband) just called and . . . and the x-rays came back from his physical, and . . . well, they're not sure what they've found. The doctor said they want to do a complete scan to verify what they think. Hank's been so careful to take good care of his health, and we've made so many plans. I'm *worried; scared.* We're both going to take the afternoon off and have lunch together and talk. Oh, I'm so *scared.*

A colleague in your department sits down with a cup of coffee, and in the course of a casual conversation says,

> That new office procedure for checking out equipment is a real pain. All it's done is add another level of administrative bureaucracy and double the amount of time and paper work to get a job done. What used to take me ten minutes to get what I need, now takes three or four days. I'm *disgusted* and *frustrated* about being ignored around this place. They give me deadlines and then make it impossible to get anything done on time. I'm really *overwhelmed* with all the nonsense they give me.

You are having lunch with a friend who is separated from his wife and going through a divorce. In the course of the conversation he says,

> I'm really *disappointed* that things didn't work out. After twelve years you'd think there would be something left to build on, but I guess there isn't. I feel *hurt* that I've invested so much time and energy into a relationship only to see it go down the drain. I go home at night and feel so *lonely* and *forsaken.*

You are a supervisor and one of your employees meets with you and shares some of her thoughts,

> Well, as you know, I submitted my plan for the new operation, and it was rejected. Maybe I didn't take enough time researching it, I don't know.

> But I spent almost four months on that project, and I think it was a good one. Anyway, that's all history, and I'm pretty *demoralized* and kind of *insecure* about submitting any other proposals. I feel *inferior* and *inadequate* at this point. Maybe I should just turn my attention to something else.

You and a fellow worker are driving to a meeting. Since the meeting is about an hour's drive away, a number of subjects are discussed. As you get to know each other better, your passenger brings up something that has been on his mind.

> Did you see the amount of money they spent on the new City Hall? I really think the mayor went way off the center line on this one. We've got potholes in the streets that will destroy anything but a truck, and he spends seven million on refurbishing six offices. I'm really *annoyed*. No. I'm *enraged* about this misspending of taxpayers' money. I'm also *resentful* that he got the money appropriated without a public hearing. But I guess I'm not the first one to be *mad* about it; there have been three *bitter* editorials in the last three weeks about the situation.

❑ The Therapeutic Listening Role ❑

In each of these situations the words and nonverbal messages indicate that the listener should be in the therapeutic listening role, a role *that focuses on the sender* and allows him or her to talk through concerns and problems. The therapeutic listening role encourages the sender to unburden problems and concerns and possibly arrive at some solutions.

❑ Listening for Feelings ❑

The therapeutic listening role is concerned with the sender's *feelings*. For example, in the first conversation, the woman unburdened her feelings of *fear* regarding the uncertainties of her husband's health. In the second, the man disclosed the *stress* he was feeling with the new procedures. In the third scene, the man going through the divorce revealed his feeling of *sadness*. The fourth example, with the woman whose plan was rejected, left a feeling message of *inadequacy*, and the fifth, in the car revealed the passenger's strong feelings of *anger* at what he considered inappropriate spending of tax money. In each of these conversations, the feelings in the messages are at least as important as the topic of the message.

The measure of success in the therapeutic listening role is more than the retention of information as it is in the comprehensive listening role. We are successful at therapeutic listening when we create a climate where the sender is able to express feelings about his or her concerns. Success in therapeutic listening hinges on *empathy*, the degree to which the listener becomes a rational and emotional mirror that invites the troubled speaker's discussion of a problem without judging. Carl Rogers, a psychologist, offers a succinct definition of empathy:

> It [empathy] means entering the private perceptual world of the other and becoming thoroughly at home in it. It involves being sensitive, moment by moment, to the changing felt meanings which flow in this other person, to the fear or rage or tenderness or confusion or whatever

> that he or she is experiencing. It means temporarily living in the other's life, moving about in it delicately without making judgments. . . .[1]

To the extent that the empathic climate encourages a free and open expression of feelings, therapeutic listening is successful.

People involved in all phases of business, professional, and family activities need to recognize the importance of therapeutic listening. Preoccupation with problems by clients, coworkers, supervisors, employees, and family members can lesson their overall effectiveness. Someone who understands the therapeutic listening role can help increase the concerned person's efficiency by allowing him or her to unburden the problem.

Therapeutic listening should stay within the bounds of normal, everyday problems: relationships, anger at a procedure, mild financial problems, illnesses, and so on. A listener in the therapeutic role should be sensitive to serious problems that might be life-threatening or have other serious implications. *If problems of this magnitude exist, the listener should refer the sender to a professional counselor.*

Therapeutic listening *focuses on the sender and his or her feelings.* To emphasize this idea, listen to this message from a junior in college who started the conversation by talking in general terms about his college experiences. Changes in the content of the message indicate that we are no longer in the comprehensive listening role. As he unburdens his feelings, the message shifts to therapeutic.

> I'm in class maybe sixteen hours a week, but I have Tuesday and Thursday afternoons free, so there's plenty of time to study . . . but I just don't have much enthusiasm. My grades are just okay—maybe even a little below par. I know I could do better if I wanted to. I don't know why my disappointment with the school and some of the faculty members can get to me so much. It's not like me. Ever since I can remember—even in primary school, when I didn't have any idea what an engineer was—I've wanted to be an engineer. Theoretically, I should be happy as a lark that I made my third year in engineering, but I'm not.

In this conversation, this student has been exploring his disappointment with himself and with his performance in school. He is concerned with such issues as his dislike for the school and for some of the teachers. Listening empathically, what would we determine are this man's primary feelings? What, if anything, would we say to him? Can we sense how listening to him and letting him unburden his feelings can improve his productivity at school? Psychiatrists, psychologists, and counselors are professional therapeutic listeners, but as this example shows, the need for therapeutic listening enters the lives of all of us who interact with people.

Typically, our educational backgrounds are more focused on comprehensive listening for content than on empathic listening for feelings. Consequently, in therapeutic listening, it is important to understand how some content words are in fact expressions of feelings. Some examples of content words and the feelings they reflect are presented in the following list.[2] With this list in mind, we can reread the five conversations at the beginning of this chapter and understand how the sender's words alerted the listener to the fact that s/he was in the therapeutic listening role, and we can also determine how the emphasized words revealed the feelings being expressed:

Feelings of Anger

Aggravated	Hostile
Angry	Intolerant
Annoyed	Irritated
Belligerent	Mad
Bitter	Mean
Bugged	Peeved
Cool	Perturbed
Cruel	Resentful
Enraged	Spiteful
Furious	Vengeful
Hateful	Vindictive

Feelings of Sadness

Abandoned	Grief(stricken)
Alienated	Hopeless
Alone	Humiliated
Ashamed	Hurt
Awful	Lonely
Blue	Low
Crushed	Neglected
Defeated	Rejected
Depressed	Sad
Despondent	Small
Disappointed	Sorrow
Down	Unhappy
Forlorn	Unloved(able)
Forsaken	Worthless

Feelings of Fear

Afraid
Alarmed
Anxious
Apprehensive
Desperate
Embarrassed
Fearful
Frightened
Horrified
Insecure
Intimidated
Nervous
Overwhelmed
Panicky
Restless
Scared
Shy
Tense
Timid
Uneasy
Worried

Feelings of Inadequacy

Broken
Cowardly
Crippled
Deficient
Demoralized
Disabled
Feeble
Helpless
Impotent
Inadequate
Incompetent
Ineffective
Inferior
Insecure
Paralyzed
Powerless
Small
Useless
Vulnerable
Weak

Feelings of Stress

Ambivalent
Anxious
Baffled
Bewildered
Bothered
Caught
Confused
Conflicted
Disgusted
Dissatisfied
Distressed
Disturbed
Doubtful
Exposed
Frustrated
Futile
Helpless
Hopeless
Nervous
Overwhelmed
Perplexed
Puzzled
Skeptical
Trapped
Uncomfortable
Unsure
Upset
Vulnerable

Becoming familiar with the feelings these words express will help alert us to the fact that we are in the therapeutic role and give us insight into the nature of the sender's concern.

Being alert to the therapeutic listening role can help people work through problems and improve their outlook. Not attending to important therapeutic cues could allow problems to grow out of proportion.

In this example, a drill instructor recalls the impact of therapeutic listening.[3]

> As a Drill Instructor at the Marine Corps Recruit Depot in San Diego, it was my duty to deal on a very personal level with a wide variety of people in some very unusual circumstances. Because of the very nature of Marine Corps boot camp, misunderstanding due to faulty listening and culture shock was more the rule than the exception. What follows is one of the more memorable events of my tour of duty.
>
> My role as a therapeutic listener was extensive. Although it was my duty to administer discipline in an almost inhuman manner, it was just as much my responsibility to listen to their problems and try to find an answer or refer them to someone who could.
>
> During my first period of a new platoon, I was faced with one of the usual "whiners." These are Privates who want to go home; boot camp didn't turn out to be what they thought. Our usual answer was, "Too bad, you're here for the duration." It was no different with this one.
>
> I sincerely wish that I had taken the time to listen. It wouldn't have hurt me, and it might have saved this kid's life. The next morning he dove out a third story window to the concrete below.

Listening therapeutically extends into family as well as work related interactions. For example, listening empathically to children can nurture healthy psychological and emotional development and further their contributions to society. When we think of adults who influenced our lives as we grew up, we can learn about the impact of their therapeutic listening by asking: "Did they listen to us without judging?" "Did they spend time attending to us; allowing us to talk?" *People Reading*, a book about listening, highlights the need to listen to the feelings of children.

> Listening to a young person can easily be an act of love. Listening with concern but without judging is an art, and it helps the child explore his motivations, his style, and the accomplishments he has so far achieved. . . . It means giving him a safe place where he can speak at his own speed and explore new options, however unrealistic they may appear to us.[4]

❑ Therapeutic Listening Guidelines ❑

When we have determined that the listening role is therapeutic, we can practice some behaviors that make this role effective in helping someone.*

1. Allow time to think. We should reflect on what the person has said and resist the temptation to respond quickly. We should ask ourselves, "What feelings are there?" "What is the basic message?" Taking time to think does not mean that the conversation loses its spontaneity. We should speak any time to help, but we should be sure we have thought before speaking. For example, if we are trying to clarify what the sender has said, rather than saying, "You're telling me that you hate school," we might say thoughtfully, "Let me see if I understand what you're saying."

---

* Much information has been written on therapeutic listening. This brief discussion is meant as a guide in dealing with normal day-to-day problems.

2. Short responses are usually best. We should keep the communication going back and forth, and avoid giving speeches. We should also try to keep the speaker from rambling.

The therapeutic listener needs to think things through and respond frequently, but the responses should be short and to the point. *Remember, we are helping by listening, so our talking should be kept to a minimum.*

3. Responses should be adapted to the speaker, by trying to share the emotional tone or climate with the person. We avoid imitating, but try to recognize and adapt to the mood of the speaker. If someone in the course of a dialogue says, "Ya, and to top the day off, I got notified that I'm being audited for last year's taxes." We should avoid a response like, "You should use my tax accountant; I never get audited." A response like that will just send the sender into a lower state, making him or her feel even less competent.[5] Instead, the listener should make a general comment: "It sounds like you're under a lot of pressure."

4. As therapeutic listeners, we need to decide when it is time to end the interaction. Someone discussing a difficult problem may become emotionally drained and need a break. At this point, it might be wise to suggest a break; get a cup of coffee; set up a time to visit again.

5. Avoid the impulse to talk. With most problems being discussed, we are listening to let the sender find solutions. Except to paraphrase part of the message for understanding, the listener should remain silent and attentive.[6]

6. Be sensitive to shifts in listening roles. When the content of a message tells us that our role is therapeutic, we form an empathic bond with the sender and act as sounding boards to help the sender unburden problems. We avoid evaluating and offering solutions. No decisions by the listener are made during a therapeutic interaction.

❑ Shut Up and Listen! ❑

Interactions in our daily lives will frequently put us in the therapeutic listening role. To be effective therapeutic listeners, we build a climate of acceptance and trust, so the sender is comfortable talking about feelings. Once feelings are expressed, the sender can often gain new insights into problems. Jennifer Kubik, a student of psychology, shares her thoughts about therapeutic listening in this essay, "Shut Up and Listen!"

In preparing for the essay I have written down times within the past few months where I have been in the therapeutic role, and times which I have sought out a therapeutic ear. After recording these situations I analyzed them trying to decipher which factors were important in allowing therapeutic listening to take place. I also looked at the factors that led to the situation having a positive or a negative outcome.

I will first discuss the factors I found to be important and influential. I will then give a few examples of good and bad situations which occurred throughout the last couple months involving therapeutic listening. Finally, I will analyze these situations and conclude with what I learned from taking a closer look at therapeutic listening.

There are several factors that play into the role of therapeutic listening. Many of these factors have the common thread of safety. I found that if the sender did not feel safe, he or she simply would not unburden. There are nine other factors that I found to be the most important and influential. Many of these factors are very closely related, work hand in hand with each other, and overlap each other. The nine factors are the following:

1. Time and Availability

The listener must be in position where he/she has enough time to sit down and really listen to the sender. I found that usually the sender has a very good sense of how available the listener is. Listening to someone is much more productive if it is not contending with time factors or hurried mannerisms.

An example of the shortened time factor hindering listening happened in the following situation: A friend knocked on my door when I was getting ready to walk out the door. I could tell she looked stressed and wanted to talk. I said, "What's up, I only have a few minutes because I have to leave for class, but let's talk." She responded, "No, Jenn, it's no big deal. I will just talk to you when you get back." I found out later that day that she had gotten a bad grade on a test that she needed to get a good grade on in order to pass the class, and she needed to tell someone. I simply could not be an effective listener because I didn't have much time I could devote to her.

2. Confidential Environment

This is an environment where both the listener and sender feel safe from anyone having the ability to "overhear" or "eavesdrop" on the conversation. This is an environment that is safe from interruptions.

Examples of the lack of confidential environment getting in the way of therapeutic listening are the following situations: My friend Ericka and I are at dinner when she starts to unburden, but sees that there are girls from our floor sitting around us and Ericka says, "Maybe we should talk about this another time." Just because the environment was not "safe" my friend felt like she could not unburden. Another example of an environment that didn't encourage therapeutic listening was the following situation: There always seems to be a lot of people in my room right after supper because all my neighbors like to use my computer for e-mail. My roommate and I have just learned that this isn't a good time or place to talk because our conversation will always be interrupted.

3. Established Trust

In seeking out a therapeutic listener I found that I always sought out someone that I knew I could trust. If the sender has already had a positive experience with the listener they are seeking, the chances are good that the person will return and feel confident about her decision. This is merely the trust that the person is a wise choice to confide in.

4. Non-Judgmental Listener

This is a listener who is not there to judge the sender or the message. In addition the listener is not there to solve the problem or offer too much advice. This concept is mentioned in this chapter as being one of the most important factors in being a good empathetic listener; I found the same to be true through my observations. I found out that when I myself got any type of advice or judgment from the listener, it lessened my chance of continuing to disclose, and ever to come back to that person to unburden.

5. Listener Reaction

I found that a listener who is not in a hurry (time/availability), not too emotionally involved or aroused, avoids judging, and one that can easily accept emotions that aren't always rational and well thought out, are the most effective therapeutic listeners. I found that when I listened to others, how I reacted to their emotions made a great deal of difference as to how much they would disclose. As much as I thought their emotions in a situation were immature, irrational, or just plain crazy, I tried not to convey that thought in my facial expressions or body language. When I showed it, they were less likely to disclose and sometimes not even willing to restate what they felt to make it fit into what I would think was appropriate. On the other hand, when I just stayed calm and showed no judgmental emotion they continued talking and disclosed more. As a result, people disclosed openly to me.

6. Confidentiality

This is where the sender is assured that the message will not be spread to anyone else. This is a lot like established trust, but different in that the sender believes that his or her feelings won't get broadcasted. I felt this factor deserved a category of its own because it is more than trusting in the personality of the listener, it is *trusting in the confidentiality of the situation.*

7. Undivided Listener Attention

This is where the listener is not distracted by any noise internally or externally. I found it hard to listen therapeutically when I was preoccupied with my own internal struggles. Many times my mood dictated how good I was at giving my attention to the sender. An example of how inattention led to unsuccessful listening is the following: I was getting ready for school when a friend of mine wanted to talk. I welcomed her in, but warned her that I had to finish getting ready while she was talking. She started to tell me about her day, but I could tell it was hard for her to continue because I was not giving her my full attention.

8. Out for the Good of the Sender

This factor also goes along with the non-judgmental factor. This is when the sender believes that the listener will be on their "side." If the listener does make a judgment, it will be in the sender's benefit if any advice is given.

9. Receiver/Sender Commonality

I found that many times when I sought out people with whom I could unburden, I looked for people that may be in my same situation or could easily relate to what I was feeling. An example of this was when I was in a position where I felt overwhelmed by a supervisor's demand to have all the phone calls made by Thursday. I knew that I had three tests that week and that I also had many other commitments. The first person that I sought out was a friend and fellow college student who was also involved in a lot of things. I knew that she would be able to see where I was coming from, because her experiences were similar to mine.

The first part of this essay focused on nine factors that I found to be most important in good therapeutic listening. Next, I will give examples of a positive and negative listening situation. After each situation, I will analyze it and try to explain what factors were present, making it positive or negative.

The setting is about 10 o'clock in the morning. I have already showered, gotten ready for class, eaten breakfast, cleaned my room, and written in my journal. I am now just relaxing until my class at 11. One of my friends who had class early in the morning knocks on my door. I answer it, and she greeted me with "Jenn, I am burning inside." I welcome her in, shut the door, turn off my stereo, move the blanket off of the chair, and pull it closer to listen. "I am getting so tired of Beth setting her alarm for 6 o'clock in the morning when she doesn't get up until 8. I am about to say something to her. She is always so inconsiderate." There is a pause.

I respond, "I get frustrated with my roommate sometimes too." This statement gives her freedom to continue to disclose.

"Jenn, she is a nice person and all, we just don't click. The things I am interested in, she's not. I can't understand her way of thinking. She has class at 8 and she doesn't go . . . ever. She'd rather spend three hours getting ready . . . it's to be cool and all, but I just want to sleep. I am so angry!"

I felt that this situation was very positive in terms of therapeutic listening. When we learned that "All you are for yourself, is only what you can be for others," I am finding to be very true. When my friend came to the door, all my needs were met and I had time to give her. I was able to give her my full attention, because I had no internal or external noise that was overpowering my ability to listen. We already had established trust in each other, along with being in a similar situation (we both lived in the dorms with a roommate). The situation took place in a confidential environment, free from distractions.

The setting is in my room after dinner. My roommate and I are discussing what our next semester class schedule will look like. My roommate, Lisa, states, "I am going to hate my schedule; it is going to be so hard. I am never going to be able to get good grades."

I responded by saying, "Well, then don't take so many hard classes. The ultimate choice is yours." Our conversation was over.

In this situation I spoke before I realized that I was in the therapeutic role. The conversation did not continue because I am sure my roommate felt like I was judging her, and that I wasn't listening, since I was too quick to talk and offer my own advice. My reaction dictated whether she would continue talking or not. She probably felt that I wasn't out for her own good. It would have been a more positive situation if I would have realized I was in this role right away.

As I look closer at therapeutic listening, I became more aware of the listening roles I was in at different times. I was surprised how many times I just said "Hi" to someone I knew in passing and we'd stop and talk and very quickly one of the two of us were in a therapeutic role. I also became aware of my own level of complaining, so I found myself trying to unburden in a less negative fashion.

In putting this essay together, I learned that being a good therapeutic listener will greatly enhance chances of people coming back to you and liking you. In some situations I consciously tried just to listen and do as little talking as possible. I was surprised that many people didn't even notice that I wasn't talking at all. Hours would pass, and as long as I was listening attentively, the other person was satisfied, even if I wasn't in the therapeutic role any more.

As I looked at some of the factors that I described, I started to think about how intelligently designed a counselor's office is. The environment is comfortable, safe, free from interruptions, and confidential. The other factors come into play when a counselor's personality is introduced as calm and nonjudgmental. Also in a counseling session the sender has the listener's full attention. As I observe and analyze different situations involving therapeutic listening, I get excited about my future. I know that if I realize when I am in the therapeutic listening role, I can practice these helpful skills every day.

❑ Summary ❑

The therapeutic listening role is listening to help, and it focuses on the sender's need to unburden problems. This role emphasizes empathy and nonjudgmental listening. Empathy is the listener's attempt to experience the same feelings that the sender is expressing, and nonjudgmental listening means suspending evaluation, that is, not judging the goodness/badness, or rightness/wrongness of the message. The sender's feelings are an important part of therapeutic listening, and certain words and nonverbal behaviors can help us understand these feelings.

On the job, at home, or in other relationships, we often interact with people who can be helped by talking about their problems. Within limits, we can listen therapeutically to help someone reach decisions about problems, and as a result increase productivity. Some guidelines for therapeutic listening include, taking time to think, offering short responses, adjusting to the sender, knowing when to end the interaction, avoiding the impulse to talk, and being sensitive to listening role changes. The person who takes the time to listen to help another unburden problems will experience strengthened relationships and improved morale and productivity.

We Listen with Our Hearts

When I listen with the heart
I stop playing the game of non-listening
In other words,
I step into the other's skin;
I walk in his shoes;
I attempt to see things from his point-of-view;
I establish eye contact;
I give him conscious attention;
I reflect my understanding of his words;
I question;
I attempt to clarify;
Gently,
I draw the other out
as his lips stumble over words,
as his face becomes flushed,
as he turns his face aside.
I make the other feel that
I understand that he is important,
that I am grateful that he trusts me enough
to share deep, personal feelings with me.
I grant him worth.

Awareness Exercises, Chapter 7

Name ____ **SS#** ______-_____-______

Before responding to these questions, spend some time paying attention to your therapeutic listening and the therapeutic listening of others. Notice how much time you spend listening therapeutically.

Listening awareness exercise. Please answer these questions thoughtfully.

1. Describe a situation in which you were a therapeutic listener.

   A. The setting

   B. The nature of the problem

   C. How you listened

   D. The outcome

2. When you share your problems with someone, describe the characteristics of that person.

   A. Personality

   B. How s/he listens

   C. The outcome

3. Describe a person with whom you would not want to share a problem.

4. Describe a person who listens to your problems

Awareness DataBase, Chapter 7

Name ______________________________ **SS#** _____-____-_____

1. People come to me with their problems.

   A. seldom B. C. D. E. often

2. I am comfortable talking about my problems.

   A. seldom B. C. D. E. often

3. I understand someone else's point of view.

   A. seldom B. C. D. E. often

4. I am comfortable listening to people's problems.

   A. seldom B. C. D. E. often

5. When I hear something I really disagree with, I keep my opinions to myself.

   A. seldom B. C. D. E. often

6. I express my feelings.

   A. seldom B. C. D. E. often

7. People tell me their feelings.

   A. seldom B. C. D. E. often

8. Listening to problems helps me understand my own problems better.

A.	B.	C.	D.	E.
seldom				often

9. Men find it more difficult to express feelings than women.

A.	B.	C.	D.	E.
seldom				often

10. Problems can be solved without talking about them.

A.	B.	C.	D.	E.
seldom				often

8 Listening Critically

This chapter discusses critical listening. Unlike the comprehensive and therapeutic roles, the critical role requires the listener *to evaluate a message and decide to do something or believe something.* When listening critically, we need to consider speaker credibility, the logic of the message, fallacies of reasoning, and the quality of data.

❑ The Critical Listening Role ❑

Communication situations might cause the listener to change from one listening role to the critical role. Unless the listener is alert to the critical nature of the message, s/he might make a decision without giving it sufficient thought. For example, someone calls for an appointment to inform you of a new system of recording and reporting information. You anticipate and prepare for a comprehensive listening situation, and at the appointed time, she arrives and begins her presentation.

As the information is being discussed, you become a bit uncomfortable and eventually realize that this "informative" interaction is a persuasive appeal to buy a computer data system. Once you realize that your listening role is now *critical* rather than *comprehensive*, you activate the critical listening behaviors necessary for a responsible decision.

A conversation might move from the therapeutic to the critical listening role. For example, someone stops by your home to tell you what a difficult meeting he had at work the previous night. His peers and his supervisor rejected an idea he had been working on for the past month. His self-esteem is low, and he needs to talk about the matter. You realize that you are in the therapeutic role and listen empathically. You talk for an hour, and when he is ready to leave, he comments that he feels much better, and is going home to do some gardening. On his way out to your yard, he notices a stack of old bricks, and asks if he could buy some from you to put a border around his garden. His request makes you uncomfortable, because the listening has just shifted from the *therapeutic* to *critical* role.

If you had not been aware of this shift from the therapeutic to the critical role, you might have decided to help him by selling him the bricks. However, since you really want to keep the bricks you reply, "No, I want to keep them for a sidewalk I'm making." This example emphasizes the idea that we must be alert to listening role changes, especially when the change goes to the critical role. If we are not alert to the critical nature of the message, an unsatisfactory decision could be made.

Critical listening can occur in a variety of settings. Some of them are obviously persuasive, and some of them may have little or no apparent persuasive intent. Our lives are filled with persuasive messages from sales people, telephone solicitations, problem solving discussions, friends trying to get us to go somewhere, requests to donate to one group or another, appeals asking us to volunteer for certain activity or clubs, and appeals for new procedures. All of these messages are pushing us to make decisions. The decisions may be short-term and relatively unimportant—"How many boxes of Girl Scout cookies should I buy," or they may be decisions that impact the rest of our lives—"Should we adopt the child?"

When we are in the critical listening role, we are acting as judges hearing arguments. The arguments may not be as formal and dramatic as an actual trial, but the considerations are similar. In making a decision, we ask, "Can I believe this person?" "Do I share the values being expressed?" "Are the conclusions reasonable and logical?" "Does the proposal meet *my* needs?" "Can I afford this?" "What are the long-term implications of this decision?" "Should I be exploring alternatives?" "Who else will be involved by this decision?" "Can I take more time to decide, or is it a 'one time only' chance?"

In order to make the best decision, we need to listen holistically. We listen to the believability, or *credibility*, of the sender, the logical structure and arrangement of ideas, the reasoning patterns, and the validity of evidence.

❑ Speaker Credibility ❑

"What you are speaks so loudly, I can't hear what you say," is an idea that demonstrates that frequently we listen to the person more than to the words being spoken. As critical listeners, we pay attention to the credibility of the speaker. A speaker with a long-standing reputation, who is a well-known authority, is more believable than a speaker who is unknown.

In judging whether to believe a speaker, we need to examine five aspects of credibility: competence, character, intention, personality,[1] and dynamism.

1. *Competence.* Competence is the product of the knowledge, background, and achievements of the speaker. A person who has spent years exploring a topic through research and practice would be considered competent. However, competence in one field of experience is usually not transferable to another. For example, a famous pilot endorsing a specific brand of air conditioner may be relying on his expertise as a pilot to transfer to an unrelated subject, air conditioning. Consequently, one might make a poor decision to purchase a certain type of air conditioner based on the testimony of someone who is an expert at flying airplanes but who actually knows little about cooling equipment.

2. *Character.* Character comes from the speaker's honesty. We ask: "Do I *trust* the speaker?" When critically listening to someone we trust, we will generally accept that s/he has *our* best interests in mind. Trust is difficult to measure and understand, but it is central to many of our decisions. Recall decisions you made because of people in your life that you trust, that is people who follow through on their promises and commitments. Think of how you listen to them. Picture how you listen to those you do not trust, and the influence they have on your decision.

3. *Intentions.* The intentions of the speaker are closely related to character and trust. We ask: "Is the persuader's intent genuinely to make my life better, more comfortable, easier?" "Is the coach really concerned about me, as a person?" "Does the coach want to win at any cost?" "Is the sales person working for a sale or really interested in my needs?" We listen critically to the intentions of the speaker and make decisions accordingly.

4. *Personality.* Personality encompasses the traits that make a person socially appealing. Is the speaker positive and optimistic, or negative and pessimistic? In general, we prefer to agree with *positive* and *affirming* people because they recognize our good qualities, see the fun in life, and affirm and respect us.

5. *Dynamism.* Dynamism is the energy behind the message. It is not necessarily volume or animation, but it is intensity, sincerity, and genuineness. It is a willingness on the part of the speaker to let the strength of his or her feelings come to the surface. Someone who is shy and totally introverted is viewed as less dynamic and less credible than a sender who has a high level of intensity and energy behind the message.[2]

In making judgments about the credibility of an unknown speaker, we listen for indications of expertise and knowledge. The role of critical listener is to listen for messages which establish the believability of the speaker. We ask, "Can I rely on this speaker for this decision?" "Has the speaker had success with the topic being discussed?" "Did the speaker answer my questions with depth, knowledge, and wisdom?"

Certain groups and professions are automatically judged to have higher credibility and believability than other groups. Harris pollsters concluded in the mid 1980's that Americans viewed universities and colleges, the medical profession, the supreme court, and military personnel with high credibility. The credibility of the White House, organized religion, and TV news ranked second. Law firms and unionized labor were at the lowest tier of credibility.[3]

Credibility, then, is a measure of the believability of the sender. The first step in the critical listening role is to determine the level of credibility by examining competence, character, intentions, personality, and dynamism. *Next, we examine the logic being used in the decision-making message.*

❑ Logic ❑

As critical listeners we listen to the structure, or logic, of persuasive messages. To help understand logical structure, Stephen Toulmin, a logician, defined six parts of logic that should be critically examined by the listener: data, claim, warrant, backing, rebuttal, and qualifier.[4]

Data

In the structure of a persuasive message, data are used as the basis of proof for an assertion. They are tangible, measurable, and can be examined and verified. Facts, opinions, statistics, and testimony fall under the heading of data. Some examples of data are:

Fact: The temperature fell to -30 degrees last night.
Opinion: I think she would be a good addition to our staff.
Statistics: Between forty and forty-five percent of the crops are planted.
Testimony: My twenty-five years in forecasting leads me to believe that we'll have a cool, dry summer.

Claims

Claims are what the sender wants us to do. They are the solutions, conclusions, or actions to be considered. A claim is the goal of the persuasive message. Examples of claims are, "Try this plan to solve the problem"; "There can be no other choice"; "Let's have one more for the road"; "I'm pretty sure it's going to rain"; "Buy this car before the new models arrive." Claims are drawn from analogy, sign, cause-effect, induction, or deduction. As critical listeners, we determine the validity of a claim by examining how it was reached by the sender.

Claims from Analogy

An *analogy* infers that if two things are alike in some respects, they could be alike in others. For example, an analogy could be used by an electrician who claims that a house needs new wiring. The electrician uses an analogy comparing electrical systems, which the homeowner knows very little about, with the use of water, which the homeowner *does* understand. In this dialogue in which the electrician compares electricity with the flow of water, the homeowner decides not to replace her wiring because the analogy is not valid where electrical fuse protection is involved. Here is a persuasive dialogue that might take place between the electrician and the homeowner. The electrician is the first to speak:

> "Picture a new house with a swimming pool," he says. "Great water demands, right? Now picture the pipes coming into the place; they're small, about this big." He closes his thumb and finger to about a quarter inch. "What's going to happen when the owner tries to fill the pool and the hot tub at the same time?"
>
> "You didn't tell me there was a hot tub," the homeowner mentions.
>
> "Well, there is, anyway. Sorry about that. But what's going to happen?"
>
> "Not enough water can get through the pipes."
>
> "Precisely," says the electrician, nodding and smiling. "So the pool and tub take three weeks to fill. Or . . . "
>
> "Or what?"
>
> "Or the pipes coming into your place break. Pipes can handle only so much water, and wires can handle only so much electrical current."
>
> "And my wires are too small? They need to be replaced with bigger ones?"
>
> "Excellent thinking," again, he smiles. "They could get hot and cause a fire."
>
> "But do pipes have fuses or circuit breakers to protect them?" asks the homeowner.
>
> "No," the electrician answers.
>
> "There's where your analogy between plumbing and electricity fails," the homeowner tells the electrician. "If my wires got overloaded, a fuse will save them from getting too hot and starting a fire, but pipes will just burst."

We must listen carefully to analogies to be sure the comparisons are valid, because the key is to determine if the analogy is similar in all of the aspects involving the decision. The analogy above was only partially valid since some water systems lack protective devices found in electric systems.

Claims from Signs

Signs suggest facts, conditions, or qualities that are not immediately evident; they are indications of something. An example of a claim from a sign is, "You're carrying an umbrella [sign], it must be raining [claim]." The critical listener must listen carefully to be sure the signs support the claims being drawn, that other signs point to the same claim, and that contradictory signs are explained.

We frequently look for signs to arrive at claims or conclusions. In this example we have a case of contradictory signs pointing to different claims:

> I could tell by his dirty bib overalls and unkempt appearance [signs] that he was out of work [claim]; as he walked toward me [sign], I guessed that he was probably going to ask me for some money [claim]. When I saw him walk over to the limousine as his driver opened the door for him [sign], I realized that perhaps I had drawn the wrong conclusions from his clothing and behavior.

As critical listeners, we must carefully explore the validity of claims drawn from signs. We listen to determine if the signs are really pointing to valid conclusions, or if several claims could be drawn from the same sign.

Claims from Cause-Effect

Claims from *cause-effect* argue that "This, and only this, caused that." For example, "Cigarette smoking causes lung cancer [cause-effect], so stop smoking [claim]." "Getting a university education [cause] assures a high paying job [effect]. Therefore you should continue your education [claim]." "The price of oil [cause] is slowing the economy [effect]. We must work to lower oil prices [claim]." The critical listener needs to determine if the stated cause is a *real* cause, and if it is the *only* cause. We may reject the idea of working to lower oil prices, because other data indicate many causes of a slow economy.

Claims from Induction

A message that uses specific instances or facts to draw a general conclusion is using *induction*. An example of a claim drawn from inductive reasoning is: "I talked to the girls at my table [specific instance], and everybody's going to Joe's after the game [claim]," or "I contacted three of the guys who took that seminar, and there's nothing worthwhile to be gained from going to it."

In both cases the speaker is making a general claim (". . . everybody's going to Joe's after the game," and ". . . there's nothing worthwhile to be gained from going to it.") derived from specific details: the girls at the table and three who attended a seminar. In cases of induced claims, the critical listener must listen for the number of individual testimonies that have led to the claim. Do the instances represent the whole? That is, how many is "everybody"? And are three opinions enough to determine the value of a seminar? Do the people polled represent the entire group?

As active critical listeners, we need to question the speaker to determine the kind of sample used. Also, we need to determine if significant exceptions are being explained. Maybe some of the girls not going to Joe's have gone before and found it a real waste of time and money. Maybe those who *are* going to Joe's have never gone before and do not know what to expect.

The generalized claim about the seminar that has "nothing worthwhile" needs the same scrutiny. What are the standards for "worthwhileness"? The number of jokes the seminar leader tells? The number of friends in the seminar? The fact that someone received a bad experience in another seminar could even prompt that generalization.

Claims from Deduction

Deduction structures a message from general information to specific conclusions. For example, "Our basketball games are always exciting, so I'm sure tonight's basketball game is going to be exciting!" is a specific claim about tonight's game based on the speaker's general knowledge that the team plays exciting, fast-paced basketball. However, as critical listeners, we need to be aware that in spite of the general exiting character of the games, this one could lack excitement. Even great teams have occasional let downs.

We are basing a decision on deduction if we stop for a cup of coffee ". . . because," says our traveling companion, "all of the service areas have good coffee." Obviously, she has not tried all of the service stops, but has apparently sampled some of them and found they served good coffee. From these favorable experiences she has formed the general idea that all the service areas have good coffee, and she infers by deduction that this specific stop also serves good coffee.

In this inspection of critical listening, we have looked at data—the facts and proof being used—and we have examined claims and conclusions, and how we arrive at them. Now we will explore *Warrants* which are the link between the data and the claim.

Warrants

Warrants are statements that are generally believed by the listeners. They connect the data and the claim. Often warrants are not stated by the sender, so as critical listeners we need to study the structure of the arguments to determine the warrants. Once we understand warrants, we have made substantial growth in analyzing decisions made from critical listening.

Claim and Warrants from Analogies

The *warrant* is the link between the data and the claim, and it is a general statement. In the earlier analogy about water and electricity, the electrician is persuading a homeowner to rewire her house; he uses an analogy, saying that substantial use of water requires larger pipes.

His arguments goes like this: You are using substantial amounts of electricity [data]; therefore your house needs to be rewired with bigger wire and more circuits [claim].

The unstated warrant in this argument is, "The physical activity of water is the same as the physical activity of electricity." This warrant links the data to the claim with a general statement that encompasses both the data (which involve water) and the claim (which involves electricity). In addition to claims and warrants from analogies, we will examine four additional claims and warrants that are found in persuasive messages. These are claims from: 1) signs, 2) cause-effect, 3) induction, and 4) deduction.

Signs suggest facts, conditions, or qualities that are not immediately evident; they are indications of something else. Under the discussion, Claims from Signs, we used this paragraph to illustrate that signs can lead to faulty claims.

> I could tell by his dirty bib overalls, and unkempt appearance [signs] that he was out of work [claim]; as he walked toward me [sign]. I guessed that he was probably going to ask me for some money [claim]. When I saw him walk over to the limousine as his driver opened the door for him [sign], I realized that perhaps I had drawn the wrong conclusions from his clothing and behavior.

The logic in this paragraph looks like this:

Data [sign]: dirty overalls, unkempt appearance.

Warrant, unstated: personal appearance is related to employment.

Claim: He is out of work.

Data [sign]: walking to limousine; driver opening door.

Warrant, unstated: expensive possessions and support employees indicate success.

Claim: He is a successful, well rewarded person; the first conclusion was not correct.

Claims and Warrants from Induction

Inductive logic builds from specific instances to a general claim. The claim discussed earlier, "Everybody's going to Joe's after the game," has the warrant:

Warrant: More than 85 percent of a sample, means "everybody."

Data: Eighty-six percent of those I talked to are going to Joe's after the game.

As critical listeners, we can examine this warrant by questioning the sampling techniques: Why is eight-five percent representative of the whole population? How many people were sampled? Was it a random sample? Why aren't the other fifteen percent going?

Claims and Warrants from Deduction

Claims that go from the general to the specific are arrived at through deduction. Our enthusiastic speaker in this category claimed:

Claim: Tonight's home basketball game is going to be exciting!

Warrant: All home games are exciting.

Data: We are playing a home basketball game tonight.

Listening critically, you find that you are uncomfortable with the claim, so you question the validity of the warrant. You might not accept the warrant that all home games are exciting. So you reject the warrant as stated and recast it:

Warrant: "*Some* of our *conference* home games are exciting."

You reject the speaker's claim and change it to:

Claim: "Tonight's game *might* be exciting."

And based on the changed claim, you decide not to go to the game tonight.

Data, claims, and warrants are the backbone of critically listening to logic, Toulmin adds three more parts for logical analysis: Backing, Rebuttal, and Qualifier.

Backing

Backing is data that prove the warrant, because sometimes, as critical listeners we might reject a warrant at face value. The electrician in the earlier example needed to offer more backing for his warrant: "The physical activity of water parallels the physical activity of electricity." To increase the believability of the warrant, backing can be added, which might include some testimonials from qualified experts. The electrician could have provided backing in the form of a picture showing similarities between electricity and water. If possible, he could have given examples that show that some water systems have safety plugs that release when the pressure becomes too much for the system. This would certainly have helped in his persuasive efforts when the homeowner mentioned the fuse/circuit breaker information.

Notice how understanding warrants—a job that takes a good deal of thought and energy on the part of the critical listener—can help us get to the core of a persuasive message.

Now we move to the appeal to go to Joe's house after the game. The answers to the questions we posed as critical listeners can provide the foundation for the backing. The warrant, which was unstated by the sender, was "More than 85 percent of a sample means 'everyone.'" What kind of backing would we listen for to accept this warrant?

Here is some backing that we might find acceptable:

Backing: According to a widely used book on survey statistics: "when a sample exceeds 85 percent, the survey is said to include virtually the entire population."

This backing might help us accept the warrant, and the data might be sufficient to persuade us that "Everybody's going to Joe's house after the game," and, of course, we should go, too.

Next, we move to the basketball game. We critically listened to the enthusiastic sender and generated this warrant: "All State home games are exciting." We heard the data: "State is playing at home tonight," and then the claim: "Tonight's game is going to be exciting."

We have disagreed with the validity of the warrant, saying, "Some of State's home conference games are exciting." If we were to mention that only *some* of the games are exciting, the speaker could respond by providing Backing for the warrant:

> *Backing*: A poll in the state's major newspaper showed that 90 percent of the state's population thought that their team played hotly contested, competitive home conference games, which was exciting.
>
> *Backing:* John Filborne, the president of the student body, believes all of our home games are exciting.

Given this backing for the warrant, we as critical listeners might accept the claim that tonight's game is going to be exciting.

Backing is a special form of data that support the warrant, and a warrant is a generalized claim, often unstated but central to the effectiveness of critical listening.

The last two parts of Toulmin's model are Rebuttal and Qualifier; they are fairly simple and apply to the Claim.

Rebuttal

A Rebuttal is an escape hatch that puts certain restrictions on the claim: "There's a *chance* the game won't be exciting. The rebuttal takes this "chance" into account, and modifies the claim. So now we hear a claim with a rebuttal:

> *Claim with Rebuttal.* Tonight's basketball game is going to be exciting [claim], *unless a key player is sick or misses the game for some reason* [rebuttal].
>
> *Claim with Rebuttal.* Everybody's going to Joe's house after the game [claim], *unless it goes into overtime and gets too late* [rebuttal].

Qualifier

A qualifier gives the listener the degree of probably, either in actual percentages or with words like, "possibly," "more than likely," "probably," "almost certainly," "there is a good chance," and so on. The qualifier does just what it means, it qualifies the claim.

> *Claim with Qualifier.* Eighty-five percent [qualifier] of the group is going to Joe's after the game.
>
> *Claim with Qualifier.* There is a good possibility [qualifier] that tonight's game will be exciting.

Claim with Qualifier and Rebuttal

Of course claims can have both a qualifier and the rebuttal.

> I think there's a good chance [qualifier] that tonight's game is going to be exciting [claim], unless Johnson's elbow isn't healed [rebuttal].

Here is a summary of Toulmin's system of logic as adapted to critical listening.

Toulmin's Model of Logical Structures

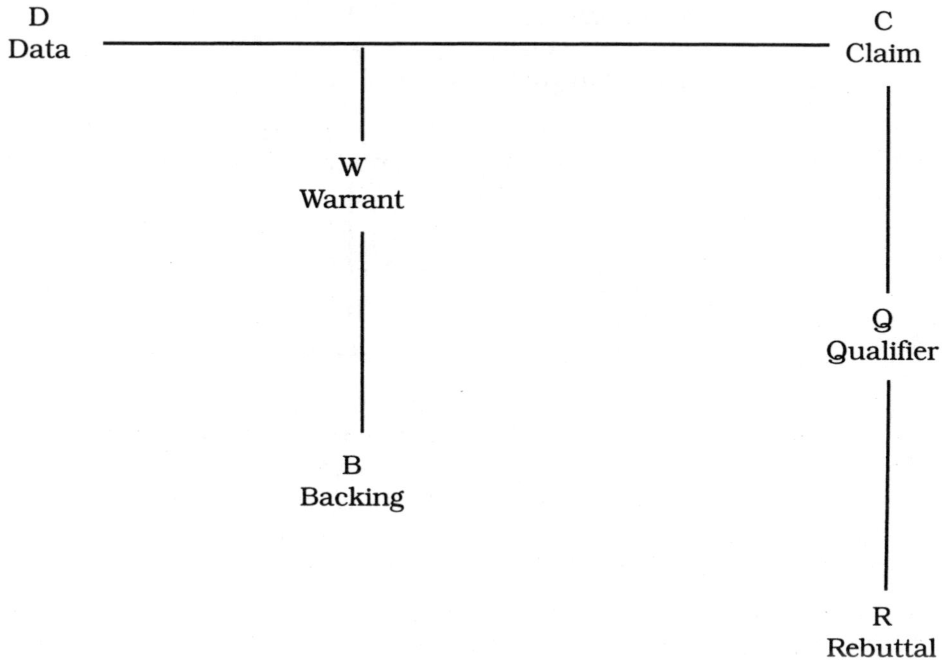

1. **(D) Data:** what we have to connect us with reality: facts, opinions, comparisons, statistics, testimonies, examples, illustrations, analogies, narratives, observations, any forms of proof.
2. **(C) Claim:** the solution or conclusion drawn from the Data. To a lesser or greater degree the claim is potentially controversial.
3. **(W) Warrant:** the bridge or "mental jump" from the data to the claim. How we get to a conclusion. Often not stated by the sender.
4. **(B) Backing:** data that strengthen the acceptability of the warrant. Sometimes listeners will not accept a warrant at its face value, so backing could be used as proof of the warrant.
5. **(R) Rebuttal:** an escape hatch which modifies the Claim. The claim may not be true under all circumstances, so the rebuttal acknowledges those circumstances. (For example, "Unless the game goes into overtime.")
6. **(Q) Qualifier:** gives the degree of probability to the Claim. "Possibly . . . Probably . . . sixty-five times out of one hundred . . . 70 percent chance."

Toulmin's Model of Logical Structures

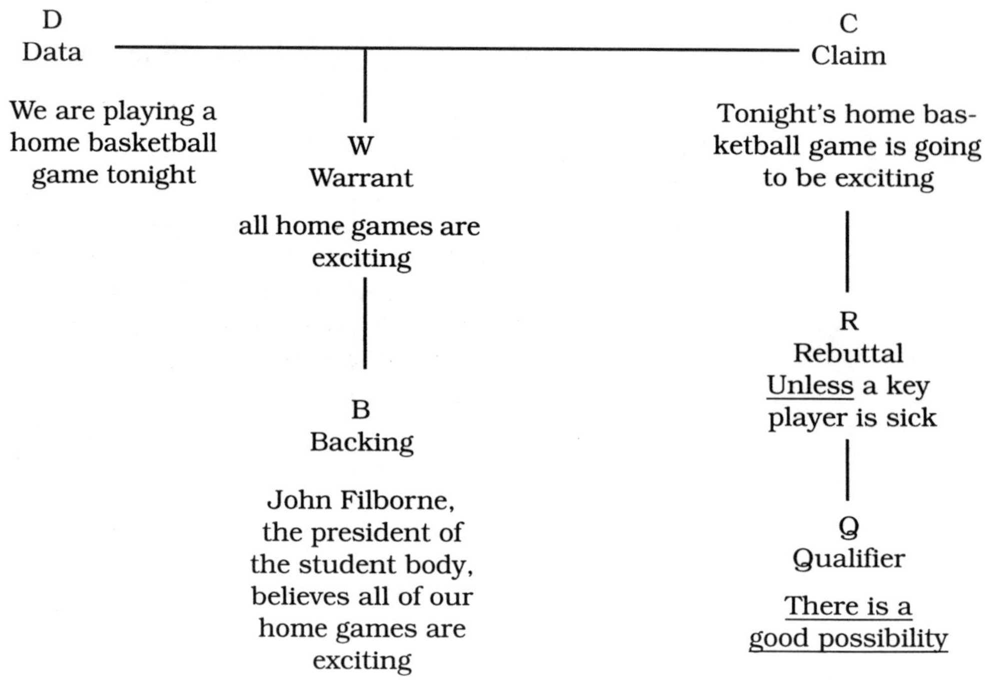

Now that we have explored critically listening to logic, which is the *structure* of persuasive message, we turn our attention to ten fallacies of reasoning that can occur within the structure. The fallacies to be discussed are: 1) Ignoring or shifting the burden of proof, 2) Begging the question or assuming, 3) *Argumentum ad hominem* or attacking the person, 4) Straw man or red herring, 5) Unjustifiable emotion appeal or pulling on the heartstrings, 6) Hasty generalization or faulty induction, 7) Stereotyping or they are all the same, 8) Disjunctive reasoning or either/or, 9) Oversimplified cause or it is obvious, and 10) Unexamined analogies or these are really the same.[5]

❑ Fallacies of Reasoning ❑

Fallacy #1, Ignoring or Shifting the Burden of Proof

The critical listener needs to be sensitive to the sender's responsibility to prove assertions that s/he makes. The assertion might be non-controversial: "I think it's going to rain," or highly controversial: "The depletion of ozone will destroy life as we know it in ten years." In every case, the responsibility to prove an assertion lies with the sender.

Listen to these arguments to understand how the burden of proof has been ignored by the sender and shifted on to the listener. In each case where the proof is ignored or shifted, the active listener needs to shift the burden back to the sender with feedback and questions:

Daughter: "Dad, just give me one good reason why I can't have the car tonight."

Dad: "No, Honey, you need to show me why you should be able to have the car."

Friend: "I'll never be able to quit smoking. How can I?"

Friend: "I don't know, how can you?"

Fallacy #2, Begging the Question or Assuming

A question or issue has been "begged" when *a portion of the assertion being given is assumed, without proof, to be true.* Here are some examples of question begging:

> **Professor:** Students accused of cheating on exams should be thrown out of school, no "ifs," "ands," or "buts." They shouldn't get any of this appeal to the next level stuff, because when they cheated, they gave up their rights as responsible students on this campus, PERIOD.
>
> **Student:** But it's *assumed* I've been cheating; I was just looking out the window.

Listening critically, we notice that the sender equates being *accused* of cheating with actually cheating. Begging the question or assuming, implies that accusation and guilt are one in the same. Listen to this person trying to persuade us to give him a ride to work. He begs the question by equating the sign—cloud build-up—with actual rain.

> Man! Look at those clouds building up in the west. I think you'd better take me to work; if I don't get a ride, by the time I get there I'll be soaked.

Circular argument is a special way of begging the question by wrapping one unproved assertion around to another and coming right back to the first one:

> We need to control weapons with stiff laws. I've heard the argument against gun control for years. The groups that are against gun control say that controls will penalize and restrict the sportsmen who would comply with the control laws, leaving the criminals to wander around freely with guns. This is shabby reasoning. If we had gun control laws, the criminals *couldn't* be running all over with guns, because the weapons would be regulated by LAW.

Fallacy #3, Argumentum ad Hominem or Attacking the Person

This Latin legal term means "Argument against the man." We have all heard politicians attack their opponent rather than the issues at stake. (Such an attack might be legitimate if the opponent offers only unsupported personal opinions as proof.)

The critical listener should notice how frequently this device is used in the legal setting also. Attorneys will attempt to discredit a witness by pointing out undesirable character traits, a lack of trustworthiness, or a past criminal record. We need to listen to whether the argument rests on solid evidence and reasoning, and accept it or reject it on those terms and not on unrelated past activities. These two examples show how *argumentum ad hominem*, attacking the person, can draw the listener to faulty conclusions.

> You know, a leopard can't change his spots. We've dealt with Chester Grenspat for years and we know he can't be trusted as far as you can throw him. So, no matter what he proposes regarding this matter, vote against it; it will not be in our main interests.

> The search of my home was illegal, and the drugs and drug money that police found in my home should not be counted as evidence against me. After all, the person who informed on me has a criminal record.

Notice in both cases, the sender is asking the listener to make a decision based on someone's past record, rather than the facts and structure of the argument.

Fallacy #4, Straw Man or Red Herring

This device can decoy the listener to unrelated issues. Straw man or decoying *shifts the subject to an entirely different topic.* The sender builds a scare crow, a straw man, which can divert the listener from the intended topic to an unrelated topic.

Moreover, if this unrelated topic is discussed and finally some decision is made, the real issue has not been touched. Consequently, spending energy on the straw man does little more than waste valuable time, because the important issues have been ignored. In this example, three people are discussing the reliability of cars:

> An auto mechanic says,
>
> "In general, the Japanese cars are more reliable than most American manufactured cars."
>
> Howard, a local labor union steward nods affirmation, yes, Howard agrees with that statement, "Yes, they do seem more dependable."
>
> However, Ginger Peachley, the art teacher at the grade school who is having her car fixed by the mechanic disagrees with this viewpoint, and says,
>
> "You're just trying to put down labor and workmanship in our United States."

If the mechanic and Howard do not listen critically, they will spend their time and energy trying to show that labor in the United States is not up to Japan's standards. They will be arguing against the straw man—the unreasonable extension of the original assertion, which centered merely on automobile reliability—and will now be defending a much weaker argument about United States labor and workmanship.

Anyone who has hunted with a dog knows that competing scents can confuse the animal and get her on the wrong trail. This form of straw man distraction is sometimes called red herring because, like the dog going after the wrong scent, it can take the critical listener away from the main issue.

As critical listeners, we need to stay focused on the main issues and not get side-tracked. The best defense for the straw man or red herring fallacy is to listen carefully to be certain that the original issue stays in focus. Point out to the sender that the discussion is wandering off the original course.

Listen for the fallacy in this argument: In a discussion about the value of Transcendental Meditation (TM), one person says that she did not find it very beneficial. The other person, who finds TM valuable, continues the discussion but creates a red herring by moving into related topics that were not included in the original discussion.

All right, as long as you're discrediting Transcendental Meditation as a form of relaxing and getting in touch with yourself, we might as well do away with the benefits of other systems of relaxing and getting to know ourselves. Napping, listening to music in a quiet setting, even the peace of going to church might as well be brought into the discussion because they all have some of the same effects.

Fallacy #5, Unjustifiable Emotional Appeal or Pulling on the Heartstrings

Emotions are a natural and valuable part of human nature. There is no inherent problem with reacting to emotional messages. Emotion can be very persuasive, and the use of emotion is legitimate when it is used for the good of the listener. Emotional appeal when used to encourage someone to buckle up before driving or to get them to give up smoking is certainly legitimate.

However, emotional appeal or pulling on the heartstrings has led to poor decision making. Many tragedies are the result of emotional appeals where cautious, critical listening was abandoned to emotional ploys. What happened to critical listening in this description?

> In late 1978 the world was shocked by a horror that as a fictional plot would have been rejected by the most charitable editor of fantasy fiction as too preposterous to be considered. Who would believe that nearly a thousand adult human beings would stand by while others murdered their children and close friends and then would voluntarily drink grape-flavored Kool-Aid that they knew had been mixed with cyanide? Yet on the instructions of an egomaniac [Jim Jones] who called himself both a minister and a god—and was believed—the inhabitants of a failed utopia called Jonestown in Guyana, South America, did just that. . . .
>
> . . . the main reason people follow a Jones is that they *abandon critical judgment* (emphasis mine) on the assumption that their leader is infallible. Consider the Unification Church of the "Reverent" Sun Myung Moon. He tells his fanatical followers that a "New Messiah" is coming and that he will be a Korean male born this century. He says that this "Third Adam" will become the father of a "Perfect Family" that will redeem mankind. Moon, who has had several marriages, is certainly a father—

seven times over. When asked uncomfortable questions, Moon replies to his disciples—"I am your brain." Obviously, the busloads of young people who are daily carted off to posts throughout Manhattan (from the church's headquarters at the former Hotel New Yorker) to solicit funds for the millennium believe this statement and are happy with it. *Would they, too, drink cyanide if Moon commanded them to?*[6]

Emotional appeal when not listened to critically can, in extreme cases, cost lives; moreover, emotional messages can also be the source of poor decisions on a less dramatic scale:

> Bill looked at his car which was totally destroyed by his best friend, Jason, who had been drinking. The car had been rolled twice and landed upright in a field. Fortunately no one was hurt.
>
> Bill recalled the emotional appeals that led to the decision he had made to lend the car to Jason. He knew Jason had been drinking, but Jason assured Bill that he was all right. Bill lent him the car after an emotional scene:
>
> Tears welled up in Jason's eyes as he told Bill that he had to see his aunt (who had raised him since he was six) one more time in the hospital. "She's dying, Bill, I just want to say 'Good-bye.'"
>
> Bill abandoned his best judgment, gave in to the emotional appeal and decided to loan Jason his car.

Fallacy #6, Hasty Generalization or Faulty Induction

Inductive reasoning examines individual cases and uses them to make a generalized claim. When the sender makes a generalized claim from *too few specific cases*, or cases that are not appropriate, the fallacy of hasty generalization exists. Here are three examples of hasty generalizations:

> Men are lousy cooks [claim]. Yesterday, I asked by brother to fix some soup and grilled cheese sandwiches for the kids. Well, he and one of his buddies attempted the job, and they boiled the soup all over the stove and burned the sandwiches [generalization from only two cases].
>
> Those people from the east end of town are pleasant and helpful [claim]. Just the other day, I had a flat tire over there and a man gave me a ride to a service station right away. And about two months ago, my wife had to return something she had bought in a store there, and they were just as nice as they could be [generalization from only two cases].
>
> Miller has won the vote in Story County [generalization from only one case]. Let's hear it for our next governor! [claim]

Fallacy #7, Stereotyping or They Are All the Same

Stereotyping is a way of thinking that focuses on *similarities* rather than *differences*. It categorizes people or things without considering individual differences. For example, some stereotyping was used in explaining the straw man fallacy, when the auto mechanic, union steward, and grade school art teacher were discussing the reliability of American and Japanese cars. In this example, the union steward and the art teacher did not behave as we might expect. The union steward, who stereotypically would be a strong defender of American products, agreed that the Japanese cars were more dependable. Moreover, the grade school art teacher, who stereotypically would not have a strong viewpoint about auto reliability or labor, expressed a supportive view for American labor. These views do not fit the stereotypical picture of a union representative and art teacher.

Critical listeners need to be alert to stereotyping: all union representatives are alike; all teachers are alike. In the example of the cooking class related to hasty generalization, one might be more willing to accept the hastily generalized claim, that men are lousy cooks, because this claim fits an already existing stereotype: "Men are no good in the kitchen."

The realization that no two things or people are alike will help us avoid decisions based on stereotyping. Realizing this, when we listen to these comments: "He's a Harvard man," "She's a liberated woman," "He's a hairstylist," "She's a sorority woman," "He's an alcoholic," "He's a high school dropout," or "She's in her third marriage," we can realize that individuals within these groups are distinctly different and should not be considered the same. To make decisions based on reality rather than stereotyping, we listen, and focus on *differences*, and not similarities *within* groups.

Fallacy #8, Disjunctive Reasoning or Either/Or

Disjunctive messages place something or someone in "either one camp or another." For example, "Jake is not doing well in his new assignment in purchasing. He's *either* stupid *or* lazy." In reality, Jake might not fit into either category. When we listen to this disjunctive comment, we need mentally to add more "*ors*." For example, ". . . or, Jake has not had sufficient training," ". . . or, Jake has been sick," ". . . or, Jake is having personal problems."

Few claims are either one or the other; there is usually some middle ground, some room in between the extremes. Even when we flip a coin, a small possibility exists that the coin will not land heads or tails, but on its edge. Following are some examples of disjunctive statements that ignore the middle ground and put people in one camp or another:

"She's either a dedicated professional or a housewife."

"If the job can't be done the way I want it, then don't do it at all."

"Look at the muscles on him; he must take steroids or work out eight hours a day."

"Look at the diamond on her. She either is rich or she deals in drugs."

Fallacy #9, Oversimplified Cause or It Is Obvious

As critical listeners, we need to listen for the two most frequent oversimplifications of the cause-claim relationship: 1) mistaking a minor or contributing cause as the main cause of a problem, and 2) attaching a problem to one cause when there are *several* significant causes involved.

When solving a problem, we must be as certain as possible that we are directing our energies at the actual cause of the problem. For example, in diagnosing an illness, the physician thoughtfully listens to the patient describe the symptoms. She listens with her stethoscope and with her hands, all in an attempt to make a decision to treat the actual cause of the problem, and not a minor cause. As critical listeners, we must put the same care and attention into our listening to find the actual causes of problems we are solving. The examples below show that *apparent* causes of problems may not be the *actual* causes:

> "If you loan me $100.00 I could get myself out of this fix I'm in." (Is lack of money the cause of the problem?)

> "A new computer will really streamline your purchasing process." (Is slow computer capability the problem?)

> "You got that cold from going out without your hat." (Did the hatless head cause the cold?)

We want to listen critically to isolate all of the major contributing causes of a problem. The examples below each address a contributing cause, but ignore other causes:

> "This country would be out of debt if we could just lower oil prices." (There are other causes of debt.)

> "Just take one of these pills a day, and you'll lose ten pounds in a month." (Weight is the product of a number of causes.)

> "This new computerized thermostat will bring those heat bills right down to minimum." (Weather extremes and insulation are two other causes of high heat costs.)

Fallacy #10, Unexamined Analogies or Are These Really the Same?

We have discussed analogies earlier, but let us review for a moment. An analogy takes parallel ideas or situations and says this one is like that one in many respects. Earlier, we used the analogy of water and electricity, and we found that they were alike in some ways, but not in all ways. Consequently, in that situation, the analogy failed to persuade. We critically listen to determine if there is *one important difference in the analogical comparison.* If there is, the analogy fails, and the listener should reject the claim. For example, the following analogy makes the claim: ". . . that some intelligence smarter than the people and objects of the universe made the universe and every thing in it."

> If you were walking on a deserted jungle path and found a mat woven out of plant stalks, one over the other, to make a rectangle two feet by three feet, you would assume that some intelligence smarter than the plant stalks had worked with the stalks and formed them into the mat, wouldn't you? Well, look at the intricate design of the universe. Isn't it reasonable that some intelligence smarter than the people and the objects of the universe fashioned all of that?

This analogy suggests that the pattern and structure of a woven mat parallels the pattern and structure of the universe. Of course, no one knows that. We can recognize a mat immediately, but the limits and structure of the universe are largely unknown. Consequently, at this point in time, the analogy is difficult to accept as valid.

❑ Examining Data ❑

As critical listeners, we must constantly be attentive to the logical structure and reasoning of persuasive messages. Now we examine listening to the data within the structure of the message. We will discuss data in the forms of 1) Examples and illustrations, 2) Testimony, 3) Definition, 4) Statistics, and 5) Visual aids.

Examples and Illustrations

Examples and illustrations are specific instances that explain or clarify part of a message. An example is a short explanation; an illustration is longer and more detailed. Senders use them to make abstract ideas clearer.

As a critical listener, ask yourself—Does the example or illustration represent the whole? Is it typical? Or is it an extreme example?

Is the example relevant? It might be typical and representative, but how does it prove the assertion being make? Sometimes a speaker may tell an interesting story or joke, but as critical listeners we need to ask how it relates to the topic being discussed.

Jessica Tuchman Mathews, an environmental scientist, discusses the greenhouse effect and makes the claim that rising temperatures on the earth could greatly affect plants and animals. Notice that her examples are representative, and are not extreme. She says that plants and animals will be affected by rising temperatures,

> becausc nothing that we know about evolution suggests that plants and animals can adapt to such rapid change. There have been big temperature swings before over geological time, but there you're talking millions of years. Now we're talking decades. For example, we know something about how fast trees can move to adjust to different climates, how far the wind blows the seeds in a year, and how far they can progress. It's a tiny fraction of how far they would have to move in order to keep up with their changing habitat. So you would expect massive extinctions. Senator Bennett Johnson said he was reminded of a Baptist preacher who said that if God meant anything, He meant everything, and that if the greenhouse effect changed anything, it would change everything. In a sense, that's right. It will change everything about modern society as we know it.[7]

This illustration is relevant and is adapted to the whole concept of greenhouse effect. As critical listeners, we would probably accept the claim that the greenhouse effect would be substantial.

Testimony

There are two types of testimony that we use to make decisions. First is *expert* testimony; second is *witness* testimony. Expert testimony reports factual findings *and recommends future plans, policies, or procedures.* Witness testimony provides factual information *without recommending future plans, policies, or procedures.*

Expert testimony might range from the physician who tells us that we should be exercising more often, to the grocer who tells us that the Colorado peaches that just arrived are especially good, and we should buy them while they are fresh, to the mechanic who recommends an engine overhaul for our car. From these expert testimonies, we form our plans: Do we jog more? Buy the peaches? Get the engines overhauled? Our decision is based, in part, on the credibilitiy of those giving testimony.

We also rely on witness testimony to determine factual information. Witness testimony helps us determine whether something did or did not occur: "I saw Mr. Jacobson's car turn directly in front of Mrs. Thurman's car, causing an unavoidable situation." "The last time I ate there, I found a bug in my salad." "I saw him pouring the cheap wine into the fancy French wine bottle." Or, "Mom, I saw Suzy kick Hal on the playground." Based on our perceived accuracy of the witness testimony, we decide if we should eat here, buy wine here, or punish Suzy.

When listening to testimony, ask yourself if it is complete and objective? Are there partially quoted portions that change the overall intended meaning? If the authority being quoted or paraphrased were sitting next to you, would s/he be comfortable with what words are being attributed to him or her?

Does the testimony come from an authority *in the field* being discussed? Just because an engineer is testifying does not mean she/he is an expert in this particular area of engineering. Does the testimony come from a neutral, unbiased source? Or does the source have "stock in the company," that is, something personal to gain from the testimony?

Definition

We need to listen closely to definitions because they can prompt decisions. In this text, listening is defined as "*Using both hemispheres of the brain to assign meaning to all sense input.*" By accepting this definition, we have accepted the ideas that we listen with both sides of our brains, with our eyes, our noses, our skin, our tongues, as well as with our ears. Ultimately, accepting this operational definition is a decision to change one's outlook toward listening and to expand listening behavior to include both sides of the brain and all five senses.

When critically listening to a definition, ask yourself: Does the definition add to my understanding of the concept? Does it clarify and delineate the idea? Is there any hidden aspect of the definition that I cannot accept?

Statistics

Basically, statistics are numbers that summarize findings or data into four categories:

Central tendency. This shows the pattern of the gathered data with the mean or median. The mean is called the average; it adds the score and divides by the number of entries. The median is the middle score. That is, half the scores are above the median; half below.

Correlation. Correlation shows the strength of a relationship between two variables. For example, a high correlation might exist between cholesterol and heart disease. One caution when listening to correlation statistics is not to confuse the correlation with causation; other factors could be involved.

Differences. The range, which is merely subtracting the lowest from the highest score, can help us by showing differences. When the range is high, there is greater diversity; when the range is low, there is more similarity.

Percentiles. Percentiles help us picture the percentage of scores that are below a particular score. For example, a tire manufacturer might tell us that on a durability scale their tires scored 480 points, a score which puts their tires in the ninety seventh percentile. This means that ninety-seven percent of the competition's tire were below this manufacturer's tires in durability.

Some of the reasoning and logical cautions discussed earlier regarding data apply here. Ask yourself as you critically listen: Were the statistics taken from a large enough sample? Does the sample represent the total population? *Are the statistics current?* Currency is especially important in areas of quickly changing technology. Who collected the statistics? Was the collector unbiased?

Visual Aids

We listen to visuals with our eyes. A visual may be attractive, but is it relevant? Does it support an idea or a claim? Is the visual an important part of the message? It might be interesting, but how does it apply here? Is the visual *clear.* Can it be easily understood? The way a graph is set up can minimize or maximize compared data. Watch to determine that the scales on a graph are equal both vertically and horizontally.

❑ Listening Critically to Campaign Speeches ❑

Our lives are full of situations where listening is a part of decision-making. The decisions we make range from when and where to go shopping to which people will lead our country. In a country that has so much freedom of choice, we must be especially aware of applying our critical listening skills to government leadership. The following speech given by an expert in political analysis, Dr. Ray Dearin, highlights the importance of listening critically before voting, and it offers some suggestions to sharpen our critical listening skills before voting.

Ray D. Dearin is a Professor of Speech Communication at Iowa State University, where he teaches courses in Rhetorical Criticism and Political Campaign Communication. The following essay is based upon a lecture he gave to an undergraduate class in Listening on September 28, 1988.

Let me begin by thanking Dr. Paul Kaufmann for inviting me to speak to you this morning on a subject I have been paying a lot of attention to lately. Since I am teaching courses in rhetorical criticism and campaign rhetoric, and since a presidential campaign is now going on, I thought it might be appropriate to share with you some ideas about critical listening as it applies to the kind of political rhetoric we hear every four years at this time.

I suppose I should first tell you how I have come to know all that I intend to tell you. Whenever a person discovers an idea for the first time, that is called *originality.* When a second person comes along and uses the idea, it's called *plagiarism.* When a third person uses it, it is called *lack of originality.* With a fourth person, it is known as *drawing from a common stock*. And when you get to the fifth person who uses it, then it is called *research*. I want you to know that what I tell you this morning is based on a lot of "research" on my part. My approach will be to look at some of the basic principles upon which most campaign speeches are built and then apply some critical listening standards to these speeches.

Three Key Features of Campaign Speeches

Of all the many principles and devices that typify modern political speaking, three features are so pronounced and pervasive that they stand out sharply. These key elements are the use of *contrast*, *repetition*, and what I call the *mood of indignation*. Let's look more closely at these persuasive stratagems.

Contrast

The primary principle of political speaking is *contrast*. You might expect this, since every election contest has candidates who try to paint the bleakest, darkest picture of gloom that will surely occur if their opponents are elected, while the brightest, most prosperous times you can imagine will be likely to follow if they are elected. Although the contrast seems to be about policies or issues, when you examine the arguments closely you will inevitably find that the contrast is achieved syntactically; that is, certain words or expressions are being played off against one another in ways that emphasize conflicting ideas. Frequently this effect is achieved through the use of balanced sentence constructions, antitheses, and phrases turned around or inverted. I'll give you some examples of these devices in action.

Although most of you were probably not yet born when President John F. Kennedy delivered his inaugural address in January, 1961, you can doubtless recite one of the memorable lines from that speech: "Ask not what your country can do for you; ask what you can do for your country." When you examine this idea, you will see that its meaning is conveyed by a rather simple rhetorical device: the use of an antithetical sentence construction. "Ask *not*," Kennedy beseeched his listeners, "what your *country* (**A**) can do for *you* (**B**) ask what *you* (**B**) can do for your *country* (**A**)." **AB** forms a balanced contrast with **BA**. Exactly the same rhetorical form was used elsewhere in Kennedy's speech when he said: "Let us never negotiate (**A**) out of fear (**B**), but let us never fear (**B**) to negotiate (**B**)." Professor Kaufmann and I are old enough to remember that this same scheme was used in the Salem cigarette commercials on television in the 1960s. Accompanied by a little jingle, the ad proclaimed: "You can take Salem out of the country, but you can't take the country out of Salem." After hearing this ditty a few times, you found yourself walking around whistling the tune.

The **AB:CD** form of antithesis is probably even more common in public speeches in general, and in political discourse in particular. It involves a direct contrast between two concepts, not just an inversion of these ideas. On January 17, 1980, the Reverend Jesse Jackson came to Iowa State University to give a speech. To this day I can still remember something he said in his talk. "We need will power (**A**) to cop in (**B**)," said Jackson, "not pill power (**C**) to cop out (**D**)." This same formal principle of sentence arrangement was employed by Winston Churchill, who ranks alone as the consummate English orator of the twentieth century. For example, in a speech in 1925 Churchill sought to contrast socialism and communism. He said: "If I were asked the difference between Socialism and Communism, I could only reply that the Socialist tried to lead us to disaster by foolish words, and the Communist wished to drive us there by violent deeds." See if you can identify the **AB:CD** pattern in this sentence.

In practically every political speech the principle of contrast appears as the driving force. If you listen carefully, you can often detect it throughout the entire speech, or at the level of individual paragraphs and sentences, and often in the specific contrasts that are developed between words and concepts. It is also the basis for a lot of humor. Former President Ronald Reagan used it when he said: "Politics is not a bad profession. If you succeed, there are many rewards. If you disgrace yourself, you can always write a book."

Repetition

The second principle of campaign speaking I would like to call your attention to is *repetition*. The recurring use of particular sounds, words, phrases, or even a whole sentence has become a staple of political rhetoric. The repetition of specific sounds, or *alliteration*, is widely used by public speakers who want to hold the attention of their listeners and create a vivid, memorable effect. No contemporary political communicator has carried the device of alliteration farther than Jesse Jackson. Notice how Jackson combines the principle of contrast with the repetition of the "s" sound in this passage:

> "Both tears and sweat are wet and salty, but they render a different result. Tears will get you sympathy, but sweat will get you change."

And think of how the repeated "p" sound must have sounded to Jackson's listeners at the end of the following idea in one of his speeches:

> "We need a value system that will allow us to fulfill our essential human and humane tasks. To be producers, to be providers, to be protectors."

Sometimes Reverend Jackson gets a little carried away with his alliteration, as in this passage:

> "We must contrast the politics of the five B's—blacks, browns, budgets, busing, and balance—with the five A's—attention, attendance, atmosphere, attitude, and achievement."

But when his repetitions work, they lend a striking quality to his speechmaking. In a distinctive way of expressing the importance of personal motivation in the lives of young people, Jackson combined the repetition of the initial consonant sound as well as the last syllable of a word to produce this gem: "Children must know that it is not their aptitude but their attitude that will determine their altitude."

Repetition in political rhetoric can be used to create effects similar to those in nursery school rhymes. Thus, Senator Edward Kennedy said of the Republicans: "They lavish tax breaks on the greedy and deny bread to the needy." And President Richard Nixon once proclaimed, "The wealthiest nation in the world should be the healthiest nation in the world." These devices, while catchy, do not approach in grandeur the style and sentiment expressed in Dr. Martin Luther King, Jr.'s speech to the crowd in front of the Lincoln Memorial in Washington, D.C. in 1963. In his address King used the recurring sentence, "I have a dream," to stir the imagination of both the assembled crowd and the millions who would hear or read this speech. King's dream of racial equality was expressed in one of the most common of rhetorical forms, but the tone established in his address has given this thought a revered place in the annals of American oratory.

As long as we are talking about repetition, I guess I should point out one feature of humor—political and otherwise—that you've probably already noticed: most jokes have three lines, with the third one being the punch line. This fact is sometimes called the *rule of three*. It can be traced back at least to Julius Caesar, who is supposed to have said: "I came. I saw. I conquered." As a vehicle of humor, the rule of three appeared in the joke that was popular a few years ago that went like this: "Do you know the three most frequently told lies? They are: 'The check is in the mail.' 'Sure, I'll still respect you in the morning.' And 'I'm from the federal government, and I'm here to help you.'" This reminds me of the wit of Senator Robert Dole, who once came into a room where three former presidents were standing together. The presidents were Gerald Ford, Jimmy Carter, and Richard Nixon. Dole took one look and said, "Hear no evil, speak no evil, and *evil*." Senator Dole's sharp tongue contrasts with the gentle humor of Ronald Reagan, who went around the country giving speeches during the Carter administration. Once Reagan said, "Well, Jimmy's in the White House, Amy's in the tree house, and Billy's in the dog house." Whether the device of repetition involves the recurring use of a sound, word, phrase, or sentence, or whether it simply establishes an expectancy in the audience that a third idea will be used to bring closure to the thought sequence, the result of its use is the enhancement of an idea. You will find that repetition is one of the most common techniques used by political campaigners to drive their points home.

Mood of Indignation

The third feature of political rhetoric I will discuss does not come from a manipulation of language but from a manipulation of our emotions. Have you ever noticed how political speakers try to get us really worked up? They seek to arouse our emotions and get us to bypass our rational thought processes. Cicero recognized the importance of the passions two thousand years ago when he wrote: "For men decide far more problems by hate, or love, or lust, or illusion, or some other emotion, than by reality, or authority, or any legal standard, or judicial precedent, or statute." This seems to be the guiding assumption behind much political discourse today.

In his keynote speech to the Republican National Convention in 1988 New Jersey Governor Thomas Kean sought to arouse indignation towards the Democratic presidential nominee, Michael Dukakis, and his advisers. Kean related the following account:

> "Last week, in a rare moment of candor, a prominent Dukakis Democrat explained their strategy to a reporter from *Congressional Quarterly*

> *Magazine*. What he said shocked me, and I have to share it with you. He said Democrats' advice to special interests was, and I quote, . . . 'Just Shut Up. Gays. Women. Environmentalists. Just shut up, and you will get everything you want after the election. In the meantime, just shut up so we can win.' Now I ask you, should this country tolerate such cynicism?"

Governor Kean is trying, of course, to arouse righteous indignation not only among Republican delegates at the convention, but also on the part of the millions of viewers at home. He is indulging in a familiar practice that is used by politicians in both of the major parties. He is arousing anger and resentment against the ideas and actions of the opposing candidate.

All three of these techniques have one thing in common. They attempt to get us to go along with our speaker's thinking without analyzing very carefully what is being said. Contrast causes us to polarize our thinking. We are led to see an issue as having only two sides, only one of which is the right one. Repetition causes us to accept an idea because it is drilled into our heads. And the mood of indignation leads us to react in a knee-jerk fashion that substitutes emotion for sound analysis and reasoning as we consider an idea. With a clear understanding of these rhetorical devices, we are now in a position to consider ways to improve our ability to listen critically to the political messages that bombard us during a campaign.

Two Principles of Critical Listening

Of all the principles of critical listening that could be mentioned, two stand out as crucial in the evaluation of political speeches. These principles relate to the prudent use of the excess attention we have as we listen to a speech, and to the emotional state in which we attend to a speaker's ideas.

Using Excess Attention Wisely

This first principle is sometimes known as "capitalizing on the thought-speech differential." It derives from the fact that we can all think much faster than any speaker can talk, and that we need to put this extra thinking capacity to work. Instead of using it to let our minds wander over peripheral or unrelated matters, we can use this mental energy to examine the premises and conclusions of the speaker's arguments. Suppose we encounter instances of reasoning such as these:

> All Democrats raise taxes.
> Al Gore is a Democrat.
> Therefore, Al Gore will raise taxes.

> Republicans favor tax breaks for the rich.
> George W. Bush is a Republican.
> Therefore, he will give tax breaks to the rich.

In these cases your excess attention can be put to good use. You can evaluate the major premises and ask, "Do all Democrats raise taxes?" and "Do all Republicans favor tax breaks for the rich?" You might remember, for example, that John F. Kennedy, a Democrat, lowered taxes, a fact that Republicans often point to in order to show that the economy got a boost when this was done. And your critical evaluation of the second argument might cause you to try to think of proposals George Bush might have made to "give tax breaks to the rich." Is he actually on record as favoring such a policy?

When a speaker uses inductive reasoning, ask yourself whether the examples cited are sufficient to lead to the conclusion that is advanced. Here is a fairly typical specimen of the kind of inductive logic found in political speeches. This passage is from a speech Alexander Haig, a former U.S. Secretary of State, gave at the 1988 Republican National Convention in New Orleans. Haig contrasts the dismal state of foreign affairs under the Democratic administration of eight years earlier with the more hopeful situation of 1988:

> "When I last spoke to a Republican convention in 1980, we saw a nation thrown off balance by blunder and gloom. The Soviets were on the march everywhere. Afghanistan had been sieged. Soviet surrogates were triumphant in Campachia, Southern Africa, and Central America. A cruel war raged in the Persian Gulf. Our allies were disheartened and freedom was in retreat. And all the Democrats could offer was indecision and malaise. Today, eight years later, the policy of peace through strength has begun to pay off. The Russians are leaving Afghanistan. Their surrogates in Africa and Asia are in trouble. The Soviets are negotiating our arms control agenda of reduction and cuts, not their agenda designed to increase Soviet superiority. Democracy, not Communism, is on the march. George Bush helped to make this happen, and he is, indeed, the safe candidate for America."

Capitalizing on the thought-speech differential, you could examine the examples set forth by Haig, asking whether the instances are sufficiently numerous, representative, and accurate to lead to the conclusion he wants us to reach.

Evaluating analogies uses our critical thinking capacity in other ways. For example, George Bush likened the American economy of 1980 to a "sick patient" in his acceptance speech in 1988. He said:

> "My friends, eight years ago this economy was flat on its back in intensive care. We came in and gave it emergency treatment. Got the temperature down by lowering regulation. Got the blood pressure down when we lowered taxes. Pretty soon the patient was up back on his feet, stronger than ever. And now who do we hear knocking on the door, but the doctors who made him sick. And they're telling us to put them in charge of the case again. My friends, they're lucky we don't hit them with a malpractice suit."

Is this a good analogy? Are there similarities between a sick patient and an economy? Certainly there are more differences than similarities. As critical listeners, we can understand the point Bush is trying to make and even be amused by it while still recognizing that this "argument" offers little substantive evidence but plays upon a few superficial resemblances between two very different conditions of life.

Switching Off Emotional Attitudes

Another thing I suggest that you learn to do while you are listening to political rhetoric is to switch off your emotional attitudes that get in the way of clear, analytical thought. This habit, of course, is especially needed when the speaker is indulging in the mood of indignation discussed earlier. But each of the principles of rhetoric we examined has as its purpose the creation of an emotional link between the audience and the speaker's thesis. Especially when you are very partisan and are inclined to favor the speaker, it is all the more imperative that you retain a critical detachment. You need to resist the tendency to suspend your judgment and get swept along with the emotional currents that are being generated by the speaker.

One of the primary means political speakers use to generate an emotional response is to use a *slogan*. A slogan is always used to take the place of rational thought. Many kinds of slogans have been used in American elections. Some were promissory; they held out a promise of the good things that would follow the election of a certain candidate: "Forty Acres and a Mule," "The Full Dinner Pail," Huey Long's battle cry, "Every Man a King," and Dwight Eisenhower's promise in 1952, "I Shall Go to Korea." Sometimes slogans have used the device of *alliteration*, which we identified earlier: "Peace and Prosperity," "Ban the Bomb," "Beat the Bosses," "Love That Lyndon," "Tippecanoe and Tyler Too," and "Win with Willkie." Other slogans have issued *warnings* to the American voters: "Don't Let Them Take It Away." "Coolidge or Chaos," "Save the American Way of Life," and "No Third Term." Sometimes slogans even pretend to be *rational*, appealing to your reason: "Let's Look at the Record," "Let's Talk Sense to the American People," and "Experience Counts." But all of these slogans attempt, in one sense or another, to elicit a visceral, nonrational reaction from the audience. Occasionally, the response is contrary to the desired result. Thus, when a billboard appeared in Champaign, Illinois, favoring Barry Goldwater for President in 1964 with the slogan, "In Your Heart You Know He's Right," some wag added below, "But In Your Guts, You Know He's Nuts!" Although the response was not the one desired, it was just as emotional as the one sought by the creator of the Goldwater campaign slogan. A knee-jerk response to a slogan, whether negative or positive, is difficult to avoid in the heat of a fiery political battle, but if we are to be intelligent respondents to such speeches and advertisements, we must maintain a critical detachment that will allow us to evaluate them without the distortion that comes from the intervention of strong personal motives and feelings. In order to preserve this detachment, we must switch off our emotional attitudes toward the speaker and his or her party and message.

Conclusion

In closing, I would say that the difference in sense and nonsense is probably not any greater in political rhetoric than in other kinds of persuasion. The same kinds of communication techniques—contrast, repetition, and the use of the mood of indignation or another strong emotion—all show up in sales presentations, advertising campaigns, sermons, pep talks to athletic teams, and so forth. But the consequences may be greater—the stakes higher—in political campaign communications than in these other contexts where we are asked to form views or make decisions. If we get a lemon for a new car or a faulty freezer or television set, the results are annoying, but if we are persuaded to elect a governor, a senator, or a president, the consequences are enormously more consequential—and more difficult to remedy. As Will Rogers used to say, "When Congress makes a joke, it becomes a law." So we need to pay close and critical attention to the speeches we hear from those to whom we are asked to entrust our public offices.

I have suggested that we use our excess attention wisely to evaluate the appeals we hear from politicians, and that we need to suspend our strong emotional feelings in order to preserve a detached and critical frame of mind. From such a perspective, we will be in a better position to scrutinize both the political messages we hear and the rhetorical means used to convey them. Of course, you should apply these same principles of critical listening to what I have said in this talk. I hope you will not be like the Siamese twin I heard about who was a poor listener—everything he heard went in one ear and out his brother's. I hope that's not true this morning, but that you will be able to apply some of these principles as you try to become a more analytical and critical listener.

❑ Summary ❑

Many of life's decisions are made on the basis of the ability to listen critically. As effective listeners, we must be alert to the critical listening role and apply the appropriate decision-making skills. The quality of our decisions, and our lives, depends on the ability to listen critically.

Listening critically requires that we make decisions based on speaker credibility, logical structure, reasoning, and valid data. Speaker credibility consists of competence, character, intentions, personality, and dynamism. Logical structure includes examination of: data, warrant, claim, backing, qualifier, and rebuttal. Fallacies of reasoning are, ignoring the burden of proof, *argumentum ad hominem*, straw man, red herring, emotional appeal, hasty generalization, stereotyping, disjunctive reasoning, oversimplified cause, and unexamined analogy. Finally, listening to data in the form of examples and illustrations, testimony, definition, statistics, and visual aids is discussed as an important aspect of critical listening.

Effective critical listening can improve quality in our daily living by promoting responsible decisions regarding relationships, productivity, purchases, and use of time. Chapter 9 discusses critical listening as it applies to spending money.

Awareness Exercises, Chapter 8

Name ______________________________ **SS#** _____-____-_____

1. Describe a recent situation when you made a decision after listening to someone.

   A. The setting

   B. The decision you made

2. Describe a person whom you trust to help you make decisions. What characteristics does this person have?

3. Build an argument using data, warrant, and claim.

   A. Data

   B. Warrant

   C. Claim

4. Write an example that shows the shifting of the burden of proof.

5. Write an example that shows the straw man fallacy.

6. Write an example that shows the red herring fallacy.

7. Write an example that shows stereotyping.

8. Write an example that shows *argumentum ad hominem*.

9. Write an example that shows hasty generalization.

10. Write an example that shows begging the questions.

11. Write an example that shows oversimplified cause.

12. Write an example that shows disjunctive reasoning.

13. Describe a single interaction when your listening role changed from comprehensive, or therapeutic to critical.

14. Describe a time when you listened and made a poor decision.

15. Describe a persuasive presentation where data were used effectively.

16. Describe a time when you listened and made a good decision.

17. Build an argument using Data, Warrant, Claim, Backing, Qualifier, Rebuttal.

    A. Data

    B. Warrant

    C. Claim

    D. Backing

    E. Qualifier

    F. Rebuttal

Awareness DataBase, Chapter 8

Name ________________________________ **SS#** _____-____-_____

1. I am aware when I am in the critical listening role.

A.	B.	C.	D.	E.
seldom				often

2. I have made decisions without being aware that I was making decisions.

A.	B.	C.	D.	E.
seldom				often

3. How many decision in a day—from radio, TV, friends, salespeople, relatives, girlfriends, boyfriends—do you make as a result of listening?

A.	B.	C.	D.	E.
0-2	3-5	6-10	11-14	15 or more

4. I am an effective critical listener.

A.	B.	C.	D.	E.
seldom				often

5. When in a persuasive setting, I pay attention to the credibility of the sender.

A.	B.	C.	D.	E.
seldom				often

6. I make compulsive decisions (that is, decision with little thought).

A.	B.	C.	D.	E.
seldom				often

7. I find it easy to "go along with the crowd."

A.	B.	C.	D.	E.
seldom				often

8. I wait a day or more before making an important decision.

A.	B.	C.	D.	E.
seldom				often

9. I am impressed by visual aids.

A.	B.	C.	D.	E.
seldom				often

10. I make wise purchases.

A.	B.	C.	D.	E.
seldom				often

9 Listening as a Consumer

Applying trained, critical listening skills to purchasing has never been more important because the 21st century is finding an expansion in advertising and marketing strategies. In what is called the "Information Age," consumers are finding themselves overwhelmed not only with the amount of products on the market from which to choose, but also with new places to buy products, such as on the Internet. Using new technology, companies and organizations have expanded capabilities and are working on innovative approaches for getting their products and services to buyers. Dr. Tony Alessandra, head of Entrepreneurial Visions (Glendale Heights), said on his recent videotape, entitled "How to Become an Effective Listener,"

> Living in the "Information Age," we are bombarded with a blizzard of data bits every day. Because we feel overwhelmed, we start to block out whatever we believe is less than immediately useful. But you will never be able to sift the wheat from the chaff unless you truly listen to what is being said."[1]

This chapter on Listening as a Consumer looks at critical decisions when spending our money.

In this chapter, critical listening is considered in relation to the purchase of products or services. To reach an awareness of the key elements in making responsible purchases, this chapter discusses: the consumer listening role, listening to our motivations to purchase, listening to selling techniques, and gaining information about the purchase.

❑ The Consumer Listening Role ❑

We are in the consumer listening role when we are deciding *if, when, how,* and *where* we are going to purchase a product or service. Television, radio, telephone, newspapers, computers, and salespeople, are all in a position to persuade us to make a decision to buy. The pressure is on us to buy, and we must listen carefully to ourselves and outside messages to make sensible decisions on how and where to spend our money.

Today's businesses spend at least $4 billion per year researching consumers.[2] They want to know what buyers value, desire and need. In addition, businesses seek to know how much consumers will spend to fulfill these desires and needs, as well as what type of advertising results in the purchase of their product or service. Consumer and marketing research has evolved to a great extent over the past decade.

> As we look back at marketing business 10 years ago, and compare that snapshot to today, we see how we have evolved many of our tools—tools

that simulate real world experience and thus give us more insightful analyses and ways to appeal to an ever more sophisticated, complex, and savvy customer. We are limited only by our imagination, tempered by an understanding of rigorous research standards. We now can apply these tools and techniques to a wide variety of target groups ranging from five-year-olds to CEOs.[3]

In the 1990s there was a shift from TV advertising to appealing to customers in the marketplace. This eliminated the usual travel time used to reflect about making a purchase.

> At your local supermarket are product pitches on your shopping cart, electronic ads above the aisles, and coupon dispensers attached to the shelves. In-store radio and television deliver hit songs and news along with cues to pick up Pampers or Pepto-Bismol in aisle two. The leading hawker of the hype, Act Media, sells ad space in 26,000 stores to such companies as Kellogg and P&G much as TV networks sell commercial time. Says Chief Executive Wayne LoCurto: "Does it make any sense to spend millions of dollars talking to people in their living rooms and cars and then let them wander around a supermarket with 30,000 product choices without something to remind them to buy your product?"
>
> Campbell Soup, which has used all of ActMedia's programs, report sales increases of 7% to 10% from various in-store promotions. Says Herb Baum: "We believe there's no better time to reach consumers than when they're in the store with a fistful of dollars."

The use of the Internet as a marketplace also eliminates the time for consideration before purchasing an item or service. Through e-commerce, consumers merely have to "click" a button in order to purchase what is needed and desired. The number of customers using this service has grown since its origin. *Time* magazine states that retail e-commerce sales nearly tripled from $2.7 billion to $7.9 billion between June 1998 and June 1999.[4]

In addition to e-commerce growth, consumers in the 21st century are also seeing a growth in Internet marketing as an innovative approach to influence buyers' decisions. One may wonder "How can words on a screen influence purchasing habits?" The answer, upon which many businesses are basing their strategies, is to continue to give the customer one-to-one attention.

> The Internet is a virtual nirvana for one-to-one marketing and is becoming a key component to many organizations' communications strategy. Technology is enabling marketers to deliver specific information, products and services based on a single individual's needs. This is often accomplished by learning more about a site visitor as they travel through a site and then using a dynamic page environment to customize a home page, or show different banner ads, for example. Possibly the most intriguing opportunity in this environment is to track and archive information and tie it to a name and e-mail address.[5]

Wal-Mart added one-to-one Internet marketing to increase their sales. The Wal-Mart website, says spokesperson Melissa Berryhill, is bringing the "feeling of one of our stores online." The site has the following capabilities:

> It remembers past visitors: there's a virtual version of the familiar in-store "greeter" to hail online return visitors by name. It customizes itself—or "morphs"—to frequent visitor needs. "If a customer is a frequent visitor to the pets department," says Berryhill, "that area becomes more prominent" during future log-ins. Customers enter information only as needed, with many forms appearing pre-filled. Online customers will soon have the option of signing up for various, local e-mail alerts. If you tell us where your local store is, the site will tell you about upcoming events, like an in-store concert or appearance or perhaps the next Oreo-stacking contest, Berryhill says.[6]

The continuous "bombardment" of marketing techniques and purchasing locations mean the consumer listener must be focused and prepared before making a purchasing decision. This preparation should include, 1) listening to our motivations for shopping and, 2) researching the products or service to be purchased.

❑ Listening to Our Motivations ❑

How we communicate intr*a*personally impacts the effectiveness of all other communication. Consequently, as consumers our decisions to spend money are the result of internal motivations. These internal messages must be listened to carefully before a purchase is made to determine our reasons for shopping, which range from necessity, to enjoyment, to addictive-like compulsion:

> Studies show that perhaps as many as 24 million Americans, fully 10% of the population, can be classified as "hard-core shoppers." These shopaholics shop for shopping's sake rather than to fill real or felt needs. Browsing the aisles somehow makes them feel good. Bumper stickers proclaim: "When the going gets tough, the tough go shopping."[7]

Another reason for the increase in unwise spending is convenience. Just a generation ago, Christmas shopping was hard work. Shoppers had to bundle up, hassle with ice and snow and trudge from store to store, perhaps in different parts of town. Today, bright, warm, well-lighted malls entice the shopper into rows of stores easily accessed with only one park of the car. The shopper can virtually spend an entire day under the roof of one mall and not visit all of the stores. The Internet has brought an additional ease to shopping. One doesn't even have to leave home to buy clothes, stereo equipment, and other favorite items. With this technology, shoppers merely have to "point and click." Add to this ease of access the option of high ceiling credit cards, and all the ingredients for unwise, addictive spending come together.

The increase in marketing pressure, and the convenience of shopping intensify the need to listen to our motivations before shopping. For example, we need to ask ourselves: Why are we shopping? What personal needs are being met? Is my shopping compulsive? Do I shop to escape boredom? Is this trip to the marketplace really necessary? Is the act of spending exciting? Answers to these questions will offer insights into our reasons for spending, which might range from spending for a real need to spending for an addictive satisfaction.

> The word "addiction" is not used lightly here. There are even support groups, such as Shoppers Stoppers, in Dayton, Ohio, that help people who are trying to stop their compulsion to spend beyond their means for

things they don't need. "Shopping is an addiction comparable to drug abuse," says Evan Steffens, the group's consulting therapist at Miami Valley Hospital. "It is done without regard to the consequences."[8]

To spend responsibly, we first need to listen to our motivations. We listen to ourselves to find out if our spending is thoughtful or compulsive. Are we spending for responsible motives or for other reasons: feelings of powerlessness, worthlessness, boredom, loneliness, or a need for attention. The following two examples show how a man made foolish purchases because of boredom and how a woman spent irresponsibly because of resentment:

> I was alone and bored last Saturday. My girlfriend was out of town at a wedding, and my best friend was on a fishing trip. I was tired of reading, and the TV had nothing to offer. I didn't feel like doing anything, so I hopped in the car and wandered to the mall. I hit the electronic store and ended up getting a real "deal" on a 27 inch TV with a built in VCR which I didn't need (I already have a good TV and VCR) and couldn't afford (I put the $600.00 purchase on my already stressed credit card). On top of that, I ended up in the sports store and bought a pair of air basketball shoes for $115.00 which I didn't need!
>
> I was furious with him for leaving me for two days to go fishing. He can afford to do that, but he's so stingy when I want to go shopping. So I went shopping in a major way and bought all those goodies that I never buy myself—and I put them all on *his* credit cards. Shoes, dresses, slacks, make-up, and purse. Even a nice camera to capture those precious moments! I buy him things with my money, so I decided it's all right for me to help myself to his money. The whole shopping spree made me feel a lot better.

Consumers need to face their motivations to determine their reasons for spending. Frequently, obsessive shoppers are venting their discomfort or anger at a friend or spouse. "They tear into the racks instead of their family." Noel, a 33 year old housewife in the process of a divorce tells her story about shopping as an escape from her relational problems: "As my frustration increased with my marriage, so did my spending," which added up to $50,000. Shopping sprees can be used to cope with anger, loneliness, boredom, or depression.[9]

After listening to themselves, some shoppers might discover that they need to get the attention of someone—even a salesperson. Listening to the friendly and helpful words of a caring salesperson can be attractive and fill the need to be listened to by someone who is interested. The sales people say, "May I help you?" They "ooh" and "ah" and fuss. You become the star in your own production. In addition to getting attention, motivation to shop can be low self esteem. According to Carole Lieberman, a psychiatrist, "People shop to make up for what they don't have on the inside. They're trying to fill up because they feel empty."

Personal motivations for shopping vary from individual to individual; however, additional personal insight can be gained by understanding that women and men are different in their approaches to shopping.

Present information indicates that compulsive shopping is more common among women than men. Women spend on clothing and accessories to enhance appearance. Men spend on electronics, tools, and mechanical devices, and they also earn a sense of power by picking up the tab for the meal. "They try to boost their self-esteem by buying an image of power."[10]

Listening to ourselves can give us crucial insight into why and how we spend money. The urge to buy can come like hunger and demand satisfaction. "Once I can see it in my mind, it won't go away until I buy it," reported a woman who had seen some jewelry in a store. Some people listen to themselves and find the urge to buy "exciting," "thrilling," and "wild." One person said it was like "falling in love with a product."[11]

Most shoppers do not fall in love with products, but if we listen carefully to ourselves, we may find some purchasing is non-logical and compulsive. The following ten questions are offered as a guide to intrapersonal consumer listening.

Directions: Circle the appropriate number after each question, and add up your score at the end. Do you:

		Never	**Sometimes**	**Always**
1.	Shop to excess?	0	1	2
2.	Shop when you don't need to?	0	1	2
3.	Buy items you don't need or won't use?	0	1	2
4.	Feel guilty about your shopping?	0	1	2
5.	Shop when you're angry, depressed, or lonely?	0	1	2
6.	Get limited or no pleasure from shopping?	0	1	2
7.	Have debts that make home life unhappy?	0	1	2
8.	Hide your shopping from friends or family?	0	1	2
9.	Go to work late or leave work early to shop?	0	1	2
10.	Have a problem with alcohol or drugs when you can't shop?	0	1	2

If you scored between 0 and 4 points, you probably have your shopping under control, although you may be trying to reach for a fast remedy sometimes.

If you scored between 5 and 10 points, you should take a close look at your shopping habits. You are probably headed for two kinds of trouble. First, you are probably not taking the time you need to take care of the underlying problem behind your shopping. Second, you are creating a new problem by compulsively shopping.

> If you scored over 10 points, you do have a serious shopping disorder that will not get better on its own. It is time to take care of yourself as you would your best friend, your sister or your daughter.[12]

Once we have listened intrapersonally and analyzed our motives for shopping, we can turn our attention to the messages that are designed to persuade us to purchase products or services. These persuasive selling techniques are rigorously planned and painstakingly adapted to us as consumers; consequently, we must listen with critical intensity to assure that we are making our purchases responsibly.

❑ Listening to Selling Techniques ❑

Awareness of selling techniques will help us understand and critically analyze messages that are targeted to sell us products or services. In this discussion of selling techniques, we will explore subliminal and conscious persuasive messages.

Subliminal Techniques

Subliminal messages are designed so that we are not aware that we are listening to them. They are based on the idea that we can respond to information below the level of awareness—subconscious listening. If subliminal messages cause us to behave in the intended way, then obviously some critical listening and conscious decision-making power has been taken from us. Being educated in subliminal advertising techniques can cause us to question this loss of critical decision-making, as well as some of our unexplained purchasing decisions.

For the consumer, the choice to buy the tapes is a conscious, non-subliminal one. The tapes are marketed for what they are. Their use, however, prompts an important question for us as consumers: can subliminal persuasion cause us to buy something below the conscious level of listening? In the 1950s, a researcher flashed "EAT POPCORN" on a movie screen and claimed that popcorn sales in that theatre increased, even though the movie viewers were not aware of the message. Arguments went back and forth about the validity of these subliminal messages, and they were not used widely again until the 1970s. At this time subliminal messages reappeared in magazine ads which used pictures with hidden erotic images to catch the unaware eye of the buyer.

Subliminal audio messages also became a way of persuading. Department store music had "I am honest" messages buried in the music to discourage shoplifting. Additionally, people wanting to lose weight, relax, and stop smoking could purchase audio tapes with subliminal messages telling them, "I eat less," "I am capable," "I am calm," or "tobacco kills."

Self-help and motivational audio tapes are also a source of subliminal influence. Even though these tapes are not intended to sell a product or a service, their use provides valuable information about subliminal messages. Every month in 1987, an average of 55,000 tapes with subliminal messages produced by Potential Unlimited, Inc., were sold in bookstores for $10 each. This adds up to $6 million in tape sales for one year. An important factor with these tapes is that the buyer is aware of what s/he is buying. The tapes are advertised as having subliminal messages, but whether the taped messages change behavior is not clear. Stephanie Konicov, Potential Unlimited vice president and marketing director, maintains that the tapes do have positive results, but there is some question as to their effectiveness:

> The interesting thing is that I can find five experts who say "bunk" and you can find five experts who say it [subliminal persuasion] works. I understand both sides. The fact is, it's a $10 product, and for $10 anybody can try it and decide whether it works for them.[13]

How well these subliminal messages work seems to depend on each individual listener. For example, in one study, people were shown the word, "BEEF" for 1/200th of a second every seven seconds. When the message was finished the viewers who were shown the word "BEEF" were hungrier than those not shown the word "BEEF," but even though hungrier, few of them chose beef from the menu.

Another attempt to determine the effectiveness of subliminal messages used two pictures of Chivas Regal Scotch whiskey bottles. One picture was an ordinary bottle of the whiskey; the other had a hidden, shadowy reflection of a naked woman on the bottle. Viewers of these advertising pictures were asked to rate them in the categories of credibility, attractiveness, sensuality, and the likelihood that they might buy the product. The whiskey ad with the hidden image was rated higher in all four categories than the picture ad without the hidden images. Similar studies, however, did not receive the same responses, so the impact of subliminal advertising is still a matter of speculation. What is hidden from one person may be obvious to another.[14]

The effectiveness of subliminal advertising as a persuasive selling method is not clear. Nevertheless, it is important to understand the diligent research energy and the vast expenditures of resources that marketers will invest to get people to buy their product or service. These intense marketing efforts require intense critical listening to determine the real value of a purchase.

Conscious Techniques

Consumer listening requires that we be aware of the types of message persuading us to buy something. As illustrated above, the messages may be hidden and difficult to analyze. Conversely, they might be direct and compelling, falling into categories that fit and satisfy consumer needs: Survival (Food, clothing, shelter); Safety and Security (physical and economic); Social (a sense of belonging); Self-esteem (self respect, worthwhileness); Fulfillment (use of talents and creativity, meeting goals through our own efforts).[15]

Somewhere between meeting needs directly and the subliminal are commonly used advertising and selling techniques. These techniques are offered at the conscious level, but they may subtly manipulate the reality of a product or service. The listener's task becomes one of identifying the underlying selling technique to determine the validity of the persuasive message. These selling techniques fall into one or more of nine categories: Bandwagon, Good Ole Days, Plain Folks, Testimonials, Emotions, Transfer, New and Improved, Card Stacking, and That's Incredible or Puffery.[16]

Bandwagon

This selling technique encourages someone to buy a product, service, or idea because everyone else is buying it. The bandwagon technique is similar to hasty generalization as discussed in chapter 8. For example, recently, this author found himself in Chicago's O'Hare airport with a two hour layover. The unstructured time offered a chance to observe people finding their way to various destinations. Remarkably, many of the travelers were dressed in similar attire—men in tan slacks with blue blazers; women in blue suits with white blouses. Haircuts and hair styles were also similar for men and women.

These similar appearances were the results of subtle pressure to be like everyone else in the category, traveling businessperson. We notice similar persuasive pressures to "jump on the bandwagon" at all age levels. Children want Nintendo 64 or Star Wars figures like their friends have. College students have a particular style of backpack, sunglasses, or hats that fit the college scene.

Adapting to a particular culture can be wise, as long as we are aware of what we are doing. As listening consumers, we need to question our motives for buying a product or idea. We ask ourselves, "Is this clothing or behavior necessary for me to fit into the setting I have agreed to be in?" "Am I comfortable with the expectations of the group I am identifying with?" The intent of these questions is: "How much of my personal values am I willing to give up to conform to this group's expectations?" If buying into the clothing, hairstyle, and behaviors of a group allows one to keep a clear sense of who s/he is, then being persuaded to hop on the group's bandwagon could be a sensible choice.

Good Ole Days

This selling strategy promotes a product or service which claims to bring the consumer back to the simpler times of the past. The messages tell us, if we buy the product, we will be getting back to the basics—the recipe grandma used: that good old fashioned country flavor.

Certainly, technology has brought advancements and comforts that were unheard of just five or ten years ago. Never-the-less, an attraction for a basic, simpler, non-technical lifestyle is built into a number of consumer messages. The strong interest in antiques—be it furniture, cars, machines, or clothing—provides a viable consumer market, and what these advertisements are saying is, "Not even technology can make this better," and in some cases, this is a valid point. For example, the trend away from man-made fabrics back to cotton and other natural fabrics verifies that some time-proven products are superior. Finding a carpenter who is a craftsman in the "old style" is viewed as worth more, because the final product is beautiful, solid, and functional. However, not all products and services from the past are superior, and the consumer should weigh a decision to buy after comparing the past with state-of-art qualities.

Plain Folks

This selling technique appeals to the hard-working, grass roots, no nonsense kind of product or service. For example, promotions that tell us that their product has, "No fads or fancy stuff," or "This meets your needs head-on," or "The truck is built tough for the hard-working man," are identifying with the common person. The North American culture values practical, functional, and basic goods and services. We see these values in Western movies and the image of the cowboy on his horse backed by a mountain scene. We see the typical mother with three kids climbing into a van with functional options that assure the safety of her family along with enough room for groceries and grandmother.

Plain folk messages often compare simple, down-to-earth behavior with frivolous, elitist behavior: the everyday Jane *versus* Snobby Susan. For example, these ads might say: "Who needs to go first class. I can get there in business class just as safely." Through these messages, the listening consumer could be convinced that s/he is making a purchasing decision based on culturally approved, practical needs.

The other side of the plain folks message appeals to the fun and non-practical. These messages say the consumer is not plain or ordinary. For example, these advertisements tempt the listener to "Spoil herself." They say to the executive, "You deserve the best at the end of a trying day." "First class travel belongs to first class people." In essence, the messages are saying, "You are not a plain person; you are special. Reward yourself." A purchase based on this message would be motivated by the belief that, in this instance, I am special; I am going to dispense with practicality and do this just for fun.

Testimonials

This persuasive technique relies on a credible source to endorse a product or service. The testimonial, usually in the form of "I choose this service over all others, because . . .," may come from a well known celebrity, a professional, an athlete, an expert, or a salesperson. When listening to a testimonial, the buyer should ask: Is the testimonial complete and fair. Is it from someone with first-hand knowledge of the product? What does the source of the testimony have to gain from the product endorsement?

Emotions

Emotions appeal to our feelings—love, hate, power, freedom, fun, and, like all appeals, they can be worthwhile. Certainly, the feelings of love and caring used in promoting the use of seat belts or abstaining from drinking and driving are noble. We need to be aware of the nature of the appeal: a non-logical attempt to tap into our feelings. Services that are sold emotionally might be centered on insurance—"The greater the love for your husband, the more life insurance you will buy"—or telephone use—"Reach out, reach out and touch someone." Products sold emotionally are greeting cards: "For those who care enough to send the very best," or caskets: "The casket you buy is a measure of your caring and love." In each case, we must determine if the emotions are, in reality, a valid expression of the product or service.

Transfer

This selling technique attempts to increase the desirability of a product or service by associating it with a well known and well accepted symbol or phrase. The seller's hope is that the listener will transfer the high regard for the symbol to the product being sold.

Many logos for products and retail outlets are positive symbols that are intended to transfer a sense of fairness, integrity, quality, or economy to the consumer. For example, the Target logo of three concentric circles carries the association, "Right on target," with purchases here. The phrase, "Proudly made in the USA," implies quality and a sense of pride in the product.

During election years, consumer listening is directed toward "buying into" one political candidate or another, and one of the most impressive uses of *transfer* occurred in a political campaign of the 1950s. During this campaign, Senator Richard Nixon appeared on television to defend his use of some campaign contributions. Mr. Nixon, who was being considered for a vice-presidential candidacy, defended these contributions and convinced the American public that he should be the vice president.

Unquestionably, his success in selling the television viewers was greatly helped by the use of symbols. He sat at a massive wooden desk, symbol of solidarity and high position; his wife Pat was at his left, and periodically, the camera would pan over to her, Mr. Nixon's symbol of faithfulness, loyalty, and family. The most impressive symbol in this television speech was a Cocker Spaniel puppy named Checkers. In this speech—which has since been titled the "Checkers Speech"—Nixon acknowledges that his family did indeed receive the puppy as a political gift, but, even if it destroyed his political future, he was not going to return this puppy. Checkers became Nixon's strongest symbol; a symbol that transferred to him as being kind, caring, loyal, respectful of life and nature, highly principled, and willing to sacrifice his career for something he and his family loved.

The television viewers listened and bought the message that Nixon was acting honestly and in the best interests of the country. He went on to become vice president.

New and Improved

This technique tells the potential buyer that the product or service being sold is the state of the art. It is the product of the latest technology. Again, the listening consumer should be alert to this technique, by asking: "Should I wait until the new models come out?" or risk purchasing an obsolete model?

The discussion above about "Good Ole Days," emphasized the idea that new is not always improved, so the consumer needs to determine if the *change* in a product or service is, in fact, an *improvement*. Is it a change for the better?

One of the fastest changing products that claim *new and improved* is computers. It seems that every month new and significant changes are brought to the public awareness. When considering the purchase of one of these new and improved computers, the critical listener needs to weigh the value of the faster speeds, increased memory, and added features. Does she need these innovations, or will her current computer set-up serve her purposes just as well?

Card Stacking

This technique attempts to sell by misleading information. It offers the buyer half-truths, or does not provide pertinent information. The term "Card Stacking" means putting the playing cards in winning order for the dealer. Card stacking might use expert testimony, but only that part of the testimony which is favorable toward the item being sold. For example, a dentist is quoted as saying, ". . . the majority of dentists surveyed preferred brand Y toothpaste. . . ." From this expert testimony, the listener believes brand Y is the best; however, the testimony *not* quoted in the advertisement goes on to say, ". . . in terms of price and accessibility. "But," the dentist continues, "if decay prevention and tooth appearance are the concern—which I believe they should be—then brand X is highest on my recommended list." The advertisers have stacked the cards in their favor by omitting the last portion of the dentist's message which substantially changes the intended meaning.

That's Incredible or Puffery

This technique focuses on the language of selling. Catchy phrases and powerful adjectives and modifiers infer that the products or services are something more than they actually are. For example, the automobile that has "The awesome power of the turbo V-6" offers a message of strength, but the specific details of the power and performance are missing, to be inferred by the listener. Listener inference is also part of the incredible, puffed message: "The store designed for those who strive to bc on thc cutting edge."

Another example of That's Incredible or Puffery involves pain capsules. If all nonprescription pain capsules take about the same amount of time to give relief, one manufacturer may claim, "that no pain capsule gives relief faster than brand X." The actual meaning of the claim is true, but the wording of the claim makes it possible for the consumer to infer that brand X works faster than the other brands.[17] This selling technique uses language that puts the product or service far beyond the ordinary and gives the impression of implied superiority. Other examples of That's Incredible or Puffery are:

International Harvester: "Nobody builds a more productive line of farm equipment."

Winston Light Cigarettes: "Nobody does it better."

L'eggs pantyhose: "Nothing beats a great pair of L'eggs."

Chrysler: "The ones to beat."

These puffed-up messages may seem innocent enough, but there is a chance that the buyers may infer beyond the content of the message and make an unwise purchase.[18]

Effective consumer listening is the result of three stages of preparation. We have explored two of these: first, listening for internal reasons for buying, and second, understanding the subliminal and conscious techniques that are used to market products and services. The third step involves researching the product that we have decided to buy.

❑ Consumer Research ❑

We turn to professional experts for information and advice, because they are knowledgeable in a particular field. The physician, with her medical background, listens for information about symptoms and makes an educated decision to treat the problem; the attorney listens to a description of a situation and decides on a legal approach to the problem; the auto mechanic listens to the details and proceeds with diagnostic efforts. In each case, *before* a sensible decision can be made, these people use listening skills to find specific information about the topic.

As listening consumers, we might not become experts (such as physicians, attorneys, or mechanics) on the products or services we buy, but gaining knowledge about a potential purchase will help significantly in the final decision. With the knowledge gained from research, the consumer can listen critically to facts and ignore the irrelevant information. Depending on the type of purchase, the complexity, and the cost, this research can be finished quickly, perhaps by surveying several models of a product, or it can be a fairly detailed and lengthy effort that might require outside professional consultation.

Two readily available sources for acquiring consumer information are *Consumers' Research* and *Consumers' Digest*. These reports explore the pros and cons of a variety of products and services. More importantly, they give the consumer an organized approach for researching prior to purchasing. This organized approach involves carefully examining the range of variables that could encourage or discourage purchasing a product or service.

Under the heading *products*, we will research a relatively low cost item—mouthwash; then, one of the highest cost items—the automobile. Under *service*, we will research auto body repair.

Mouthwash.[19] Annual sales of mouthwashes are about $500 million, and one alone grossed $100 million. The two top selling mouthwashes are Warner-Lambert's "Listerine," and Proctor & Gamble's "Scope." Basically, these products are diluted water-alcohol solutions of chemicals, and on the store shelves are a number of less expensive—half the price—mouthwash products whose compositions duplicate those of the leading brands.

The question is, "Which one should I purchase?"

Several studies have determined that the private label mouthwashes are as effective as their brand-name competitors. The most effective brand in plaque-reduction is Listerine which reduced plaque an average of 25% and gingivitis, 29%. Scope and Cepacol showed a 14% reduction in plaque and a 24% reduction of gingivitis. Based on these studies, the private label imitations of Listerine, Scope, and Cepacol should be equally effective in reducing plaque and gingivitis in each of their respective categories.

With this information, the consumer is prepared to listen critically to sale messages about mouthwashes, because s/he has researched the product in a credible journal. As with any purchase, the final choice of which mouthwash to buy will be the result of the consumer's internal motivation, the sales techniques targeting the product, and the researched information. Next, we consider a research model for a large purchase—an automobile.

An Automobile.[20] This research assumes that the buyer knows in general what s/he wants and is now in the process of getting information on the more subtle details which influence the decision.

First, you as a consumer should read car enthusiast and road test reports to decide on the general model type, equipment, and price range you want. Next, start visiting dealers for test drives; perhaps rent a car you are considering. Once you start looking at specific cars, you begin a practical evaluation.

Start your evaluation when the car is parked and locked. Does it take one key for the door and one for the ignition? Are the door, trunk, and hatch smooth to open, or are they heavy and awkward?

Once inside, are you really comfortable? Does the seat adjust well? Is the steering wheel lined-up with your position in the seat? Does the seat adjust comfortably? Will you be comfortable for a long drive? Is the rear seat accessible in a two door model? Try placing packages or a child's seat in the back seat of a two door model. In a sleek hatch back model, is the hatch heavy and awkward? Is it large enough to handle packages and luggage that would fit in a trunk?

In the driver's position, are the mirrors functional? Are the sideview mirrors easily adjusted? Do they give a full and complete picture?

Next check the safety equipment. Adjust the seat and put the belt system in place over your body. Adjust the belt and take up slack. Notice if the belts "load" properly; the shoulder belt should rest halfway between the shoulder-arm joint, not too close to your neck. Determine if the belts are easy to unlatch and stow each time you remove them. Check the belt system in the rear seats. Are they easily used? Retracted seat belt systems are often an obstacle, and sometimes the use of the rear seat area is too difficult for elderly passengers. The number of passengers that a vehicle can carry is designated by its designated seating position (DSP) represented by each set of seat belts. If buying a van or recreational vehicle, notice if the number of DSP's is sufficient for your use. The safety system is like insurance. Be sure you have the best possible.

Now you can begin the road test. Be aware of the ease of latching the belt system, starting the engine, moving away from a stop, and maneuvering out of a parking space. Does the transmission move smoothly into "drive?" Is the clutch smooth in engaging first gear? How do the brakes feel? Are they solid and secure feeling? Are there any unusual noises or surges from the engine? Is the car quiet and tight? In traffic, is there adequate visibility of the front, back, and sides? No obstructions that add guesswork to parking? Can you park it easily? On the road, is the ride comfortable? Not too mushy or stiff? At night, is the instrument illumination adequate? Can you read the instruments and control markings?

Finally, research for possible hidden costs. Research insurance prices for the make and model you are considering. Full coverage on a full set of aluminum wheels might amaze you. In addition, ease of repair, frequency of theft, performance, and luxury can all add substantially to insurance costs.

The consumer who has carefully researched, is now ready to listen critically to the details presented by a salesperson and to increase substantially the probability of making a sensible purchase.

Having explored some of the research possibilities of two products—mouthwash and automobiles, we turn to a service—auto body repair. As with the products, the purpose here is to look at a format or outline to model research for the best service decision.

Auto Body Repair.[21] Automobile body repair is a service that is used by every adult at one time. The chances of getting into an accident are one in four, and even without an accident, sooner or later the car may need cosmetic work to eliminate rust and normal wear and aging.

In researching where to go for body work, here are some steps that will help guide the listening consumer toward a comfortable decision.

1. Get recommendations first. Frequently, the most reliable advertising is through people we know. A visit with friends and relatives will often lead to a reliable body shop. Referrals from a mechanic, insurance agent, or car dealer can also be helpful.

2. Watch the shop in action. Visit the shop and observe these six areas:

—Is the lot fenced in, or is it open? A shop that is concerned with security is likely to be just as careful in doing quality work.

—Do signs indicate membership in reputable associations? Memberships of organizations like the Automotive Service Association (ASA) are expected to comply to a code of ethics and responsible automotive consumer service practices.

—Are there indications that the shop employees are certified mechanics? The National Institute for Automotive Service Excellence (NIASE) offers a certification program for mechanics, including auto body repair personnel and painters.

—Are cars waiting for repair damaged from a variety of sources? Cars with rust, fenderbenders, and major collisions will give you an idea of what the shop is capable of handling.

—Is the shop relatively clean and organized? Are precautions taken such as having the painting booth well removed from the sanding area to promote contamination?

—What equipment is used? The best shops have state of the art equipment. Down-draft spray booths, and laser alignment equipment, as well as sophisticated welding and paint mixing systems are indicators of a well equipped shop.

After observing in these six areas, listen careful while you visit with the manager and repair technicians about these topics:

—Dent repair. A good shop will not usually fill major dents with body putty, but will either pound out the dent or replace the part.

—Body fillers. For little dings, hammer and dolly marks, and minor damage, body fillers should not exceed more than one-half inch.

—Sand blasting. To clean rust thoroughly, the shop should use sand blasting *and* some sanding.

—Metal protection. Metal conditioners and primers should be applied to bare metal to prevent rust.

—Preparation. Areas to be painted should be sanded first and primed, so that the paint will adhere well.

Next, get a detailed estimate. Ask that all parts and labor be clearly itemized and be sure the shop will notify you if the costs might exceed the estimate. Today, some shops offer written warranties, and a 90 day written warranty on paint is a reasonable request.

Clarify parts warranties. Get manufacturer's warranties, and be sure the highest quality replacement parts are used.

As this model shows, researching a service is more complex than researching a product, because products and workers' understanding and skills are combined to become directly responsible for the final result. With the information gained from this research, the listening consumer will be in a solid position to make the best decision on where to have the car fixed, and in more general decisions s/he will have a model to get information for any service to be purchased.

❑ Summary ❑

This chapter applies critical listening to the process of making a purchase. This consumer listening role involves making decisions on how and where to spend money. Before reasonable buying decisions can be made, the consumer should listen for: 1) internal motivations for shopping. These motivations range from need to compulsion, 2) persuasive messages which encourage the purchase of a product or service. These advertising techniques are subliminal (below the conscious level) or aimed at conscious perceptions, and include: bandwagon, good ole days, plain folks, testimonials, emotions, transfer, new and improved, card stacking, and that's incredible or puffery, and 3) information acquired through thoroughly researching the product or service. The listener who attends to these details will enjoy the satisfaction of responsible consuming.

Awareness Exercises, Chapter 9

Name ______________________________ **SS#** _____-____-_____

Review Chapter 9, and respond

1. Describe an *in-store* promotion you have observed.

2. Describe a situation where you or someone you know made an unnecessary purchase.

   A. Why was the purchase unnecessary?

   B. What were the *real* reasons for the purchase?

3. Describe subliminal advertising.

4. Give an example of subliminal advertising that you have been told about or have observed.

5. Describe thee examples of Bandwagon advertising:

   A.

   B.

   C.

6. Describe three examples of Good Ole Days advertising.

A.

B.

C.

7. Describe three examples of Plain Folks advertising.

A.

B.

C.

8. Describe three examples of Testimonial advertising.

A.

B.

C.

9. Describe three examples of Emotional advertising.

A.

B.

C.

10. Discuss three examples of New and Improved advertising.

    A.

    B.

    C.

11. Discuss three examples of Card Stacking advertising.

    A.

    B.

    C.

12. Discuss three examples of That's Incredible advertising.

    A.

    B.

    C.

13. Describe a product or service you plant to purchase in the future. Outline, in detail, the steps you will follow to research this purchase.

10 Listening Appreciatively

Listening appreciatively is listening to enjoy. Each day, we have the chance to take little vacations that may not involve travel, but give us time to leave our daily responsibilities and give us a different perspective. We close the office door, turn on some music, look at a favorite picture on the wall. We jog and enjoy the sounds of spring, or are entertained with head sets; we relax and visit with a friend; we share jokes and stories. Perhaps we go to the theatre, a concert, a movie, a production featuring an entertainer or a comedian, or an exhibit that centers on a favorite hobby. We might watch TV or listen to the radio, or rent a movie or an audio cassette. To add further understanding to appreciative listening, this chapter discusses: 1) the appreciative listening role, 2) the steps of appreciation, 3) the individual nature of appreciation, 4) knowledge and appreciation, 5) the link between appreciation, learning, and fun, and 6) humor and appreciation.

The Appreciative Listening Role

Appreciative listening is listening for enjoyment and pleasure. This role differs somewhat from the comprehensive, therapeutic, critical, and consumer listening roles, because the appreciative listening role is *initially* based on a nonrational and intuitive *attraction*. The attraction, at first, can happen by chance, but as our interest grows, the steps that lead to the appreciative listening role can lead to choices that substantially affect our enjoyment in life.

The Steps of Appreciation

Interviews with a variety of people show that appreciative listening develops in three steps which progress from casual interest to a deep-felt appreciation.[1] Awareness of these steps can help us understand how we come to appreciate, and how we can prepare for the appreciative listening role.

Step one is *Attraction*. This step draws our attention to something or someone, and is primarily a function of the right brain: it is non-evaluative and non-logical. It is an emotional reaction that pulls us. As a result of this attraction, we *might* have a desire to gain knowledge about the subject and move to the next level.

The second step of appreciation is *Contact*, which is a combination of right and left brain functioning. Because of the emotional right brain attraction, we become interested in this subject and begin to learn about it through continued listening, observing, involvement, or participation. In this step, we are learning about what attracts us, and we are using the right and left brain to add to our understanding about this attractive person or topic.

The third step is *Critical Evaluation*. Here, the left brain hemisphere dominates. As we learn more about the subject, we begin to judge it; we rely on int*ra*personal messages and we prioritize our own internal values—"Is this good or bad for me?" "Is this a wise way to spend my time?" "Is this exciting to me?" Next, we might survey the accepted social norms—"Is it an acceptable or unacceptable interest?" This step in appreciative listening takes continual information from step two—Contact—to provide a basis for comparison and evaluation, and it takes sustained energy from step one—Attraction—to supply the motivation to pursue the interest.

Following is an example of the three steps of appreciative listening: Step one, Attraction. You see a glider flying overhead. Step two, Contact. You think it is interesting, so you watch it. You begin to take note of all the times you see gliders and watch them. The more you watch, the more interested you become, so you read about gliders and possibly take a ride in one. Soon you can identify different types of gliders. Step three, Critical Evaluation. Even without riding in a glider, you decide it would be fun, so you attend an air show or take a class to learn more about flying. This whole process is based on ideas from past experiences about what you like, what you think is difficult, and what you think is exciting.

The simple act of seeing the glider is preparation for the Attraction step. If you had chosen (most likely subconsciously) not to watch the glider you would have never reached the first step. However, something stimulated you to take interest in the glider, causing you to be attracted. The stimulus could be anything and could have been there for you hundreds of times, but for any number of reasons, this time you were attracted to it. It may have been a type of glider you had never seen before, or you could have simply been noticing it against a sky that you thought was especially beautiful.

As you continue to watch, you proceed to the Contact step. At this step you watch the glider and learn about it. This initial knowledge can be as simple as just seeing that it flies and can actually gain altitude.

If you decide that it is fascinating, you have made a judgment about the glider and have reached the critical evaluation step. With each sighting of a glider you compare it to your past experiences and become a critical judge, deciding whether you like or dislike what you are listening to.

Another example of a situation leading to appreciative listening could have happened to you as a gradeschooler attending your older sister's band concert. At the concert, you become fascinated by the drums. You watch the drummer and notice his contribution to the music. In high school, you are asked if you want to play in the band, and you decide that you want to play the drums. As you go through your school year playing in the band, you are just an average drummer, but later as an adult you still can appreciate the drummer's contribution to music.

This example shows how you may be "forced" into a listening environment, since, as a child you probably had little choice in deciding whether to attend the concert or not attend. When you saw the drummer, you reached the Attraction step. Your listening to him that night was Contact, and even though it may not have been extensive contact, you learned more about the drums. Next, you moved to the Critical Evaluative step, which led you to conclude the drums were fun and interesting. At this point in the process, you made a temporary exit, or pause, until you were asked to play in the band.

As you play in the band, you go through the three steps as many times as you feel are necessary. Years later, you still probably watch drummers in bands, and you notice mistakes that most non-drummers miss. Again, this is the critical evaluation step surfacing. You also appreciate a drummer's playing a difficult passage well, and you make this evaluation through a comparison to your past knowledge.

We can choose to appreciate and to stop appreciating. If we find someone attractive, we will follow the three steps—attraction, contact, critical evaluation—repeatedly, until we approach a level of desired appreciation. This level might never be reached, as in the case of lifetime relationships with special people. Moreover, if our attraction decreases, we can exit the appreciative listening process, deciding that we have taken it as far as we desire. When we decide to exit or pause appreciative listening, we usually do it at the attraction step. That is, based on the knowledge we have, we are no longer attracted to this person.

This model summarizes the appreciative listening process:

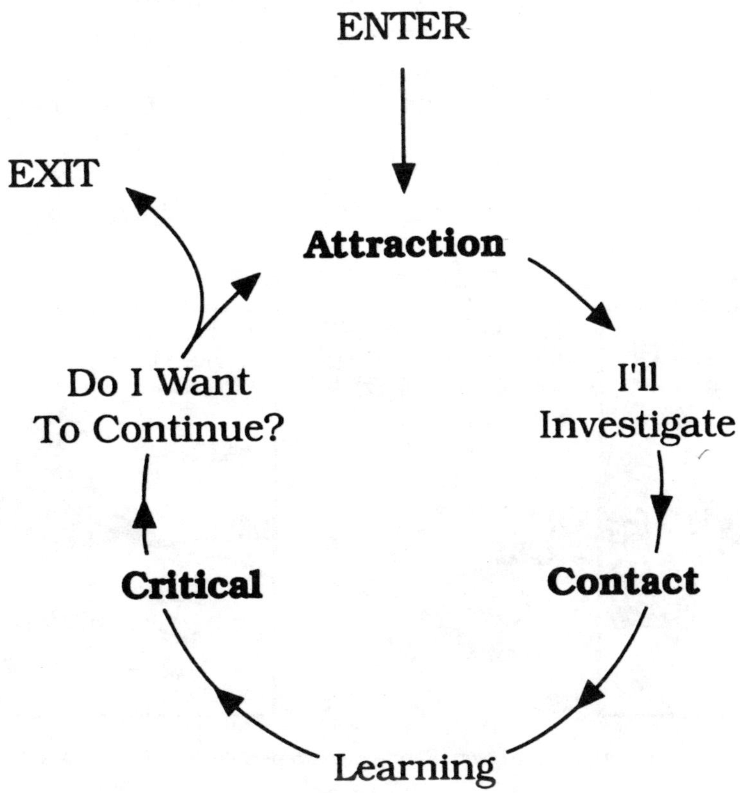

❑ The Individual Nature of Appreciation ❑

Appreciative listening is highly individualized. In a *comprehensive* listening setting, two efficient listeners would be able to compare notes after a lecture and find that they understand and recall the same central ideas. Two listeners discussing something they appreciate, say, a play or concert, however, can have differing impressions of the event. Music, for example, will impress people in different ways; some may find it stimulating and exciting; others might find it loud and meaningless; still, others might not react to it in any way whatsoever.

Appreciation is individualized and is noticed early in life. The baby in her crib listens to her music box and is quieted and soothed. She listens and assigns some meaning to the music box tune. Another child might listen to the same music box and not be soothed at all. Rather, it might stimulate the child to want to touch and play with it. Appreciation varies from person to person. Some are more prone to appreciate color and design, while others appreciate the workings of machines. In this author's view, we come into the world with certain predispositions regarding what we appreciate.

Diverse appreciation is part of life. Every newspaper advertises a variety of different events that involve appreciative listening—concerts, ranging from hard rock, to jazz, to symphonic; intimate dinner theatre or grand productions from early Greek, and Shakespeare, to modern comedies and musicals, and movies ranging from animated musicals to horror.

Some appreciation tendency is inborn, but we also *learn* to appreciate. In the process of growing up, we tend to value what our family valued. The interests enjoyed by our parents often are enjoyed by us. As we grow through life, we form our own set of criteria for appreciation. Our friends introduce us to new entertainments, different art forms, and hobbies. Perhaps we take a course in music appreciation, art appreciation, geology, or oral interpretation. Inherited differences combine with learning to help us listen in a variety of situations.

❑ Knowledge and Appreciation ❑

Appreciative listening is linked closely with knowledge, because we need some knowledge to appreciate. In general, we want to know more about what attracts us. We may listen to a musician because she is unique, and has a style we have not heard before. She possesses a knowledge that we appreciate, just as a classical artist can be appreciated for her knowledge. The idea that knowledge is needed for appreciation is true with any topic of appreciation. For example, the mechanic who appreciates a smoothly running engine understands the engineering and care which went into its development and manufacture.

Appreciation also comes from comparative knowledge. For example, we see a sunset, and we compare it with other sunsets we have seen, and we evaluate it as one of the most beautiful. We see a play performed, and we compare it with other performances and make a judgment. To appreciate someone or something, we compare them with our past knowledge, and we evaluate based on this comparison.

The amount and type of knowledge can also affect appreciation. A person may have knowledge that leads him to judge something as unattractive. For example, someone who has the idea that opera consists of loud singing in a foreign language will probably never go to an opera and have the chance to appreciate it. A friend invites him to go to a performance, but he refuses to go. He says he has heard bits and pieces of that opera, and it is "not for him." His friend knows he dislikes opera, and is aware that he knows very little about it, so the friend explains the plot and some aspects to listen for: humorous scenes, interesting music, and intricate costumes. With this knowledge, he might be attracted enough to attend an opera and *begin* to appreciate some of its qualities.

In this example, we see that some knowledge about opera can increase attraction. However, if we know more about opera, will we enjoy it more? There is no clear-cut answer to this question, and the question leads to other questions. If listeners are knowledgeable about opera, is the probability greater that they will activate the left brain and be in the critical listening role? With this added knowledge, will they make decisions on how it *should* be played, and consequently, not appreciate it? Or does appreciation increase with knowledge?

A dilemma exists in the relationship between appreciative listening and knowledge. As one poet wrote, "We murder to dissect," that is, once we have studied a topic thoroughly (dissected it), we cannot listen and appreciate it any more (we have murdered our ability to appreciate; we are too critical). With knowledge comes the possibility that appreciative listening will become more critical.

However, knowledge does not always lead to critical assessment. Someone with considerable knowledge can understand the difficulties in staging the performance. Even though the performance might be less than perfect, this mature critic can appreciate the efforts and difficulties involved in the production. Knowledge and appreciation work together. Some knowledge is needed to sustain attraction, and as the knowledge increases beyond the initial attraction, the listener tends to judge the details of the appreciated subject. In time, knowledge becomes a source of mature appreciation.[2]

❑ Appreciative Listening: Learning and Fun ❑

Appreciative listening comes initially from attraction to something that is fun—listening to music, going to a play, a concert, or a movie. In the process of having fun, we learn about people, life's peculiarities, or a favorite hobby.

Richard Bach, in his book, *Illusions: The Adventures of a Reluctant Messiah*, expands the idea that appreciative listening is fun and learning. In this excerpt, one of the main characters, Don Shimoda and his new friend, Richard, have decided to relax for an evening by going to the movie, *Butch Cassidy and the Sundance Kid*. The author uses this scene to illustrate that appreciative listening is fun and learning. At an exciting part in the movie, Don touches Richard on the shoulder and asks him:

> "Why are you here?"
>
> "It's a good movie, Don. *Sh.*" Butch and Sundance, blood all over them, are talking about why they ought to go to Australia.
>
> "Why is it good?" he said.
>
> "It's fun. *Sh.* I'll tell you later."
>
> "Snap out of it. Wake up. It's all illusions."
>
> I was irked. "Donald, there's just a few minutes more and then we can talk all you want. But let me watch the movie, OK?"
>
> He whispered intensely, dramatically. "Richard, *why are you here*?"

After the movie, Donald and Richard discuss the reasons for appreciative listening: fun, learning, or both.

> "The other people, any people anywhere who go to any movie show, why are they there, when it is only illusions?"
>
> "Well, it's entertainment," I said.
>
> "Fun. That's right. One."
>
> "Could be educational."
>
> "Good. It is always that. Learning. Two."
>
> "Fantasy, escape."
>
> That's fun, too. One.
>
> "Technical reasons. To see how a film is made."
>
> "Learning. Two."
>
> "Escape from boredom . . ."
>
> "Escape. You said that."
>
> "Social. To be with friends," I said.
>
> "Reasons for going, but not to see the film. That's fun, anyway. One."
>
> Whatever I came up with fit his two fingers; people see films for fun or for learning or for both together . . .[3]

Once we have decided that a diversion from our daily demands and responsibilities is in order, we need to survey the arena of possible appreciative experiences available to us. We might appreciate the vivid message of a polished speaker; a casual talk about a hobby; the humor of a comedian; a story dramatically told. We might be listening to life's joys and problems when the lights go down in the theatre as the play begins. We might appreciate the vigor and energy of a rock concert; the soothing mix of tones at a symphony. The choices available for appreciative listening are as varied as people's interests; one need only to explore them. Here are some appreciative listening choices gathered from people of all ages:[4]

visiting museums	going to the restroom after being in the car three hours
soap smell after a shower	nice wet juicy kiss
silence of snow and it hitting you in the face	sound of chopping wood
the feeling of clean sheets in a freshly made bed	hitting a bull's-eye
eating gummy bears	coming to a swishing stop while snow skiing
bees	rippling water under a dock at night
sound of working with wood	creaminess of French silk pie
computer printer	smell of cologne
crowd and band at a basketball game	champagne and roses
baked bread and cookies	well tuned sport bike
Poplar trees blowing in the wind	fresh cut grass
sound of water	sound of cooking steaks
impressionists' paintings	apple trees in bloom
smell after a rainstorm	thunderstorms
heat of the sun	smell of pine
sleet hitting a window	sunsets
feel of soft fur	smell of wife/husband
changing of seasons, budding trees	taste of pure, clean water
walk in a snowy woods	chocolate
taste of fresh bread with butter melting on it	proportion of Victorian houses
taste and sight of fresh vegetables and fruit	feeling her cat
the chatter of a happy child	sound of loons
feel of squeezing a hand	feel of velvet
fresh ground coffee	petting her black Lab
smoking a pipe after a meal	hearing what the customers want
feel of a soft woman	hard bike tires
new car smell	crackling fire
feel of his muscles flexing	good golf shot
voices of grandchildren	feel of soft leather

❑ Humor and Appreciation ❑

What we appreciate is usually learning or fun. Humor—those scenes that we find amusing and make us laugh—is a rich source of fun and learning, and being attracted to humor is the start of an appreciative interest that is healthy and can keep life's worries in perspective. Appreciating the humor in life can help us stop worrying.[5]

Worry can contribute to high blood pressure, rheumatism, stomach ulcers, the common cold, thyroid complications and many other physical ailments.[6] One authority on arthritis listed five of the most common conditions that contribute to arthritic problems: marital failure, financial disaster, grief, loneliness, and long-held resentments.[7] Moreover, it is suggested that one-half of all hospital beds is taken for patients with nervous and mental troubles.[8] The negative effects of worry are clear, and one way to minimize the effects of worry is through appreciative listening to humor.[9]

Humor plays three important roles in lowering the effects of worry. It improves health, increases learning, and helps solve conflict. Health research has found that laughing has a positive effect on blood pressure, oxygenating the blood, massaging vital organs, facilitating digestion, and causing release of endorphins in the brain. (Endorphins produce feelings of well-being.) Moreover, humor is suggested as a possible help in prevention and recovery from illnesses.[10] Not only does humor reduce the effects of worry, it is also a key to learning. Laughing and learning seem to work together, helping the listener pay attention and remember the message.[11]

One final aspect of appreciative humor is that it adds to professional effectiveness. For example, students judge humor a high priority in effective teachers,[12] and managers with a sense of humor are judged more effective leaders.[13]

Listening appreciatively to humor has the benefits of minimizing worry, increasing learning, and contributing to professional effectiveness. To increase listening appreciatively to humor and realize these benefits, we should look for humor in everyday happenings and see ourselves as sources of humor.[14] Moreover, we can increase our sense of appreciation for humor by adapting an attitude of playfulness and by listening for the humorous incongruities in situations involving ourselves and others.[15]

❑ Listening Experience ❑

The following essay, entitled, "Listening Experience," was first constructed as a lecture about appreciative listening. Notice how the author emphasizes the idea that listening to a performance is a group listening experience, with each listener coming for different reasons with a variety of backgrounds and experiences.

The late David P. Hirvela was Associate Professor and Director of Theatre at Iowa State University. He taught acting, directing, and arts management. He directed and acted professionally with regional theatres. He authored THE PERFORMING ARTS: AN AUDIENCE'S PERSPECTIVE.

As defined earlier, listening in the performing arts includes receiving both aural and visual stimuli. Listening, a complex behavior, involves all our senses. It encompasses more than what passes through our ears. Although we listen each day of our lives, listening as a part of an audience presents different demands than our usual daily experiences. What are the components of the performing arts listening experience?

Performing arts listening is a *group experience.* Most often a person responds to the performing arts as a member of a group. And, the nature of how we respond will be influenced by the group's behavior. Unfortunately most of our group listening is associated with sitting in classrooms for 12 to 16 years.

The positive and negative behaviors we have learned from classroom listening many initially transfer to the audience experience. Classroom listening has taught us how to remain attentive over relatively long periods of time; how to engage ourselves with the instructor and with our fellow classmates; how to concentrate. However, we have also learned how to *look* attentive, but *think* about other things; how to escape boring instructors or lessons through daydreaming; how to focus on the most insignificant distractions.

Each audience member has *different purposes for attending a theatrical event.* The assumption that an audience has a single unified purpose for attending—to respond to the performance—ignores the reasons people attend any performance. Our purposes for being in the audience impact our listening. They affect our attention to the performance and our interest in listening. If you listen with less attention and interest, you reduce the chances that the performance will make its desired aesthetic impression.

Performing arts listening occurs in a *restrictive communication environment.* Sitting in a theatre with other people restricts the freedom of your response to what you see and hear. The group discourages verbal response among audience members or with performers. Other audience members may quiet anyone who disturbs the performance by talking. Therefore, you have little opportunity to respond verbally, an uncomfortable condition for some people. Consequently the audience's situation offers even more restrictions than the classroom listening.

Performing arts listening emphasizes *physical passivity.* Audience members of theatre, dance, and music performances (excluding most popular music events) have little opportunity to move. The formal theatre environment and group expectations encourage *listening while sitting.* Only extraordinary emergencies permit leaving the theatre during a performance.

This physical passivity contrasts with the freedom of movement allowed with the more informal performing arts. At a rock concert you feel free to stand and shout, dance in the aisles, or even stand on the seats. The rock performance stimulates this activity, and the whole audience participates actively. As you watch a film in a theatre, you can get up and leave for more popcorn at any time. This action is accepted by other audience members and encouraged by the theatre management, who show commercials promoting, "Have a snack" and inform audiences that the snack bar is closing in five minutes.

Even greater informality exists with television and radio listening; viewers move whenever and wherever they please during these performance events. Since most of your performance models for listening behavior are typically informal, you may feel uncomfortable and limited in an audience of the formal performing arts. This physical passivity affects your listening.

The listeners to the performing arts have a *shortened attention span.* Most audience members have an attention span for sitting and listening to the performing arts that is significantly shorter than our ancestors'. Audiences even as recently as the 1950's expected Broadway plays lasting at least two and one-half hours, attended double bills at the movies, or listened to the radio for 3-4 hours in the evening. In the early 1900's audiences felt cheated if their theatre evening was not a 4-5 hour experience, which might include an orchestral overture and between-act music, a full-play, variety acts, and a short play as an after-piece. Why has our attention span for the performing arts shortened?

Our individual tempo-rhythms, i.e., our internal responses to time, reflect the pace of our technological society. Information speeds around the world in seconds; at work, computers process information in milliseconds; we even expect restaurants to serve our food *fast* and *on demand.* We even have less patience with performing arts which do not engage us immediately.

With entertainment we have developed concentrated attention spans of eight to twelve minutes from our watching television since childhood. The average American spends over five and one-half hours each day watching television. This television experience teaches us to concentrate on the performance only eight to twelve minutes. Longer concentration is impossible, because commercials interrupt the performance. Television does not permit focusing on the performance for longer time periods. Therefore, we develop a shortened attention span for the performing arts from the very influential early years of childhood. Because of the short attention span, theatre performances of two hours, broken only with one intermission, may seem unbearably long. They strain an audience member's concentration. This shortened attention affects how you listen and therefore how you *receive* the performance.

The performing arts experience places new demands on your listening skills. Your listening techniques must adjust to performance situations. New approaches to listening must develop. These adjustments and changes will enhance your reception of the performing arts, and ultimately increase your enjoyment and appreciation.

An Individual's Experience with the Performing Arts

Every time you attend a performance, you bring along your accumulated experiences with that performing art. As each person in an audience is unique, likewise each person's experiences with performing arts vary. Some audience members will have attended many performances; some will be attending for the first time. How does this variation in experience affect audience responses?

The greater your experience, the greater the likelihood that you will involve yourself in the aesthetic elements of performance. Aesthetic involvement increases the range and intensity of your reactions. These reactions feed back directly to the performers and your fellow audience members. If your experience is limited, the range and intensity of your aesthetic involvement with the performance will decrease, which affects feedback.

If intense aesthetic appreciation requires knowledge and experience, how can the exuberant reactions of first-time viewers of any performance be explained? If you remain open to receiving any new experience, you have the potential of being caught up in its energy, excitement, and aesthetic. "Remaining open" in the performing arts usually means allowing your right brain to receive the experience and avoiding left brain impulses to evaluate. Even a first-time viewer of ballet will be captured by the movement, the spectacle, the beauty of the performers, and the music, without understanding the intricacies of ballet choreography.

As we experience more performances of any art, our aesthetic appreciation grows. We walk into performances more knowledgeable, ready to respond emotionally and thoughtfully. Accumulating performance experiences may reduce our right brain responses to the immediacy of the performance. We could become left-brain cognitive evaluators of the arts. Be wary. Remember: our first pleasures in the arts were right brain—intuitive, spontaneous, simultaneous, non-verbal. No matter how many experiences we may have, we must never lose this way into appreciating performance.

❑ Summary ❑

This chapter defines the appreciative listening role as listening to enjoy and to learn. The process of appreciation occurs in three steps: Attraction, Contact, and Critical Evaluation. We can exit this three step process at any time, but exiting is usually at the Attraction step. Appreciative listening is unique to each individual's experiences and personality, and it encompasses a wide range of activities. Knowledge of a subject plays a central role in appreciation, and this knowledge might encourage or discourage appreciative listening. To increase sources of appreciation, the listener should actively explore a variety of experiences. Appreciating humor is discussed as a way to improve health, learn, and improve professional effectiveness.

Chapter 11, "Listening in a Partnership," discusses the variables in the five listening roles as they function in the building of a partnership.

Awareness Exercises, Chapter 10

Name ________________________________ **SS#** _____-____-_____

Recall activities you enjoy.

1. List six events where you were an appreciative listener.

   A.

   B.

   C.

   D.

   E.

   F.

2. Discuss a situation where you went expecting to relax and appreciate, but it turned into a critical listening event.

3. Discuss a situation where the expectation was critical listening, and it became appreciative.

4. List four forms of entertainment that you do not appreciate.

   A.

   B.

   C.

   D.

5. List four forms of entertainment that you do appreciate.

   A.

   B.

   C.

   D.

6. What is the best movie you have seen in the last month? Why did you appreciate it?

7. What is your favorite TV program? Why do you appreciate it?

8. What hobbies do you have that you appreciate?

9. Why do you appreciate them?

10. Which radio station(s) do you listen to most often? Why do you listen to them?

11. Which TV station(s) do you watch most often? Why do you watch them?

12. What time of the day do you usually do your appreciative listening? Why?

13. What is you favorite music group?

14. Who is your favorite vocalist?

15. What is your favorite song?

16. Who is your favorite actor?

17. Recall someone you appreciate. Briefly describe what led to the appreciation using the three steps:

    A. Attraction

    B. Contact

    C. Evaluation

18. Recall something you appreciate. Briefly describe what led to the appreciation using the three steps:

    A. Attraction

    B. Contact

    C. Evaluation

19. Describe a time when humor helped reduce worry.

20. Who is your favorite comedian?

21. Who is your favorite author?

22. Who is your favorite painter?

23. Who is your favorite poet?

24. Who is your favorite playwright?

25. What is your favorite short story?

11 Listening in a Partnership

In the previous chapters of *Sensible Listening*, we have discussed a background for effective listening and emphasized the ideas that we listen intrapersonally, interpersonally, and holistically to comprehend, to help, to decide, to purchase, and to appreciate. As we become competent in these roles, we increase the probability of making responsive connections with others, and some of our most meaningful connections are partnerships. In this chapter, the importance of listening in the development and maintenance of partnerships is considered by first discussing partnering in our lives, second, by defining partnering, and third, by clarifying the link between listening and partnering.

❑ Partnering in Our Lives ❑

We go through life in a series of partnerships. Some of them may last thirty minutes or less; some thirty years or more. Short-term partnerships might be between people on the phone discussing a meeting or problem; a neighbor visiting about a community issue; someone asking for directions. In these cases, the partnership may not continue after the goals are reached—the meeting is set; the issue resolved; the directions given.

Longer partnerships exist between couples, family members, professional colleagues, owners and contractors, contractors and subcontractors, or any people who share common interest and goals. Whatever the duration, a partnership is formed whenever shared goals, values, and cooperation are needed for productivity and satisfaction. A partnership, to be effective, develops a culture of cooperation.

❑ Partnering Defined ❑

A partnership is an agreed-upon process to listen actively and work together to reach common goals. In the workplace, partnerships are frequently formed around projects for development, design, management, or construction. In fact, this kind of project partnering is the most frequent type of partnering in United States' organizations today, because it has significantly helped reach the goals of reducing legal confrontation and saving resources.

In business, partnering begins with a commitment from the leadership. It is an assurance by the owner and management of the project to treat the contractor as a trusted team member; moreover, partnering is a commitment by the contractors to a relationship of fairness and openness with the owners and managers. By definition, partnering is not a legal agreement with joint liabilities, but rather an informal relationship—with listening at the core—that leads to mutual acceptance without exploiting either party. A partnership is not necessarily a friendship (although partnerships do occur between friends), but it is a commitment-process to treat those involved with dignity and respect.

Below is the definition of partnering developed by Partnering Task Force of the Construction Industry. Notice that the definition stresses a process with commitment, equality, trust, and respect for each partner's dignity.

> Partnering is a long-term commitment between two or more organizations for the purpose of achieving specific business objectives by maximizing the effectiveness of each participant's resources. This requires changing traditional relationships to a shared culture without regard to organizational boundaries. The relationship is based upon trust, dedication to common goals, and an understanding of each other's individual expectations and values. Expected benefits include improved efficiency and cost effectiveness, increased opportunity for innovation, and the continuous improvement of quality products and services.[1]

The development of Chrysler's sub-compact car, the Neon, provides rich examples that fit this definition of a working partnership. In the development of the Neon, management first listens and commits to the project, and the project leaders nurture a partnership based on commitments, teamwork, trust, and fair play.

The beginning of the Neon partnership began in a test track garage where Robert Marcell, the head of Chrysler's small car team, met with Lee Iacocca, then chairman of the board at Chrysler. Iacocca listened as Marcell built his case to gain Iacocca's commitment to the Neon project.

> He began showing slides of his home town, Iron River, a decaying mining community in Michigan's Upper Peninsula. Up flashed the now-shuttered Homer-Wauseca mine, where Marcell had worked summers during college. Then the abandoned yard, where 1,000 railcars a day were once loaded with ore. And the hospital where, because of the flight of the young from Iron River, five people die for every one that is born. "The town is crumbling," he said, his voice shaking, "because we couldn't compete."
>
> Detroit, Marcell argued, was slowly heading toward the same fate, and abandoning small cars would speed its demise. But if Chrysler could become the first U.S. company in decades to make a profitable subcompact, it could help reverse the trend. It could prove that American carmakers, in toe-to-toe combat, can outmuscle the Japanese. Marcell uttered what became his team's rallying cry: "If we dare to be different, we could be the reason the U.S. auto industry survives. We could be the reason our kids and grandkids don't end up in fast food service." As he ended his pitch, he thought he saw a tear in Iacocca's eye.[2]

As a result of this speech, Marcell gained Iacocca's commitment to the Neon project, and one of the most remarkable partnership efforts in auto manufacturing history began. It was a partnership made up of over 1000 people—150 managers, 600 engineers, 289 suppliers, and a number of blue collar workers who contributed to the effort.

Once the first partnership step—commitment to the Neon project—was completed, Marcell proceeded to the next step—building a team. He and twelve engineers first assigned to the project began a process called "concurrent engineering." This meant building a listening team of engineers, marketers, purchasers and financial experts to work together from the beginning to avoid later delays from disagreements or misunderstandings.

Marcell knew that team building was crucial inside the Chrysler organization and with *outside* vendors and suppliers who would supply nearly 70% of the value of the finished car. Consequently, in October, 1990, the Chrysler team invited 25 suppliers of crucial components such as seats, tires, and suspensions to send engineers to Chrysler's proving grounds in Chelsea, Michigan. These meetings helped those outside Chrysler understand the project needs, and they also helped secure the *trust* needed to build a working team.

> At first, the suppliers were skeptical of the partnership Marcell envisioned, which called for sharing sensitive financial data and ideas in a mutual effort to slice costs. They had all been burned before by customers professing brotherly love. But Marcell's earnestness won them over.[3]

With *commitment, team development*, and *earned trust*, the partnership was well under way to meeting its goals of developing a marketable sub-compact automobile in a timely manner.

Central to this partnering process was listening. Iacocca listening to Marcell, engineers and suppliers listened to each other, and of course, Chrysler constantly listened to their most important partners, the potential buyers of the Neon.

> One thing Marcell did know was that the Neon wouldn't sell if it scrimped on features or performance. So the team focused on cutting costs where customers wouldn't notice, or wouldn't care. For instance, small-car owners told researchers power windows weren't important, so the team chose the crank variety. Market research also showed that buyers saw nothing special in the four speed automatic transmission most competitors offer. So engineers adapted an existing Chrysler three speed, saving more than $300 million. The team also decided to sell identical cars at Chrysler and Dodge dealerships instead of offering two slightly different versions, as Ford did with its Escort and Tracer. That saved about $10 million in engineering and tooling. Stylists did away with all but one exterior molding, chopping parts costs $50 per car.[4]

In addition to listening to potential customers, early in the partnering process, Marcell also listened to the workers who would be building the Neon, and he included the United Auto Workers as team members.

> As early as November, 1990, he had asked union members there to help engineers make the car easy to build and to streamline production methods. The result, in theory, will be fewer defects. "Engineers are great, but they've never built a car," says Bob Dunlavy, a United Auto Workers quality coordinator.
>
> In January and February, 1992, Marcell enlisted the UAW full-time. Chrysler bused about 90 Belvidere workers to suburban Detroit to help assemble the first production prototypes and suggest how to do the job better.[5]

The trust and teamwork, which was developed throughout the partnering process, created an atmosphere where partners would listen openly to criticism and evaluation. Ideas for improvement were considered, and if a team believed goals could be better reached, the ideas were incorporated into the process.

> Among the many ideas they came up with: a height-adjustable assembly line, so assemblers can fasten on components without fatiguing body contortions that lead to mistakes. Two workers, Ron Swain and Cary Smoot, suggested changes to Neon's door installation equipment so window glass would fit perfectly. That's crucial, since there's no upper door frame to guide the glass, and the slightest gap can cause wind or water leaks. So far, workers have proposed more than 4,000 changes in the car and production process, and many have been implemented.[6]

A review of the Neon project shows that the key steps to effective partnering were considered: commitment to the project and the process of listening in the partnership, as well as the development of trust and respect for the partners. Perhaps the most meaningful comment about this partnering process comes from United Auto Worker Bob Dunlavy:

> "We're proud of what's going on."[7]

In order for partnering to work, it needs to become an integral part of the culture which is valued and totally supported by the key players in the organization, whether they are the CEOs and owners of multi-million dollar enterprises, family members at home, or friends who enjoy a hobby together. In all cases, effective partnering uses the full range of listening theory: an understanding of the communication process, intrapersonal, interpersonal, holistic, and the five listening roles: comprehensive, therapeutic, critical, consumer, and appreciative. Partners listen comprehensively to the details of the partnership; they listen therapeutically to the feelings and concerns of the partners; they listen critically to test the credibility and logic of the partnership and to decide how resources might be used, and they listen appreciatively to enjoy the many aspects of the partnering experience.

Effective listening is an integral part of partnering, and listening plays a key role in developing the six criteria of a working partnership: 1) Commitment, 2) Communication, 3) Conflict Resolution, 4) Trust, 5) Teamwork, and 6) Evaluation.

❑ Listening and Partnering ❑

Commitment

Achieving goals begins with commitment at two levels. At the first level, potential partners must be genuinely committed to the project. At the second level, they must be committed to the positive effects of partnering in reaching the goals of that project. As discussed in chapter 4, "Listening to Ourselves," all communication begins within ourselves. In order to become committed to a project, we first listen to determine how this project can meet our needs and goals. For example, we might ask if the project will fulfill our need for *survival* by assuring a paycheck? Conserving resources? Saving time and money? Will it fulfill our need *to belong*? Will it bring us together with people who respect us? Will it fulfill our need for *power*? Will we be empowered to make important decisions? Will this project fulfill our need for *freedom*? Will we be allowed to create solutions to problems? Will we be free to be ourselves? Will it fulfill our need for *fun*? Will we be able to appreciate our achievements? Will we be able to pursue aspects of the project that we enjoy?

Commitment says that we accept the project goals, and we share these goals with our partners. Consequently, we will listen as partners to reach the goals. The goals can cover the range of human endeavors: building a bridge, painting a house, rebuilding a plane, being married, planning a vacation, raising children, making money, keeping warm, making a dress, keeping healthy, losing weight, and so on.

Once we have made our commitment to project goals and to partnering as a means of achieving these goals, we are ready to develop a productive relationship with our partners through effective communication.

Communication

One of the first steps in establishing effective communication is to promote interaction in the partnering culture. Regular meetings, discussions, even newsletters and posted material encourage communication. Just keeping office doors open encourages two-way interaction. Moreover, communication is supported when the culture supports equality. Equality means listening openly, without judgment, and empathically to feelings; listening with interest to comprehend facts and information, and listening to appreciate the insights, interests, and humor of partners.

A partnership, by definition, is based on communication—the act of sending messages and listening to each other. This substantial part of partnering says, "I will give the energy to connect with my partners. I will take the time to listen to them and listen to my own feelings, so that I can share with them."

Conflict Resolution

The definition for *conflict* is "the interaction of interdependent people who perceive incompatible goals and interference from each other in achieving those goals."[8] Basically, this says that conflicts are disagreements that come from having different goals or different approaches to reach goals. Conflict resolution is a structure to solve these disagreements. For example, two people might agree on a goal to go to Chicago to see a play. Within this overall goal are sub-goals which might cause disagreements and require a plan for conflict resolution. Which play should they attend? The matinee or the evening production? Should they drive, take a plane, a bus, Amtrak? Where should they stay? What time should they leave? Without some established method of conflict resolution, this partnership could become bogged-down in conflicts that waste time and energy.

Any effective partnering process needs an agreed-upon, readily available procedure to resolve conflicts quickly and satisfactorily. *Without a system of conflict resolution, many of these conflicts become adversarial and are dragged-out in expensive and time consuming proceedings.* In interpersonal relationships as well as business dealings, un-partnered conflicts often find their solutions in legal battles that cost substantial amounts of time and money.

The importance of an understood and agreed-upon method of resolving conflicts is basic to effective partnering. When issues go unresolved, they fester and increase in magnitude and if unchecked could end up in court. In order to resolve problems quickly and satisfactorily, a responsive problem resolution plan is necessary at the level closest to the problem. The resolution plan will also help keep unproductive, adversarial roles from developing in the first place. Here, again, alert listening to conflicting facts and feelings can ward off potentially disruptive conflicts.

In the case of the two playgoers, conflicts are simply resolved by an agreement to meet over lunch to discuss any differences: which play to attend, the mode of transportation, and lodging. In more complex relationship, such as marriages and other couple commitments, conflict resolution is necessary to meet the goals of the relationship. Over time, many couples work-out ways to resolve differences. In the Bob Newhart television program, Bob and his TV wife Emily tried to solve conflicts by agreeing not to go to bed when they were angry at each other. Certainly, not all conflict resolution plans are that simple, and couples might spend a good deal more time and effort building ways to solve problems, but even a plan this simple could work.

Many couples consult therapists to explore and build conflict resolution programs for their relationships. Therapists help the couple listen to themselves and to each other, and ultimately develop a plan to solve relational problems. Below is an example of a couple who worked out a conflict resolution plan which helped their marriage partnership reach some of its goals. The plan they developed was specific and tailored to their partnering needs. Here is their story.

Susan and Ted are psychology teachers who fell in love. They started living together and after eight months started having serious relational problems. Ted, who had been abused as a child, was full of anger and had an explosive temper. Once he punched a hole in the wall, breaking his hand. He never hit Susan but did push her and, needless to say, often frightened her. Their relationship was punctuated with fights, and the week after their engagement, Susan threw the ring at him.

The therapist they consulted helped them work on two conflict resolution plans: one which helped Ted resolve his temper flare-ups and another which helped them fight symbolically. The conflict resolution program that they developed for Ted's temper was simple and creative; it forced Ted to listen to his anger and share his problem with some of his less intimate partners.

> In the last session, Belson [the therapist] addressed Ted's violence. He had Ted bring three male friends to therapy and explain the problem to them. He told Ted to buy a red phone, to serve as his violence hot line—if things got out of control, he was supposed to call his friends. The hot line worked as a deterrent. "I had always kept my temper a secret," says Ted. "This exposed it, made it more real. And if I gave in to it, I would lose face with my friends."
>
> Belson also suggested that the couple find a safe way to fight. They bought a squirt gun; they haven't used it much.[9]

When partnerships involve more people, the conflict resolution becomes proportionally more complex, but the *keys to resolving conflict remain the same: listen and agree on the goals and the methods of reaching them.*

To function effectively, a partnering organization needs a conflict resolving system that fits the culture of the organization. For example, a commonly used method of resolving conflict in decision-making discussions and debates is a system called, *Robert's Rules of Order*, which are carefully structured procedures designed to solve differences. When a group agrees to abide by these rules from the beginning, the members understand that Robert's rules will be the basis for conflict resolution in this group, where ideas will be moved and seconded, and discussion limited to a specific time and topic.

All successful groups have established ways to solve conflicts. For instance, in basketball, when conflict arises regarding the possession of the ball, the method of resolving the conflict is the jump ball, or alternate possession. In all conflict cases, the referees resolving the conflict must first listen carefully to the facts and feelings and then apply the resolution fairly.

Established, fair rules for resolving conflicts help keep partners from becoming adversaries, and these rules naturally make the work environment more productive. Coors Brewing Company of Golden, Colorado provides a valuable model for conflict resolution that has built trust and minimized lawsuits for the past thirty years. An article in *Personnel Journal* first provides some background and then the specifics of Coors' conflict resolution program.[10]

> In 1975, the brewing company created the Peer Review System, a process that guarantees employees fair treatment by allowing them to bring their grievances in front of a group that includes their coworkers. It was an innovative move back then, and it has proved successful.

This conflict resolution system has effectively brought management and workers together in a reasonably equal relationship, and has diminished major conflicts and litigation. The conflict resolution system Coors uses is based on active comprehensive, therapeutic, and critical listening. Below is a summary of the nine step conflict program. The program is clear and definitive, and its application is understood and equally applied in all conflict circumstances:

1. An employee who is dissatisfied with a company policy decision—not the policy itself—may file an appeal with his or her employee-relations representative within seven working days after the incident.
2. The employee-relations representative then sets up an appeal board by randomly selecting two members of management and three employees from the same job category as the appellant.
3. A hearing is scheduled by the employee-relations representative.
4. At the hearing the supervisor describes the circumstances surrounding the discipline.
5. The employee explains why the supervisor's action was unfair.

6. Board members listen and ask questions of both parties, and may listen to other witnesses, if requested.
7. When the board members have listened to all the information they need, they privately discuss the case.
8. They vote on one of three outcomes:
    a. To uphold the action.
    b. To reduce the severity.
    c. To overturn the action completely.
9. The decision of the board is final, and a signed, written summary is given to the supervisor and the employee.[11]

As the examples of the playgoers, the fighting couple, and the Coors brewery point out, a partnership needs listening, commitment, communication, and *a clearly understood system to resolve conflicts*. The fourth requirement for a successful, working partnership is trust.

Trust

Trust is difficult to define, but it correlates closely with speaker credibility as it is discussed in chapter 8, "Listening Critically." Basically, trust in a partnership is a blend of 1) Competence—which comes from knowledge, background, and achievements, 2) Character—honesty, 3) Intentions—concern for others, 4) Personality—positiveness and optimism, and 5) Dynamism—intensity, sincerity, and energy. Additionally, the way partners listen seems to affect trust. A recent poll which asked "What builds trust with your partners?" produced these response categories:[12]

> Listening objectively to the facts involved.
>
> Listening openly, without judgment to a partner.
>
> Listening that gives the speaker dignity and respect.
>
> Making decisions after listening to all of the information, including the *feelings* involved.
>
> Appreciating and enjoying the partner for who s/he is.

Trust develops when the partners *know they can depend* on each other. It grows with the knowledge that a partner will follow through on commitments and will act reliably and helpfully; that s/he will listen openly and objectively to understand, and when decisions and judgments are made, the trusted partner will consider all input and weigh the alternatives fairly and equally before coming to conclusions.

The fact that fair and equal treatment builds trust is emphasized in the closing discussion about the Coors conflict resolution system. In this discussion, an employee relations manager for Coors, emphasizes the idea that partners will use a resolution plan only after experience has shown them that the people responsible for operating the plan are trustworthy.

> Despite the fact that the majority of decisions favor the supervisors, employees trust the system. It took a while, however. "At first, employees' use of the system was low." says Edward Cruth, employee-relations area manager. "The first few years that the system was in existence, less than eight appeals per year were held. But then, as the employees gained trust in the process, the numbers steadily grew. For the last several years, we have been averaging approximately 60 appeals per year."[13]

After relationships evolve through commitment, communication, conflict resolution, and trust, interdependent teamwork begins to unfold in the partnership. This teamwork creates the activity that leads directly to measurable productivity.

Teamwork

Our discussion so far has provided the basis for a practical definition of *teamwork*. In fact, the terms *partnering and teamwork are nearly synonymous*. Partners are committed to a project and to each other. Moreover, they have developed processes to communicate and resolve conflict. However, *the idea of teamwork takes partnering one step further by adding a sense of dynamic activity*. People can be partners even when they are doing nothing together—not interacting at all. For example, two partners could be alone in the library researching ideas for a common project. At this point, they are partners working independently to find some ways to reach their goal. Moreover, it is possible to have a "silent partner"—someone who is committed to a program but is not active with other partners in the process of reaching program goals. Even though these people are partners, their lack of interaction keeps them from being team members. It is not possible to have a silent or non-interactive team member, because, by definition, a team member is *interdependent* in working toward the partnership goals. Consequently, when partners discuss and merge their efforts to reach a goal, they are acting as team.

Teamwork, then, is a partnership in action. When the team is functioning at its best, all of the partners are utilizing the diverse skills and talents of each partner to the fullest. We have all observed teams when they are functioning at their optimal level: a basketball team that is quickly and carefully listening to nuances of voice, movement, and eye contact, moving down the floor like a flawless machine: a partnership of managers, supervisors, production workers, and vendors combining their thoughts to find a solution to a product design problem, a couple discussing how they are going to take care of the kids during a business convention. In each case, teamwork is partnering in action. It is listening and interacting, and arriving at solutions *that probably could not have been found independently*,

These synergistic solutions which build interdependently are based on the understanding that each partner has valuable and diverse contributions to make, and *if they are actively listened to as team members, the best solution will be generated*. Like holistic listening where all the senses combine like a team to give a fuller picture than any of the senses operating independently, synergistic solutions incorporate a range of diverse ideas that is greater than the sum of all the individuals involved in the process. Teamwork, then, evokes a stimulation that energizes each partner to contribute and create beyond what could be done independently.

With the components in place—listening, commitment, communication, conflict resolution, trust, and teamwork—the partnering process now needs monitoring and evaluation. Partnerships grow and mature, and to assure optimal growth, systematic evaluation is necessary to monitor the process.

Evaluation

Partnering is a process of commitment, communication, conflict resolution, trust, and teamwork. The process of partnering—like any process—needs to be examined and evaluated regularly. *Evaluation is defined as a process of gaining information and using that information to make goal oriented adjustments.* Many partnering projects perform a final evaluation when the project is finished, and this evaluation is extremely valuable in comparing partnered projects with unpartnered projects. However, evaluation is also necessary *during* the project.

Ongoing partnering evaluation should consist of regular time-outs to listen to the progress of the project. These listening time-outs might be established at four levels. Level one focuses on Comprehensive Listening to the status of deadlines, costs, and procedures. Level two, Therapeutic Listening, gauges the current feelings in the partnership. This level is concerned with feelings of trust, comfort, satisfaction with relationships, communication, and conflict resolution. Feelings of mistrust, discomfort, dissatisfaction, frustration with the communication, the relationships, or conflict resolution might be expressed at level two, as well. Level three uses Critical Listening to evaluate decisions. The thoroughness and clarity of decision-making is considered here. Questions related to decision input and the quality of decisions in saving time, money, and other resources are considered. Level four incorporates Appreciative Listening. At this level, the reward system and feelings of satisfaction, dignity, and respect are discussed and evaluated. The four evaluation levels can be summarized as the four C's:

1. Comprehend	Comprehensive Listening
2. Care	Therapeutic Listening
3. Critique	Critical Listening
4. Commend	Appreciative Listening

These evaluation time-outs can be formal or informal discussion or written surveys and questionnaires. The evaluation should first be a system of gaining feedback—information and feelings—about goal achievement and the partnering process. This feedback should then be used to make adjustments in the partnering process. The evaluation process is needed for keeping a project on course. Regular time-outs for comprehensive listening to adjust the group's directions and appreciative listening to monitor self-esteem and feelings of worthwhileness will help insure effective evaluation. Process evaluation says: "Take time out to see how we're doing in reaching our project and partnering goals."

❑ Summary ❑

Partnerships are agreed-upon, carefully structured arrangements to listen actively and work together to reach common goals. At the center are active listening, shared goals, and respect for the dignity of each partner. By definition, partnerships are non-legal and non-adversarial agreements which focus on reaching goals through cooperation and compromise. Partnerships can be short-lived and exist between any number of people who are willing to listen actively and: 1) commit to goals and the partnering process, 2) work on effective communication, 3) develop a plan for conflict resolution, 4) build trust, 5) work as a team, and 6) establish systematic evaluation of the process.

Awareness Exercises, Chapter 11

Name ________________________________ **SS#** _____-____-_____

1. Describe a partnership that affects your life.

   A. age of partnership—how long have you been in it?

   B. number of partners

   C. levels (example: owner, board of directors, general manager, production manager, line supervisor. Mother, father, children, roommate, and so on.)

2. What are the goals of that partnership?

3. What form of commitment has been made in that partnership?

   A. to goals

   B. to the partnering process

4. What system of communication is used in that partnership?

5. How do the partners resolve conflicts?

6. How would you judge the level of trust in that partnership?

7. What signs of teamwork do you observe in the partnership?

8. What steps are taken to evaluate the partnering process?

9. Evaluate the partnership in these areas.

    A. listening

    B. commitment

    C. communication

    D. conflict resolution

    E. trust

    F. teamwork

    G. evaluation

10. List three large—ten or more people—organizations that you believe function as partnerships (possibly regional or national).

    A.

    B.

    C.

11. List three small—fewer than ten—organizations that you believe function as partnerships (possibly local).

    A.

    B.

    C.

12. List three two-person partnerships.

    A.

    B.

    C.

12 Listening Improvement

Awareness of the variables that contribute to active listening is the first step in becoming an effective listener, and the goal of each chapter in *Sensible Listening* is to bring about this awareness. With this goal in mind, the five chapters in the first half of the book are organized to: 1) examine the importance of listening, 2) develop a model to understand and analyze the listening process, 3) expand the model to include nonverbal, holistic listening, 4) show how communication movement affects listening, and 5) stress the importance of listening to ourselves. These first five chapters give the background for practicing active listening. Chapters 6 through 10 focus on specific listening roles: Comprehensive, Therapeutic, Critical, Consumer, and Appreciative. Chapter 11 addresses a common, yet complex form of listening—"Listening in a Partnership." This final chapter, "Improving Listening," summarizes ideas which can be realistically used in all settings to improve our listening.

❑ Listening Analysis and Preparation ❑

Any difficult task—whether it is performing in a play, a concert, or in athletic competition—takes analysis and preparation. Listening is no exception, and the reason for preparing to listen is to become effective active listeners. This preparation is done *before* listening, *while* we are listening, and *after* listening. In our listening analysis, we examine the parts of the communication model: sender, listener, message, culture, climate.

❑ Analysis before Listening ❑

Sender

Before the listening interaction, we should acquire as much information as possible about the sender. This information can come from a variety of sources: people who know the sender and the sender herself. We should organize our research to gain information in these six categories:

1. How the sender spends his/her occupational time. Is the sender a manager, a coworker, a student, a new employee, a physician, a sales person, an attorney, a police officer?
2. The cultural, social, and educational background of the sender.
3. The reason for the interaction.

4. The political orientation of the sender. Knowing this ahead of time will signal possible differing viewpoints.
5. The age and sex of the sender.
6. The economic level of the sender.

By knowing the sender and the reasons for the interaction, we can prepare for the listening role. If the interaction is primarily informative, one would take the comprehensive role; if the sender indicates personal problems, the therapeutic role; if the sender's goal is persuasion or to sell, the critical or consumer role; and, if the goal is enjoyment, the appreciative role.

Listener

Before we listen to others, we need to monitor and regulate our own internal noise. Chapter 5, "Listening to Ourselves" discusses the idea that effective *interpersonal* communication—listening to others—begins with intr*a*personal communication—listening to ourselves. Preparing ourselves to listen involves regulating our level of self-esteem—our feelings of worthwhileness and confidence, and deciding to accept or reject these perceptions and feelings about ourselves. If we find fears or anxieties, we modify them or put them aside to focus on *what we want* from the interaction: "I want to understand completely the information the sender is going to give," "I want to help the sender come to his or her own decisions about these important personal problems," "I want to listen carefully so the best decision can be made," or, "I want to enjoy this."

Once we have monitored our own internal messages, we can continue our intrapersonal preparation by using our imaginations to picture the people and the setting where we will be listening.[1] In preparation for a listening role, we can imagine the size and location of the meeting place, the decorations, the lighting, the temperature, the colors, the furniture, the noises, and the smells. Next, we can imagine the people. We picture where they are sitting or standing, the sound of their voices, their faces, eye movements, gestures, and clothing. Once we have listened intrapersonally to our feelings and have imagined the setting and the people in the listening scene, we are ready to prepare for the message.

Message

Whenever possible, we should determine the general nature of the upcoming message. Perhaps the sender sent a memorandum indicating the goal of the meeting. For example, the memo might read: "Jen, I would like to discuss the Bolger contract at 9:00 on Monday," indicating a comprehensive listening role to share information. If the memo read: "We need to look at some changes in the routing slips," we could expect some decision-making in the critical listening role. A salesperson's appointment would indicate consumer listening. Someone requesting time to visit about a problem would predict a therapeutic message. A smiling friend stopping us to share an event from the last weekend would be appreciative.

If the listening is with a group, an agenda may be available which shows the topics to be discussed, and the content would alert us to the type of message to expect. A public speech, lecture or workshop might have a title or explanation of the content or intent of the message. In each case, if we are alert to the general ideas to be discussed, we can prepare for the listening role by adjusting for the nature of the expected message.

Culture

It is important to know ahead of time if we are going to be in listening situations where two different cultures are operating. As discussed in Chapter 2, every organizational unit has its own culture: its own set of values, traditions, rules, rewards and punishments. If the sender is from another culture, we need to remind ourselves of the cultural differences, and allow extra time to become comfortable with each other's cultures. For example, when a union steward has made an appointment with his supervisor to discuss a production problem, the steward and the supervisor need to be aware that two different cultural systems are functioning. The union culture values clear and precise technical and production information. The management culture values increased production while maintaining high quality.

The *setting* where the listening takes place is also a reflection of cultural values. If we are to be listening to another cultural setting, we should try to imagine it or visit it ahead of time. We might be listening in a noisy, busy production unit, a quiet, tastefully decorated private office, a seminar room with ten or twenty other people, or an auditorium with three hundred people.

The setting will reflect cultural values. In the example with the union steward and the supervisor, cultural values are an integral part of both workplaces. In fact, most workplaces offer valuable cultural information. A physician's office and examination room reflect cultural values through pictures, degrees, instruments, and diagrams explaining various aspects of health and health care. A restaurant's decorations, server's clothing, pictures, type of menu, silverware, and tablecloths will tell the listener what that restaurant values. In private or public places, if the culture values listening, the setting will reflect this value: comfortable chairs and spacing of furniture, a place to hang coats, a quiet, relaxed atmosphere; a closed door for privacy. Cultural values will also be reflected in the meeting time, formality, and preparation:

1. The time of day. Will the meeting occur at the beginning of the day, when minds are more likely to be active? Or will we be listening at the end of the day when we could be tired and more easily distracted?

2. The formality of the setting. Is the occasion a formal interview to assess the quality of work or offer a promotion? Or is it an informal routine visit?

3. Time constraints. Is the time limited? Do we need to get down to business quickly? Is there plenty of time? Time to get a cup of coffee and relax with the sender?

4. Interruptions. Are phone calls put on hold? Are other interruptions controlled?

Climate

Culture can be analyzed over a period of time before the interaction, since culture is a fixed part of the communication setting. The communication *climate*, however, is more difficult to analyze ahead of time, since it can change quickly, without warning. As listeners, we should be in touch with the prevailing climate, whether it is joy, frustration, optimism, anger, or despair, and adapt to the climate. For example, you are on your way to an appointment with a coworker, when you find out that he has just been promoted. With this information, you mentally prepare to listen in the happy climate that awaits. In fact, because of the climate, much of the discussion might be about the promotion and not the originally planned agenda.

However, the climate might affect listening without advanced warning. You may walk into a room, listen to the nonverbal messages and realize that the atmosphere is not what you expected. At this point, you adjust your listening to get a sense of the climate and adapt to it.

Movement

As discussed in Chapter 4, all communication is accompanied by movement: Place, Push, Pause, Please, or Pull. By understanding the sender, the nature of the message, and the culture and climate, we can anticipate and prepare for the kinds of movement we might find in the communication setting. For example, we know the sender to be a calm and controlled person who has asked for a meeting to clarify a procedure. His cultural values are objectivity and fairness, and nothing has happened to change the climate. In preparing to listen in this setting, we can reasonably predict Place moves, where facts, figures, and ideas are placed in a non-threatening atmosphere.

On the other hand, we might know a sender who is upset about some delays in production. He has called for a meeting to "streamline this operation," and we know the climate is highly energized. His cultural values center on "getting things done," and so we prepare to listen to a series of Push moves in the meeting.

❑ Analysis while Listening ❑

Communication is a dynamic process; it involves the interaction of a number of elements and interdependent variables, which change as the communication progresses. We analyzed before listening, and we analyze *while* we listen to adjust to any changes and to reduce noise coming from: sender/message, listener, culture, climate, and movement.

Sender/Message

While listening, we need to activate holistic listening, because the sender will be encoding messages that are read by all of our senses. As discussed in Chapter 3, while we are listening to words with our left brain, our right brain is actively processing the nonverbal elements of the message.

As we listen to the sender, we listen to vocalics—the pitch, rate, and pauses. We listen for vocalizations which might indicate what the sender is thinking or is in agreement with some feedback being offered.

We listen with our eyes to the sender's use of space. Does he prefer to be close or distant? We listen to the sender's body communication. Does she seem relaxed, comfortable, and confident, or nervous, disinterested, and uninvolved? We listen for messages from eye movement and facial expressions. Is the eye contact direct and natural? Does the eye movement reflect interest and vitality? Does the sender look away in thought or disinterest? Does the facial expression indicate sincerity, confidence, enjoyment, intensity, confusion, indifference, or are you getting a blank look that tells you the sender is mentally somewhere else?

We listen to touch. Is the handshake firm and sincere? Is the touch on the back or arm friendly, a genuine expression of warmth and concern? Is the touch appropriate for the situation?

We listen to smell. Does the sender smell of smoke or alcohol? Are there smells that might add to the noise in the listening situation? Perhaps the meeting is right before lunch, and the smell of popcorn enters the office, or the smell of something burning distracts us.

We listen to the sender's concern for time. Does s/he seem in a hurry, under time pressure? Or relaxed, having all the time in the world? One of the most obvious clues concerning time can be sensed by how often the sender glances at a watch or a clock.

We listen for immediacy, power, and responsiveness. Immediacy tells us how much the sender wants to communicate with us. The sender's smiles, frowns, distance, touches, words, and attention give an overall indication of how much s/he wants to be in this situation.

We listen for how much power the sender is using. Does the sender lean over us and physically dominate? Does s/he ignore the accepted norms of space and push into our personal space? Does s/he ignore questions and feedback.

While we are listening, we try to evaluate the overall responsiveness of the sender. Is the sender sensitive to our feedback, and nonverbal cues? Is the sender alert, aware, and focused? Responsiveness is the most important variable in an interaction.

Listener

The nature of the message that the sender transmits determines our listening role. As listeners, it is crucial that we be aware of what role we are taking. Being sensitive to different messages alerts us to subtle listening role changes that may take place *while* we are interacting. For example, we might begin an interaction in a comprehensive listening role, only to have the message shift to a critical listening role. Being aware of this shift is necessary because it takes the listener from being an *information gatherer* to a *decision maker*, and the listener will need to change the perspective from one of understanding information to one of critical analysis for a decision. The steps to remain effective *during* a interaction are to: 1) monitor the message to determine the current listening role, and 2) activate listening behaviors appropriate to that listening role.

To monitor the message we must be constantly alert to the listening role we are taking: comprehensive, therapeutic, critical, consumer, or appreciative. Next, we need to behave appropriately for the role by keeping the goals of each role in mind: Comprehensive, understand and retain information; Therapeutic, allow the sender to unburden; Critical/Consumer, understand and evaluate; Appreciative, enjoy. Following are some guidelines for each of these listening roles.

Comprehensive Listening Guidelines

1. We can take accurate notes. This gives us a written record to review later. We can record key words, outline the message, or write periodic summaries. Any note-taking system devised should record enough information to reconstruct the message.
2. It is helpful to remember items in sequence. First, second, third, and so on. "First she said this, then this. . . ."
3. Asking relevant questions is an important part of *active* listening. As listeners, we have an *obligation* to ask questions to clarify a message.

Sometimes when we are in a group, important questions are not asked because of fear of being looked upon as "inattentive" or "slow thinking." This is usually not the case. Granted, an interrupting question, or one that has just been answered, may be out of place at that time, but as listeners, we must realize that the responsibility of accurately receiving a message is our own. Consequently, we must work to be comfortable about asking reasonable questions. Questions should be placed before the speaker genuinely and appropriately.

Therapeutic Listening Guidelines

When in the therapeutic listening role, we can follow guidelines that will help adapt our listening to the sender. These guidelines might find application in other listening roles, but they are more appropriate in the therapeutic setting:

1. Provide an appropriate setting. This involves minimizing distractions with a quiet atmosphere without interruption, so the entire focus can be on the speaker.

2. Develop active, attending behaviors. In the therapeutic role we need to shift the focus to the sender. Attending involves looking at the sender in a relaxed, non-threatening way; having direct body orientation which faces the sender; leaning forward; and having close (but not uncomfortably close) interactional distances. In addition, while attending to the sender, the therapeutic listener should not initiate new topics, but make comments or ask questions about some aspect of the sender's message.[2]

3. Establish a supportive communication climate. This means that a safe and comfortable climate is provided for the sender to disclose and talk out problems. Support is shown by being considerate. For example, by offering the sender a chair, a drink of water, or a tissue, we show concern and support. Being supportive tells the sender, "I care about you. I accept you for who you are. I am interested in your feelings and thoughts. I respect you."

4. Offer supportive responses. Supportive responses are usually Place Moves that are: 1) *Descriptive*, "I sense that you're troubled about the new accounting procedure." 2) *Problem-Oriented*, "If possible, I'd like to help you deal with the procedure." 3) *Spontaneous*, "The options give you a good deal to consider, don't they?" 4) *Empathic*, "I understand the concern and worry you're feeling as a result of the change." and 5) *Equal*, "I respect your concerns about this and am willing to listen as you work out your options."[3]

Our responses can help keep continuity in the communication by minimizing interruption, or sending unrelated messages. Morcover, appropriate responses give the sender an opportunity to focus on her or his own concerns because we are *responding in a supportive manner* that encourages the speaker to unburden problems.

Critical/Consumer Listening Guidelines

We must be aware of the critical listening role. Gradually or abruptly, the sender might switch to a persuasive message by asking us to loan something, approve a policy, buy something, or do something. Listener awareness is vital here, and we can apply our listening knowledge to make the best decision. We need to be aware of:

1. *Speaker credibility*. Is the sender trustworthy and knowledgeable? Does s/he have my best interest in mind?

2. *Logic*. Is the message structured in a straight forward pattern? Are the claims drawn from valid data? Are the warrants clear?

3. *Reasoning*. Is the message responsibly constructed? Does it stay on the topic? Does emotion dominate the persuasive appeal?

4. *Persuasive techniques.* What techniques are being used? Bandwagon, Good Ole Days, Plain Folks, Testimonials, Emotions, Transfer, New and Improved, Cardstaking, or That's Incredible?

Appreciative Listening Guidelines

We usually know when we are in the appreciative listening role. Someone comes into our office with a smile on her face and says, "Hey, I just heard a good one," and starts to tell the story or joke. We turn on our favorite TV show, put our feet up and relax; we walk into the theatre, concert hall, or auditorium to spend an evening away from usual activities; we take a walk or a jog and enjoy the scenes and sounds around us.

While listening appreciatively, we activate the right hemisphere of the brain; take in the whole scene, and relax, letting our listening carry us into the plot of the play or movie, or the environment around us.

By trying not to evaluate, we can experience involvement in the activity. The goals of appreciative listening are to have fun and learn something. While listening, we occasionally try to remind ourselves of these goals. If we find ourselves drifting into a critical role, we need to bring ourselves back to the reasons for the diversion: fun, learning, or both.

Culture

While listening, we need to be sensitive to cultural cues—messages that indicate traditions or values. We can compare expressed values with previous impressions of the culture before the listening took place. Was the cultural perception accurate? Are there some differences in values, rewards, or punishments that need to be incorporated into a new cultural picture? For example, perhaps cultural analysis prior to the interaction led us to believe that *people* in the organization were the highest concern, but as the interaction continues, we get message cues that the *stated* culture values people, but the r*eal* value is based on numbers and profit. In short, the organization *said* people were valued when, in fact, production and profit were the actual cultural values. Gaining this insight into actual cultural values can help us adapt to more subtle ideas about the organization's culture.

Climate

The sender and/or the setting can alter the climate. The sender may begin the interaction in a high state of energy, and as the message unfolds, she becomes more calm and at ease, changing the climate from tense to relaxed. The setting can also impact the climate. For example, two people are communicating in a quiet office with comfortable chairs, and soft music in the background. The message is on a thoughtful topic, and progressing smoothly and productively. A knock on the door from a technician working on the ventilation system interrupts the interaction and distracts the sender. The technician asks a few questions about the temperature and comfort of the room and proceeds to adjust some of the controls. This five minute interruption significantly changes the climate from productive to nonproductive.

After experiencing this change in climate, we might try to bring the conversation back to the earlier climate by summarizing the message, or we might say to the sender, "Let's see. Where were we?" Through careful listening and responding, we can help bring the climate back to one that is productive.

Movement

While listening, it is important that we be sensitive to communication movement. We listen for the sender's placing, pushing, pausing, pleasing, and pulling. If uncomfortable, we can analyze the source of the discomfort. Is the sender pausing some important issues? Is the sender constantly pushing? Is the sender trying to pull us into an inappropriate topic? By monitoring and analyzing the movement in the interaction, we can give the sender feedback that we are uncomfortable. The feedback should usually take the form of place moves: "It seems that you keep ignoring the part the weather played in the accident." "I think that's an interesting topic, but I'd like to stay with our original agenda." "I realize that you want me to do something, but first I need to know exactly what happened." While listening, we need to be sensitive to the moves being used to communicate. The moves indicate the kinds of force in the message.

❑ Analysis after Listening ❑

It is over. The meeting, the lecture, the seminar, the production report, the conversation, the presentation, the interview, the movie—whatever we have been listening to—is finished. A natural temptation is to move on to the next responsibility. Before we move on, we should ask ourselves, "What have I learned from this about listening? What behaviors would I repeat? What would I change?"

Future listening can be improved if we take some time to analyze the listening we just finished. To correct problems and reinforce positive aspects, successful people take the time to analyze the details of an event: the doctor talks with her colleagues after a surgical procedure; the attorney meets with his peers after a court presentation; the pilot discusses with other pilots after an unusual flight. Likewise, we should take the time to debrief after a listening experience. Every time we listen, there is something to be learned about increasing listening effectiveness and reducing noise. To organize our analysis after we have listened, we can use a check list.

Listening Check List

1. Sender
   - ______ Comfortable?
   - ______ Given the opportunity to talk?
   - ______ To listen?
   - ______ Internal/external noise reduced?
2. Listener
   - ______ Comfortable?
   - ______ Attentive?
   - ______ Gave feedback?
   - ______ Internal/external noise reduced?
   - ______ Appropriate listening role(s) taken?
     - ______ comprehensive
     - ______ therapeutic
     - ______ critical
     - ______ consumer
     - ______ appreciative
3. Message
   - ______ Clear?
   - ______ Questions answered?
   - ______ Adequate feedback?
4. Culture
   - ______ Conducive to listening?
   - ______ Visible to the sender?
   - ______ Understood by the sender?
5. Climate
   - ______ Conducive to listening?
   - ______ Non-interfering?
6. Movement
   - ______ Sender
     - ______ place
     - ______ push
     - ______ pause
     - ______ please
     - ______ pull
     - ______ varied
   - ______ Listener
     - ______ place
     - ______ push
     - ______ pause
     - ______ please
     - ______ pull
7. Result
   - ______ Information understood? Remembered?
   - ______ Sender unburdened?
   - ______ Decision considered?
   - ______ Purchase considered?
   - ______ Enjoyable time?

❑ Summary ❑

This chapter emphasizes the importance of analyzing listening interactions before, during, and after they happen. The analysis centers on topics discussed in the preceding chapters of *Sensible Listening*, focusing specifically on the elements in the communication model: sender, listener, message, climate, culture, and movement. The purpose is to increase listening effectiveness by reducing noise in the listening interaction. *Before* the communication happens, the listener should find out as much as possible about the sender and the setting. Moreover, the listener should intrapersonally explore self-esteem and motivations. With this information, s/he can prepare for listening behavior by imagining the details of the meeting. *While* listening, the listener is flexible to changes in the message and the setting. S/he keeps constantly aware of shifts to the critical or consumer listening role. *When the listening is finished*, the listener analyzes what went well and what should be changed. S/he uses a checklist to help in this analysis.

When these guides to effective listening are functioning, the listener will experience strengthened interactions with colleagues, clients, managers, friends, and family members; improved morale and productivity; responsible decisions and purchases; efficient use of time; clarified information, directions, and procedure; increased economic and personal rewards; and the satisfaction of being a responsible person contributing to a productive culture.

Awareness Exercises, Chapter 12

Name ______________________________ **SS#** _____-____-_____

You are ready to plan for your next listening interaction.

1. What will be your listening role?

2. What preparations will you make prior to the interaction? Respond in these categories.

   A. Sender

   B. Listener

   C. Message

   D. Climate

   E. Culture

   F. Noise

   G. Movement

3. What reactions do you have after the listening interaction? Respond in these categories.

   A. Sender

   B. Listener

   C. Message

   D. Climate

   E. Culture

   F. Noise

   G. Movement

❑ Chapter Notes ❑

Notes: Chapter 1 Listening in the Organization

1. Leland Brown, *Communicating Facts and Ideas in Business,* Englewood Cliffs, New Jersey: Prentice-Hall, 1982, p. 380.
2. William F. Keefe, *Listen, Management!* New York: McGraw Hill, 1971, p. 10.
3. Ron Karg, Production Manager, Armstrong Rubber Co. personal interview, Des Moines, Iowa, April 7, 1985.
4. Lee Iacocca [with William Novak], *Iacocca An Autobiography,* New York: Bantam, 1984, pp. 54-55.
5. Thomas J. Peters and Robert H. Waterman, Jr., *In Search of Excellence: Lessons for America's Best-Run Companies,* New York: Harper and Row, Publishers, 1982, p. 193 (also a program aired on public television).
6. Carl R. Rogers, A *Way of Being,* Boston: Mass., Houghton Mifflin, 1980, p. 142.
7. Russ Canute, Counselor, personal interview, Ames, Iowa, October 5, 1983.
8. Paul J. Kaufmann, *Selected Communication Variables and Their Effect Upon Advisee Satisfaction with Adviser-Advisee Conferences,* unpublished doctoral dissertation, Iowa State University, Ames, Iowa, 1975.
9. Peters and Waterman, pp. 311-312.
10. Iacocca, p. 58.
11. Scott Miller, Marketing Analyst, Winnebago Industries, Personal Interview, Forest City, Iowa, November 11, 1987.
12. Peters and Waterman, p. 195.
13. Harold J. Leavitt and Ronald A. H. Mueller, "Some Effects of Feedback on Communication," in Alfred G. Smith, *Communication and Culture: Readings in the Codes of Human Interaction,* New York: Holt, Rinehart and Winston, 1966. pp. 344-353.
14. Paul J. Kaufmann, "Classroom Instruction and Listening," unpublished monograph, Ames, Iowa, 1989.
15. *Ibid.*
16. Sylvia Porter, "Poor Listening Is Big Problem for Businesses," *The Washington Star,* November 14, 1979, pp. F-B.

17. From: http://www.speaking.com/articles/articles,d/direstaarticle1.html, "Empowerment Comes From Learning Listening Techniques" by Diane DiResta.

18. Peters and Waterman, Public Broadcasting Program.

19. "What's He Doing? He'll Kill Us All!" *Time*, April 11, 1977, pp. 28-35.

20. Kristi Koebke, "Engineer says unethical call led to disaster," Iowa State *Daily*, March 4, 1993.

21. From: http://www.otsma.com/advisory/publish/Listening.htm, "Are you Listening," November 24, 1999 from a Customer Support Management Magazine, January/February 1999 issue.

Notes: Chapter 2 Listening and the Process of Communication

1. William H. Miller, "More than Fish Stories Now," *The Business Management Magazine,"* vol. 234, no. 4, August 24, 1987, pp. 39-41.

2. Warren Weaver, "The Mathematics of Communication," *Scientific American*, vol. 181, pp. 11-15, 1949. Reprinted in *Communication in Culture*, Alfred G. Smith, editor, New York: Holt, Rinehart and Winston, 1966, pp. 15-24.

3. Del Marth, "Keeping all the Lines Open," *Nation's Business*, October, 1984, p. 85.

4. Thomas J. Peters and Robert H. Waterman, Jr., *In Search of Excellence: Lessons for America's Best-Run Companies*, New York: Harper and Row, Publishers. 1982. pp. 75-76.

5. Charles E. Beck and Elizabeth A. Beck "The Manager's Open Door and the Communication Climate," *Business Horizons*, vol. 29, January-February, 1986, p. 15.

Notes: Chapter 3 Listening Holistically

1. Dave Benson, Attorney. Personal Interview. May 7, 1987.

2. Betty Edwards, *Drawing on the Right Side of the Brain: A Course in Enhancing Creativity and Artistic Confidence.* Los Angeles: J. P. Tarcher, Inc. 1979.

3. Albert Mehrabian, *Silent Messages*, 2nd ed. Belmont, California: Wadsworth Publishing Co., 1981.

4. Stephen Michael Kosslyn, *Ghosts in the Mind's Machine: Creating and Using Images in the Brain.* New York: W. W. Norton & Company. 1983.

5. Gerard Egan, *Exercises in Training Skills: A Training Manual to Accompany The Skilled Helper.* Monterey, CA: Brooks/Cole Publishing Company. 1985.

6. Mark L. Knapp, *Nonverbal Communication in Human Interaction*, New York: Holt, Rinehart and Winston, 1972, p. 12.

7. Alfred G. Smith, *Communication and Culture: Readings in the Codes of Human Interaction.* New York: Holt, Rinehart and Winston. 1966.

8. Daniel Goldman, "Can you tell when Someone is lying to you? *Psychology Today*, August, 1982, pp. 14-23.

9. Jean Stockard and Miriam M. Johnson, *Sex Roles: Sex Inequality and Sex Role Development.* Englewood Cliffs, N.J.: Prentice-Hall, 1980.

10. Stephen Thayer, "Close Encounters," *Psychology Today.* March, 1988, pp. 31-36.

11. Doug Harms, *The First Thirty Seconds.* Unpublished Monograph. Ames: IA, 1985, pp. 27-31.

12. Mehrabian, pp. 43-47.

Notes: Chapter 4 Listening to Communication Movement

1. Paul J. Kaufmann, *Basic Communication Behavior: the Impact of Movement on Interpersonal Communication,* Ann Arbor, MI, Management Dynamics Corp., 1980.

2. T. Boone Pickens Jr., "Restructuring America: Focus on the Core Business" General Partner, Mesa Limited Partnership, Speech delivered before the Economic Club of Detroit, Detroit, Michigan, May 2, 1988. *Vital Speeches of the Day.* Vol. LIV, Sept. 1, 1988, No. 22, p. 676.

3. *Ibid.*, p. 678.

4. Theo Pitt Jr., "The Truth About Savings and Loan Institutions: State and Federal Bungling," Speech delivered at the Third Regulatory Policy Conference of the U.S. League of Savings Institutions, Washington, D.C., June 28, 1988, Vital *Speeches the* Day. Vol. LIV, September 1, 1988, No. 22, p. 674.

Notes: Chapter 5 Listening to Ourselves

1. William Glasser, *Control Theory, A New Explanation of How We Control Our Lives,* New York: Harper & Row, Publishers, 1984, pp. 5-15.

2. Glasser, pp. 9-10.

3. Glasser, p. 10.

4. Russ Canute, "Listening and Counseling," Lecture given October 14, 1982.

5. Dorothy Corkille Briggs, *Your Child's Self-Esteem,* Garden City, New York: Doubleday & Company, Inc., 1975, p. 29.

6. Sveri Wahlross, *Family Communication,* New York: Macmillan. 1974, p. xi.

7. Caroline Donnelly, "Writing an Advertisement for Yourself," Money, vol. 4, January, 1974, p. 308.

8. Nathaniel Branden, *How* to *Raise Your Self-Esteem,* Toronto: Bantam Books, 1987, p. 48.

9. Virginia Satir, *Making Contact,* Millbrae, California: Celestial Arts, 1976.

10. Glasser, pp. 13-16.

Notes: Chapter 6 Listening Comprehensively

1. William A. Welker, Ed.D. "Listening Skills: Learning to Actively Pay Attention," http://wphs.ohio.k12.wv.us/warwood/skills34.htm. November 24, 1999.

2. Guy H. Lafrancois, *Psychology for Teaching,* 3rd ed., Belmont, California: Wadsworth Publishing Company, 1979, pp. 168-170.

3. A. Paivio, *Imagery and Verbal Processes*, New York: Holt, Rinehart and Winston, 1971, p. 332.

4. Kittie W. Watson and Larry R. Smeltzer, "Barriers to Listening: Comparison between Business Students and Business Practitioners," Paper presented at the Fourth Annual International Listening Association Convention, St. Paul, Minnesota, March 4, 1983.

5. Russ Canute, Counselor, Iowa State University, Ames, Iowa, Personal interview, October 5, 1983.

6. George F. Tuttle and Johnny I. Murdock, "A Competency-Based Model for Teaching Listening within Organizational Environments." Presentation made at the Sixty-Ninth Annual Speech Communication Association Meeting, Washington, D.C., November 10, 1983.

7. *Harvard Milton College Study Skills Program Level HI,* Reston, Virginia: National Association of Secondary School Principals, 1983.

8. Robert L. Montgomery, "How to Improve Your Memory," *U.S. News and World Report,* August 23, 1979, p. 55.

9. Roy M. Berko, Andrew D. Wolvin, and Darlyn R. Wolvin, Communication: A Social and Career Focus, 2nd ed. Boston: Houghton Mifflin Company, 1981. p. 76.

10. D.E. McHenry, "The Effects of Certain Learner, Task, and Response Variables on Immediate and Delayed Aural Comprehension of Meaningful Verbal Material," Ph.D. dissertation, University of Denver, 1974, cited in Paul G. Friedman, *Listening Processes: Attention, Understanding, Evaluation,* Washington, D.C.: National Education Association, 1983, p. 11.

11. Francis J. DiVesta and G. Susan Gray, "Listening and Notetaking: II. Immediate and Delayed Recall as Functions of Variations on Thematic Continuity, Note Taking, and Length of Listening-Review Intervals," *Journal of Educational* Psychology, vol. 64, 1973, pp. 278-287.

Notes: Chapter 7 Listening Therapeutically

1. Carl R. Rogers, *A Way of Being,* Boston: Mass. Houghton Mifflin, 1980, p. 142.

2. *Active Skills for Staff Development. A Cognitive Viewpoint,* St. Paul MN. Department of Education, pp. 8-9.

3. Stephen E. Nicol, "Some Thoughts on Listening," unpublished report, Iowa State University, Ames, Iowa, 1993.

4. Ernest G. Beier and Evans G. Valens, *People Reading,* New York: Stein and Day, 1975, p. 154.

5. Gerard Egan, *The Skilled Helper: A Systematic Approach to Effective Helping,* 3rd edition. Monterey, California: Brooks/Cole Publishing Company. 1986, pp. 105-106.

6. William McCormack, pediatrician, personal interview, Ames, Iowa, November, 1989.

Notes: Chapter 8 Listening Critically

1. James C. McCroskey, "Scales for the Measurement of Ethos," *Communication Monographs,* Vol, 33. 1966, pp. 65-73.

2. *Ibid.*

3. Louis Harris, "Confidence in Institutions Rises Slightly," New York: The Harris Survey, November 17, 1983, pp. 2-3.

4. Stephen Toulmin, Richard Rieke, and Allan Janik, An Introduction to Reasoning, New York: Macmillan, 1979.

5. James M. McCrimmon, *Writing with a Purpose.* Boston: Houghton Mifflin Company. 1980. pp. 236-242.

6. James Randi, *Flim-Flam! Psychics, ESP, Unicorns, and other Delusions,* Buffalo, New York: Prometheus Books, 1982, pp. 94-97.

7. Bill Moyers, *A World of Ideas: Conversations with thoughtful men and women about American life today and the ideas shaping our future,* Betty Sue Flowers, Editor. New York: Doubleday, 1989, p. 292.

Notes: Chapter 9 Listening as a Consumer

1. Robert E. Guzik, "Are You Listening?" http:www/svobodamag.com/features/0720are.html.

2. Barry Sheehy, "Are You Listening?" *Across the Board.* V. 36, no. 4, April 1999, pp. 41–46. Copyright ISSN: 0147-1554, No. BBP199023888. (magazine publisher).

3. Marion Plunkett, "Learning Through Listening," *Marketing (Maclean Hunter),* V. 103, no. 39. October 19, 1998, p. 29. ISSN: 0025-3624, No. BBP198092378. Copyright (magazine publisher).

4. Rebecca Winters, "Tales from the E-Commerce Front," *Time* magazine. Oct. 4, 1999, vol. 154, no. 14. http://www.pathfinder.

5. Interview—Rob McClelland (Technology) and Marianne Kocal (VP)—Meyocks & Priebe advertising, Des Moines, IA, November 11; December 18, 1999.

6. Don Peppers, "Wal-Mart Clicks on Main Street."

7. Jeffrey A. Trachtenberg, "Shop until you drop?" *Forbes,* vol. 141, January 11, 1988, p. 40.

8. *Ibid.*
9. Anastasia Toufexis, "365 Days Till Christmas," *Time*, vol. 132, no. 82, December 26, 1988, p. 82.
10. *Ibid.*
11. Anne H. Rosenfeld, "Mind Openers: An All-Consuming Passion," *Psychology Today*, vol. 22, no. 12, May, 1988, p. 12.
12. Georgia Witkin, PhD, "The Shopping Fix," *Health*, vol. 20, May, 1988, p. 74.
13. JoAnna Natale, "Are You Open to Suggestion?" *Psychology Today*, May, 1988, p. 28.
14. *Ibid.* p. 30.
15. "How Consumers Make Decisions," *Georgia 4-H Consumer Judging, Cooperative Extension Service*, the University of Georgia College of Agriculture, Athens, p. 6.
16. John L. Price and George Mann, "Thinking Skills and Propaganda Detection," presented at the Annual Conference of the Mid-South Educational Research Association, Little Rock, Arkansas, November 8-10, 1989, pp. 5-6.
17. Robert G. Wyckham, "Implied Superiority Claims," *Journal of Advertising Research*, February/March, 1987, p. 54.
18. *Ibid.*
19. Dr. Irving Allan Kaye, "Fresh Breath for Less," *Consumers' Research*, vol. 74, no. 2, February, 1991, pp. 29-30.
20. Richard Williford, "Do You Really Want *That* Car?" *Consumers' Research*, vol. 74, no. 8, August 1991, pp. 20-22.
21. Walter W. Watt, "Finding an Auto Body Repair Shop," *Consumers' Research*, vol. 73, no. 2, February, 1990, pp. 30-33.

Notes: Chapter 10 Listening Appreciatively

1. Steven C. Larson, "Steps Leading to Appreciative Listening," unpublished report, Iowa State University, Ames, Iowa, 1992.
2. James J. Kaufmann, professional musician, personal interview, Ames, Iowa, September 5th, 1992.
3. Richard Bach, *Illusions: The Adventures of a Reluctant Messiah*, New York: Dell Publishing Co., Inc., 1981, pp. 102-111.
4. David Meadows, "Individualized Listening to Enjoy," unpublished report, Iowa State University, Ames, Iowa, 1992.
5. Dale Carnegie, *How to Stop Worrying and Start Living*, New York: Simon and Schuster, 1985, p. 86.
6. John Morreall, *Taking Life Seriously*, Albany, New York: State University of New York Press, 1983.
7. Roger Cecil, *A Textbook of Medicine*, Philadelphia: Saunders Publisher, 1955.

8. Carnegie, p. 89.

9. Larry Peter and B. Dana, *The Laughter Prescription*, New York: Ballantine Books, 1982.

10. James Goodman, "Humor: When Health is a Laughing Matter," *Executive Fitness*, vol. 13, no. 15, pp. 10-11.

11. Anne Ziv, *Personality and a Sense of Humor*, New York: Springer Publishing, Co., 1984.

12. James Check, "Positive Traits of the Effective Teacher, Negative Traits of the Ineffective One, *Education*, vol. 106, no. 3, pp. 326-334.

13. Jeremy Abrams, "The Best Lessons I've Learned as a Superintendent." *The Executive Educator*, vol. 9, no. 3, pp. 20-21.

14. Goodman, p. 11.

15. Peter and Dana.

Notes: Chapter 11 Listening in a Partnership

1. "Partnering," Unit 1, Chapter 2, *Resolutions International*, 1993, p. 2.

2. "Chrysler's Neon: is this the small car Detroit couldn't build?" *Business Week*, May 3, 1993, p. 116.

3. *Ibid.* pp. 118-119.

4. *Ibid.* p. 122.

5. *Ibid.*

6. *Ibid.*

7. *Ibid.*

8. J. L. Hocker and W. W. Wilmont, *Interpersonal Conflict*, Dubuque, Iowa: Wm. C. Brown, 1985, cited in Joseph P. Folger, Marshall Scott Poole and Randall K. Stutman, *Working Through Conflict*, New York: HarperCollins College Publishers, 1993, p. 4.

9. Phoebe Hoban, "He Said, She Said: Couples' Therapy is the Flavor of the Month," *New York Magazine*, June 15, 1992, p. 34.

10. Dawn Anfuso, "Peer Review Wards Off Unions and Lawsuits," *Personnel Journal*, January, 1994, p. 64.

11. *Ibid.*

12. Paul Kaufmann, "Partnership Trust," unpublished survey, Iowa State University, Ames, Iowa, January, 1994.

13. Anfuso, p. 64.

Notes: Chapter 12 Listening Improvement

1. Doug Harms, "Mental Rehearsal Effects on Business Communication," unpublished Master's thesis, Iowa State University, Ames, IA, 1988.
2. Allen E. Ivey, *Microcounseling: Innovations in Interviewing Training.* Springfield, Illinois: CHARLES C. THOMAS PUBLISHER, 1971, p. 36.
3. Jack R. Gibb, "Defensive Communication," Journal *of Communication,* vol. 11, September, 1961.

Index

---

n denotes note